Publics, Politics and Power

DONATED BY
SAGE

Publics, Politics and Power

Remaking the Public in Public Services

Janet Newman and John Clarke

Los Angeles • London • New Delhi • Singapore • Washington DC

JN
318
.N48
2009

© Janet Newman and John Clarke 2009

First published 2009

Apart from any fair dealing for the purposes of research or
private study, or criticism or review, as permitted under the
Copyright, Designs and Patents Act, 1988, this publication may be
reproduced, stored or transmitted in any form, or by any means,
only with the prior permission in writing of the publishers, or in
the case of reprographic reproduction, in accordance with the
terms of licences issued by the Copyright Licensing Agency.
Enquiries concerning reproduction outside those terms should be
sent to the publishers.

SAGE Publications Ltd
1 Oliver's Yard
55 City Road
London EC1Y 1SP

SAGE Publications Inc.
2455 Teller Road
Thousand Oaks, California 91320

SAGE Publications India Pvt Ltd
B 1/I 1 Mohan Cooperative Industrial Area
Mathura Road
New Delhi 110 044

SAGE Publications Asia-Pacific Pte Ltd
33 Pekin Street #02-01
Far East Square
Singapore 048763

Library of Congress Control Number: 2008929610

British Library Cataloguing in Publication data
A catalogue record for this book is available from the British
Library

ISBN 978-1-4129-4844-9
ISBN 978-1-4129-4845-6 (pbk)

Typeset by CEPHA Imaging Pvt. Ltd., Bangalore, India
Printed in India at Replika Press Pvt Ltd
Printed on paper from sustainable resources

Contents

Contents

Preface

Writing a book like this incurs a variety of debts. We have no doubt that think-ing and writing are collaborative acts – and many people have done their best to help us think and write in better ways. We are fortunate to work in a university environment that (still) supports and sustains thinking and writing; and the Faculty of Social Sciences, and the Department of Social Policy within it, have provided spaces in which we have been encouraged, stimulated and supported. Particular individuals have pushed us along our way and we are especially grate-ful to Clive Barnett, Allan Cochrane, Janet Fink, Gail Lewis, Engin Isin, Evelyn Ruppert, Vron Ware, Louise Westmarland and Margie Wetherell. We also owe a great deal to the doctoral students who have inspired us to think new thoughts: Rachel Aldred, Richenda Gambles, Kim McKee and Andrew Wilkins – and especially Nick Mahony who contributed to one of the chapters here.

Beyond the strange confines of the Open University, we have been fortunate to have friends whose work has made us think new thoughts and whose comments have taught us important things: Stephen Ball, Lavinia Bifulco, Vando Borghi, Janine Brodie, Wendy Brown, Kathy Coll, Evelina Dagnino, Julia Elyachar, Paul Hoggett, Bjorn Hvinden, Wendy Larner, Ota de Leonardis, Tania Li, Vivien Lowndes, Morag McDermont, Catherine Neveu, Mirko Noordegraaf, Anu Sharma, Paul Stubbs and Evelien Tonkens. We owe special thanks to those who have taken the time and trouble to read parts of the book, and to tell us what they thought of them.

While we have been grappling with these issues we have been members of a number of networks that have provided a constant flow of engaged scholarship that has provoked us to think. These include: the ESRC seminar programme on *Emerging Publics*; the *Publics Research Group* within the centre for Citizenship, Identities and Governance at the Open University; the *ITIS (Intermediaries and Translators in Interstitial Spaces)* network based in Zagreb; Larry Grossberg and the *Cultural Studies* programme at the University of North Carolina; and the *Society for the Anthropology of North America*, not least for the 'social in social justice' debate in 2007 (Hilary Cunningham, Carmen Ferradas, Catherine Kingfisher and Jeff Maskovsky).

We have also been fortunate to be visitors in several places over the last few years where hospitable environments and colleagues have drawn us into conver-sations about the issues that are explored here. These include the Utrecht School of Governance; the Department for Intercultural Communication at Copenhagen Business School; the Zentrum für Sozialpolitik at the University of Bremen; NOVA in Oslo; and the Socialforskinninginstituttet in Copenghagen. We owe a special debt of thanks to those who have made these visits possible, pleasurable and productive: Jon Kvist, Tine Rostgaard, Hans Kraus Hansen and Dorte Salskov-Iversen in Copenhagen, Irene Dingledey and Ellen Kuhlmann in Bremen, Mark Bovens, Peter Leisink and Mirko Noordegraaf in Utrecht, and Bjorn Hvinden in Oslo.

We also want to acknowledge those with whom we have, separately or together, worked on research programmes: Kathy Coll, Evelina Dagnino and Catherine Neveu (in the *Comparing Scales of Citizenship* project based at the Columbia Institute for Scholars and the Maison des Sciences de l'Homme in Paris); Marian Barnes, Andrew Knops and Helen Sullivan (on the *Power, Participation and Political Renewal* project); Nick Smith, Elizabeth Vidler and Louise Westmarland (on the *Creating Citizen-Consumer* project); and Sue Richards (National School of Government), Michael Hughes (Audit Commission), and Chris Skelcher (University of Birmingham) for collaborative research on public management and governance.

Finally we want to thank all of those who have, in different ways, shared their experiences of the remaking of publics and public services – in responding to our interview questions, enabling us to observe what is happening, or engaging in conversations with us at courses, summer schools and conferences. Without them we would not have undertaken this project; and we hope that it helps unravel – or at least make visible – some of the contradictions, paradoxes and possibilities at stake in the remaking of publics and public service.

■ Introduction

This is an exciting time to be writing this book. Discussions of publicness and the public sphere have tended to be preoccupied with narratives of decline: public services being privatised, state funding squeezed, public culture debased, politics corrupted, and so on. Underpinning such narratives is a fundamental assumption that any wider sensibility of public connectedness and public action is in retreat in the face of the growing power of markets, individualism and consumerism. The fortunes of the state, the institutions of the public sector, and the public itself are thus deeply entangled in the dismantling of the public sphere.

But in the early twenty-first century we can see the emergence of new concerns and debates – about the environment, security, food safety, global warming, poverty, social exclusion and democratic participation – all of which require public action, both within and beyond the nation state. But what is the potential for public action given the fragmentation of state power, the demise of a public sector and the impoverishment of the public domain? Some look towards a market-based citizenship that privileges consumer power as a means of securing equality and participation through the exercise of choice. Others look to the power of the internet to create new spaces of connectedness and to mobilise public action across, as well as within, nation states. Yet others (especially in Europe) look back nostalgically to social democratic or welfare states and attempt to defend the public sphere from the incursions of neo-liberalism. All point to vital disputes about what a politics of the public might be.

The politics of the public

Questions of what is public (and thus a focus for collective action) and what is to be left to the market or the actions of private individuals have been at the forefront of current programmes of state reform. Of course, these are not new questions: the association between the public sphere and welfare states was based on relatively recent social and political settlements. But the dislocation of these settlements is troubling, not least because of the connections with neo-liberal politics. As a result, struggles have intensified around the remaking of the relationships between public, private and personal. These struggles are shadowed by a sense of uncertainty about who forms the public – and where it is to be found (Clarke, 2004b; Newman, 2005a and 2006b). At one and the same time, the public is thought to have collapsed into a loose collection of selfish individuals, while having its opinions solicited through old and new technologies of public engagement. It is seen as fragmented and fractured by divergent interests and identities, and is thought to be either complacent and complicit, or unstable, unpredictable and excessive in its expectations. At one edge, such shifting images of the public leak into concerns about populations – the problems of social demography (ageing and fertility have commanded most recent attention); the troubles of social composition (associated with multi-ethnic societies and multi-cultural governance); and the problems of social dysfunction and social disorder (the wrong sort of people in the wrong places doing the wrong things). Questions about the public also leak into controversies about citizenship: its increasingly troubled relationship to national identity; its shifting mixes of rights, responsibilities and relationships; the ways in which it is enforced and enacted in everyday life; and the contested character of access to its benefits.

In this book, we make much use of the word 'publicness' as a way of talking about the combination of things, ideas, issues, people, relationships, practices and sites that have been *made public*. Such things, people, and issues get made public by a variety of means, but all of them involve processes of making visible matters of connective concern. Public issues or problems (objects) imply publics to take an interest in them (subjects) and these are connected by institutions, relationships and practices (mediums: Barnett, 2007b; see also Latour and Weibel, 2005). Publicness is historically and socially variable – the combinations of things, sites, people, ideas and the rest are not permanently or intrinsically public: their construction as public matters involves political struggles to make them so. They may also be de-publicised, and de-politicised (taken out of recognisable public concern). Recently, publicness has become the nodal point of multiple debates, connecting arguments about civil society, community, citizenship, old and new forms of solidarity, social divisions and diversity, and the search for social cohesion, integration and identity. The health of the body politic, the frayed fabric of social order, the wealth and well-being of the nation, even the level of happiness among the population, are persistent matters of public interest, concern and debate. So too is the role that public services might play in creating such conditions and in remedying such problems. One key question about the place and role of public services concerns how their publicness is constituted. In Britain, the question was answered by pointing to an embedded chain of connections in which publicness was secured: public services served members of the public, were funded by public resources and organised in a public sector, were accountable to public bodies, and were staffed by public employees (who embodied an ethos of public service).

We want to note two things about this conception of publicness. First, it was always a piece of institutional myth-making, rather than an accurate and reliable description. Each of the links in this chain could be, and has been, challenged – from the problems of representative politics through to the difficult mixtures of power, paternalism and public accountability. Second, in the last thirty years, this chain of connections has been dismantled. Political direction has moved to an 'arm's length' relationship through the use of agencies, privatised contractors, public-private partnerships, and the creation of markets and quasi-markets in public services. Representative politics has had a shrinking hold on public enthusiasm, engagement and trust, while being supplemented by an ever-widening variety of forms of consultation, participation and 'citizen engagement'. Public resources (derived from taxation and social insurance) have been combined with sources of private (corporate) finance and with less visible but significant developments around co-payment and co-production of services, or even the transformation of some services into private matters. Public services have been fragmented into multiple providers, many located in the private or third sectors or multi-sectoral hybrids, whose employees are not 'public servants' in the conventional sense. Tracing publicness in these emergent fields is problematic: is it to be found in finance, in governance arrangements, in regulatory surveillance, or embodied in the 'end users' (members of the public)?

Such debates are taking place in a context where, while public services remain the object of reform, there seems to be a growing awareness of the problems produced by previous cycles of change. The imperatives of managerialism – captured in part in the rhetoric of the New Public Management – continue, with profound consequences for public services and for those who work in them or depend on them. But the future of public services is being shaped through arguments about new forms of governance: the rise of networks and partnerships, innovations in democratic practice, the development of 'co-production' and 'choice' as service models and initiatives directed towards citizenship and social inclusion. Such developments are producing an explosion of new public discourses: public accountability, public governance, public participation, public value, and many others. And they are producing new arguments about the public role of public services, even where these no longer form part of a public sector.

Our purpose in this book is to explore this shifting landscape of publics and public services. We start from a set of orientations: that publicness is politically important; that its old certainties have been profoundly disturbed and are now being reworked in unpredictable and confusing ways; and that attention to such emergent forms of publicness is of critical political, practical and analytical importance. We do not believe that questions about the future of publicness – and the place and character of public services – can be satisfactorily posed, much less answered, by succumbing to either the fantasies of the marketising right nor the nightmares of the statist left. Both tell stories of the opposition between markets and states. Both exclude important elements from this binary distinction. Both announce (though in very different tones of celebration and lamentation) the current triumph of the market. While we understand the simple pleasures of story-telling, such 'grand narratives' exclude or gloss over almost all that we find interesting, troubling and difficult about publics, politics and power. In this book, we try to offer a different way of looking at and thinking about publics and their relationships to services.

Public services as mediums of publicness

The subtitle of this book – Remaking the Public in Public Services – underlines our interest in public services as mediums of publicness. That is, public services can – under some conditions – act as a focus for the formation of public imaginaries and collective identities, and help sustain solidaristic attachments. Membership of a local library, participation in the governance of a school, and even commiserating with others queuing for treatment in a hospital accident and emergency unit, are all potential sources of a public imaginary. This means that public services are not only public because of their material basis in public funding or being located in a public sector. They are both constituted by, and constitutive of, notions of publicness. They are constituted because of their association with a particular set of 'public' discourses and cultural resources; and they are constitutive through the ways in which publicness is constantly being remade through the practices of public service work and technologies of public governance. There is an important argument about the diminution or erasure of the publicness of public services resulting from the introduction of markets, contracts and a consumerist focus. It is often asserted that, without collective solidarities, it is impossible to have state-funded welfare delivered through public institutions. We want to turn this on its head, arguing that collective provision and public institutions can help constitute collective belongings through the relationships and identifications they foster.

We can trace several ways in which the role of public services as mediums of publicness is being remade:

- Public service bodies act as channels through which public culture is sustained, reproduced and reframed. Many services promote, organise and regulate cultural events, and some operate their own communications media.
- The proliferation of public participation initiatives in contemporary governance regimes means that public services have become significant mediums of communication and democratic participation.
- Public services are implicated in 'place shaping' activities that influence how publics encounter each other in the public sphere.
- Public services are involved in the remaking of 'community' and 'civil society' through strategies of partnership and capacity building.
- Public service staff are implicated in emerging strategies of governing that require publics to become more responsible and self-reliant, or to change aspects of their behaviour.
- It is in the everyday dilemmas of public service work that the meaning of concepts associated with the public sphere – openness, tolerance, equality and justice – are being remade or re-inscribed.

We belive that mediums matter. For example, markets as a medium have had particular consequences for the sustainability of publicly oriented solidarities and identifications. Of course, publicness is formed and shaped through multiple mediations – the mass media and cultural organisations play crucial roles. But we want to argue that publicness is also shaped also through individual and collective experiences of, and encounters with, public services. This makes the technologies and practices of public service work, public management and public leadership critical elements in shaping publicness. Public services are engaged in the remaking of the public domain through practices of design, the policing of space, and the governance of public interactions. They deploy new information technologies as ways of engaging in dialogue with particular publics as well as a means of re-engineering systems of service delivery.

However public services are everywhere the subject of projects to reform, re-invent and modernise them. The state of public services and their proposed futures appear at the centre of current public and political debates. These swirl around a series of key terms – efficiency and effectiveness, activation, personalisation, partnership, markets, social enterprise, social justice, choice, citizens, consumers, good governance, contestability, globalisation, devolution, localism, the public service ethos, multiculturalism, diversity and inequality. Sometimes these terms behave as if they are the products of coherent political-cultural lines of thinking, such that the Right proclaims the superiority of markets in promoting efficiency and effectiveness and in creating personalised and enterprising public services, while the Left champions citizenship, social justice and democratic renewal. However, we think it is much more common for these terms to exist in unpredictable and unlikely combinations: for example, when contestability, competition and choice are seen to address diverse needs, remedy inequality and promote social justice. As the then British Prime Minister, Tony Blair, said in 2004, choice must be extended 'from the few to the many' as part of a politics of egalitarianism. Such combinations can, of course, be written off as the rhetoric of a particular government's neo-liberal turn. But such strange combinations promote both political and policy puzzles about the future of public services and about how to make sense of, and engage in, such controversies.

In thinking about futures, it seems that they may no longer be dominated by the terms of the New Public Management. The NPM has come to be viewed as an historical phase in academic literatures and in much professional/policy/political discourse. Many strands of the current reform agenda (though not all) decentre the organisation, the site which the NPM struggled to transform. Instead they look towards changing the behaviour of the public in an effort to render citizens more health-conscious, more work-oriented, more effective parents, or more active contributors to the public good through voluntary and civil society participation. This has implications for the orientations and skills needed by public service staff. While the dominant managerial logics associated with the high point of the NPM were based on economics, it seems that public services now require more therapeutic or psychological skills in order to deliver developmental and behaviour-changing strategies.

This suggests that public services are being re-assembled in multiple ways: not only as businesses, but also as complex partnerships and hybrid organisational forms, and in new kinds of relationship with the public. The drive for efficiency and performance has by no means disappeared, but overlaid on it – in what are often deeply uncomfortable ways – are new demands that public services should empower citizens and communities, develop partnerships, collaborate with 'civil society' groups, and foster 'co-production' arrangements with service users. Much of this has been cast as a new 'progressive' agenda (e.g., Diamond 2007; Pearce and Margo, 2007). The current reform agenda, then, is not a simple project of privatising state bodies and public resources. Public services are certainly implicated in governmental strategies for promoting entrepreneurship and business through commissioning practices coupled with 'market development'. Many have been 'freed' from their direct links with the state to compete for the 'customers' of public services, including customers from other nations within an enlarged European Union. But public services are also enrolled in strategies concerned with enhancing citizenship and social cohesion, supporting forms of 'civil society' based activity, and promoting democratic involvement.

Thinking paradoxically: decline and proliferation

In this book we explore some of those paradoxes inherent in thinking about a politics of the public. Much critical academic and political discussion during the last two decades has offered a narrative of decline that attributes a central role to forms of politics that one might term both 'anti-social' and 'anti-public'. Here, conceptions of the public and their institutional embodiments seem to be distinctively at risk in the current period (e.g., Marquand, 2004). But there are temptations to treat decline as the only story, ignoring two other dynamics. One is the steady expansion of the reach of the state and other governmental institutions in response to issues such as crime and security. While state welfare may be under threat, there has been a proliferation of governmental strategies concerned with the management of unruly population groups – strategies for the control of anti-social behaviour, the disciplining of the 'socially excluded', the integration of migrant populations, the management of those seeking to cross national borders and the exclusion of 'undesirable' alien populations. This dynamic involves both an extension of state powers and the construction of public/private institutions through which such powers are exercised (most obviously prisons, police forces and immigration services, but also partnership bodies concerned with producing community safety and promoting social inclusion or cohesion).

A second dynamic that challenges the picture of a declining public sphere is concerned with the extensions of 'publicness' that are taking place alongside strategies of privatisation and marketisation. Again this has more and less visible aspects. Most visible is the proliferation of public bodies concerned with the regulation of services delivered through the market or through some combination of public and private authority. Rather less visible – and rather more ambiguous in its embodiment of 'publicness' – is the proliferation of sites and spaces in which the public is invited to participate in the design, delivery or governance of institutions and services. At stake in each is a third form of proliferation – that of discourses of the public and publicness: the language of public policy is pervaded with concepts such as public value, public accountability, public scrutiny, public engagement, public empowerment and many others.

This proliferation of projects, innovations and contestations around publics and public services makes us wary of announcements of the death or decline of the public. Publicness remains a site of significance: the focus of material and symbolic investments. In this book, we hope to tease out the shifting and fluctuating fortunes of publicness, looking at the different challenges to its old institutionalisations, exploring the attempts to supplant it with new orientations – privatised, marketised, individualised - while paying attention to the ways in which the public is being re-invented, emerging in new sites, forms and institutionalisations. In the process, we try to be attentive to the processes of destruction and diminution to which publicness has been subjected, while not falling prey to a nostalgic romanticism about older institutionalisations: when were public services so great that we would like to go back to them? When was the public realm ever wholly open, accessible and inclusive? We will, at various points, be pointing to the 'dark sides' of publicness: the capacity for publics to be parochial, exclusionary and traditional in their orientations; or the tendency for them to fail to live up to the aspirations of those seeking to mobilise, engage or activate them. Similarly public institutions – and those working for them – can exhibit a bleaker side. It may be that the oppressive practices associated with bureaucratic and paternalistic forms of power are being eradicated, and the 'knowledge-power knot' that sustains professional authority unravelled; but public services are now implicated in a range of new strategies for 'governing the social' that may be regarded as coercive and punitive in their effects. They also form part of the governing apparatuses that distinguish between publics (desirable populations) and non-publics (a range of marginalised and troublesome groups), even while targeting the latter for a range of more or less disciplinary interventions, from the administration of anti-social behaviour policies to the development of programmes designed to overcome 'poor parenting'.

We take an equally sceptical view of contemporary developments – the emergent forms of publics and publicness. We think there are problems about reading them one-sidedly, either as the product of global neo-liberalism or as its antidote (the expressions of an authentically popular public). Our concern is to explore the ambiguities, uncertainties and paradoxes associated with the contemporary condition of publicness; and to draw out the conditions, tendencies and contradictory dynamics associated with the politics of the public in the twenty-first century. To do so we will be offering a series of vignettes, not as examples of a particular issue, but as a way of seeing how diverse trends and tendencies come together – with more or less strain and discomfort – in a particular site in which publics and publicness are being reconstructed. In reading them there is a need to note the specificity of each. They do not illustrate general trends, but attempt to show the complexities and ambiguities condensed in specific sites and practices. In writing this book we have not attempted to produce a comparative, text, but have tried to set our own knowledge of, and engagement in, the UK (and other Anglophone places, such as the USA) against examples, narratives and analyses drawn from various 'elsewheres' to generate both a more complex view of the dynamics of publicness and a richer analytical capacity for thinking about change – especially about new formations of publicness.

Keywords

Our interest in writing this book has been driven by the puzzle of decline and proliferation: how do we make sense of the persistence and reinvention of the public? Are bits of publicness merely the residue of earlier political-cultural times? Are they merely a 'smokescreen' for the spreading virus of neo-liberalism? Or are they new sites of public formation, investment and mobilisation, alternatives to the de-collectivising, de-socialising and de-publicising waves of neo-liberalism? This puzzle – and indeed the possibility that such emergent forms may be more than one thing – engaged us in the work that underpins this book; and in particular, drew us to the idea of *ambiguity* as a way of marking the different conjunctural possibilities embedded in the remaking of publics and public services.

Ambiguity is linked to two other keywords as orienting principles for our approach here. It has an important connection with our continuing interest in the analysis of *articulation*: the formation and mobilisation of discursive and political connections into dominant blocs (and thus the production of subordinated elements). For us, this concern with articulation as a set of political and discursive practices has been an enduring contribution of cultural studies to the analysis of contemporary processes and projects. We start from the assumption that no keyword (in Raymond Williams' sense, 1977) has a fixed or necessary meaning – not even 'public'. The language of publicness is currently highly mobile, or unfixed. We can see it being recruited to, and positioned in, different chains of meaning in which it takes on new associations – for example, public sphere, public culture, public places, public interest, public safety, public scrutiny, public value. The language of publicness can be – and is – appropriated by very different political projects.

Words are articulated into specific political-cultural projects that aim to either fix or change aspects of social formations. Such projects – to modernise government, to improve the population, to make the nation competitive – are usually contested. The concept of articulation denotes the political-cultural work that has to be done to mobilise both meanings and people in order to realise a project (and the work of dis-articulation and de-mobilisation that is necessary to close out other projects). As a result, we are particularly concerned to explore the attempted closures around dominant political-cultural logics of rule, and the attempted co-options of such logics for other purposes (not necessarily resistance – just other purposes that inflect, twist or borrow from dominant logics). Such other purposes are important because this field of meanings and mobilisations forms a site in which emergent *publics* (identifications with, or membership of, a larger and collectivity) or *publicness* (sites, practices, spaces, cultural represent-ations, and institutional norms) might be shaped.

The third of our keywords for the book's approach is *assemblages:* the idea that the institutionalisation of specific projects involves the work of assembling diverse elements into an apparently coherent form. In the context of studying publicness, the idea of assemblage points to the ways in which policies, person-nel, places, practices, technologies, images, architectures of governance and resources are brought together and combined. Assemblage does two particular things for us in this book. It draws attention to the work of construction (and the difficulties of making ill-suited elements fit together as though they are coher-ent). And it makes visible the (variable) fragility of assemblages – that which has been assembled can more or less easily come apart, or be dismantled. In a period where we have seen the vulnerability and mutability of what appeared to be solidly established institutionalisations of publicness, the idea of assemblage allows us a way of working with this double dynamic of solidity and fragility.

In the following chapter we put these concepts to work in exploring the com-plexity of transitions of ideas and institutionalisations of the public, and in teasing out different ways of trying to make sense of this multiplicity of changes.

1 Contesting publicness: decline and proliferation

In the Introduction we identified three keywords – ambiguity, articulation and assemblage – as resources for helping us to think about the paradox of decline and proliferation. In this chapter we begin to put these concepts to work in exploring the complexity of both ideas and institutionalizations of the public, and in teasing out different ways of trying to make sense of its transitions. We begin by outlining our approach to defining what we mean by publics and publicness, examining how this meaning was 'fixed' – albeit conditionally and temporarily – in specific discursive chains. Much of the work of this book focuses on how these chains have been disrupted, heralding the decline of these historically embedded associations between public, nation and state. These processes of disruption – the taking apart of earlier assemblages – have produced the sense of the 'decline' of the public (Marquand, 2004). However, alongside this story of decline we can, as we argued in the Introduction, trace a proliferation of sites and practices in which publics and publicness are being remade. Discourses of public governance, public value, public participation, public action, public responsibility, and many others contribute to this sense of proliferation. Particular publics – faith based publics, active citizens, local communities – are being summoned to participate in governmental projects or decision-making bodies. Specific kinds of policy intervention – on responsible parenthood, civil behaviour, healthy diet and other lifestyle choices – disrupt established boundaries between what is considered to be private or personal and what is a public matter. At the same time the revitalisation of ideas of citizenship, community and civil society in current policy agendas offers new inflections of what it means to be part of a public or to act publicly.

This points to the question of how the processes of decline and proliferation are related to each other. Is what we are witnessing a 'progressive' moment, in which, after decades in which business values and NPM strategies have been dominant, public services are being humanised, democratised and opened up to new forms of public involvement? Or is it politically regressive, with emergent spaces of public engagement and action immediately captured in the roll out of neo-liberal, globalising pressures? We distinguish our approach from 'epochal' narratives – especially narratives that privilege neo-liberalism as an overarching force sweeping all before it. Instead our focus on assemblage and articulation brings with it attention to processes and agents involved in 'translating' forces, pressures and ideas across multiple boundaries. In the final section we turn to the questions of politics and power that are posed in the remaking of the public.

Contesting the meaning of 'public'

Let us begin from the elusive character of the word itself: what do we mean by public? Is it a noun (the public as a collectivity) or an adjective (public interest)? Does it identify groups of people (publics); locations (public spaces, realms, spheres); or institutions (public authorities; public services)? Does it mark a sphere of collective belongings and solidarities that promotes 'public' action in the interests of the whole – and if so how is the whole to be circumscribed (the nation, the community, the global)? Is it a domain of citizenship rights and responsibilities that can be demarcated from the private domains of household, family and intimate relationships? Is there something we might call a public domain in which cultural values are contested and cultural legacies remade through the circulation of images, ideas, representations and signs?

It is, of course, all of these – and more. Indeed, Charles Taylor (2004) argues that the term is a central organising concept of what he calls 'modern social imaginaries' – a key to the mapping of aspects, domains and areas of social life. In recent years there have been debates about what the 'public' in public services, public policy, public administration, public culture and so on might actually mean. Some have attempted to get back to conceptual roots. For example, Weintraub (1997) notes how the public/private distinction figures as a central descriptive and ideological conceptualization in political and social theory. The public, here, tends to be defined in relation to its shadow opposites: it is not the private, not the family, not the market, not the personal, not the individual. These shadows have marked a series of debates about the decline of the public – the shift from state to market, the demise of collective solidarities in the face of indi- viduation and consumerism, the critique of public institutions and corruption of public culture, and so on. But the meaning of the public and private in such nar- ratives of decline is not clear cut because the public is what Benn and Gaus (1983) term 'a complexly structured' concept that contains descriptive, ideological and normative associations. This has led some to suggest that the public is not only too conceptually ambiguous to be useful, but also has problematic ideological associations. Matthews, for example, talks of its 'pinkish tinge of collectivism' and suggests that the idea of the public good is a 'hopelessly romantic concept of uniformity and consensus that is incompatible with our pluralist pragmatism' (Matthews, 1984: 121).

But meanings of the public and private are not merely descriptive and normative; they are cultural categories that help shape social identities and relationships. As Warner notes,

> Public and private sometimes compete, sometimes complement each other, and sometimes are merely part of a larger series of classifications that include, say, local, domestic, personal, political, economic or intimate. Almost every cultural change – from Christianity to printing to psycho-analysis – has left a new sedimentary layer in the meaning of the public and the private. (Warner, 2002: 28)

This means that it is important to transcend treatments of the public as an abstract category founded in the domains of law, politics and economics. Warner argues that publics are rooted in the self understandings of their participants, and as such 'the idea of a public is motivating, not simply instrumental. It is constitutive of a social imaginary' (2002: 12). The reference to 'participants' here opens up questions about publics as subjects: not the citizen-subjects of a state, but actors who shape – and sustain – spaces and sites of publicness and public action. Defining the boundaries of who is and who is not a public in these terms is not simple, precisely because publics are fluid and mobile, being assembled at particular moments for particular projects. And, as Calhoun argues, they are plural, with cross-cutting identifications and forms of agency:

> The idea of a single, uniquely authoritative public sphere needs to be questioned, and the manner of relations among multiple, intersecting, and heterogenous publics needs to be considered. ... Recognising a multiplicity of publics, none of which can claim a completely superordinate status to the others, is thus a first step. Crucially, however, it depends on breaking with core assumptions that join liberal political thought to nationalism ... we should understand the public sphere to be a sphere of publics. (Calhoun, 1997: 84, 100)

Defining the public, then, is not just a question of delineating different groups of people, models of thought or spheres of action. It is about trying to understand why and how notions of the public have taken on such a degree of cultural significance in Western thought; how they help constitute identity and social action; and how they are the focus of contestation and struggle in contemporary politics and culture. Such questions have become increasingly significant as strategies for the reform and modernisation of states and public services have moved to the centre of the political programmes of governments in many nations (Clarke, 2004a; Leibfried and Zürn, 2005; Newman, 2001; Pollitt and Bouckeart, 2004; Seeleib-Kaiser, 2008). Strategies for reform have not only re-aligned the boundary between state and market and the relationships that traverse them, but have also brought public and personal, family and state, business and government, individual and social into new alignments.

Disrupting the public

In this book we want to try to capture ways in which publicness has become the object of contestation as its meaning is reworked in the context of new social and political formations. How are Warner's 'new sedimentary layers' being laid down as strategies of governing across Europe and beyond remake publicness? But identifying shifting, contested and emergent meanings is not to say that the definition of what is and is not public is infinitely flexible. Abstract conceptions of the polysemic character of language need to be set alongside investigations of how specific meanings are inscribed or become sedimented in apparatuses, policies, people and practices. This takes us back to notions of articulation, and the specific discursive chains in which meanings and practices of publicness have been – temporarily and conditionally – fixed. There are many such chains, including those concerned with public space, public culture, public feeling or sentiment, public opinion and so on. But in this book we have chosen to focus on three chains that have 'fixed' the meaning of the public in twentieth-century discourses in many nation-states, and which have become disrupted in the recent remaking of publics and public services. The first centres on ideas of the nation – a category often missing from debates about a public sphere or domain:

$$Public = citizens = the\ people = Nation$$

Here the notion of a people united in a shared national citizenship forms the basis for collective belongings and identifications that give a rationale for the public provision of goods and services. The associations in this chain produce, however, not an emphasis on a public sector but on a population united in a shared public domain of citizenship. In Britain – and elsewhere – such notions of a people sharing national citizenship underpinned the social and political settlements of welfare states in the post-war years (Clarke, 2004a; Hughes and Lewis, 1998). This produced a national conception of social citizenship that was expressed in conceptions of citizens as 'members of the public' with entitlements to benefit from public services.

The chain of connections here has always been an 'unstable equilibrium' (Gramsci, 1971). Each of the terms has been vulnerable to challenges and contestation – whether around the implicitly racialised conception of the 'people'; the conditional and exclusive systems of citizenship; or the assumed geographical, political and cultural unity of the nation. As nations have become subject to post-colonial and globalising pressures that loosen boundaries and dislocate the sense of a coherently controlled national space, so questions of inclusion in, and exclusion from, the membership of the national public have intensified. In the following chapters we look at some of the ways in which publicness has been displaced. In Chapter 2 we examine the contested landscape of the nation, national identity and the territorial basis of governing, while Chapter 3 turns to some of the forms in which publicness has been displaced from the nation-state as civil society, community and non-governmental bodies come to be viewed as the places in which 'ordinary people' come to govern themselves. In these processes of dislocation publics are being remade in new territorial, social and organisational forms that displace – or transform – the meanings and practices of publicness.

The nation is of course deeply entangled with institutions of the state (Gupta, 1998). As well as embodying the nation, the state forms the institutional base for the provision of public goods and the regulation of private (commercial) actions. Through its policies and practices, the state inscribes the appropriate boundary between public and personal responsibilities for care, welfare and other socially valued goods. In the 'modern social imaginary', the state is viewed as both the repository and guarantor of public values (such as equality, tolerance and justice) and as the defender of a collective conception of a public interest. This equivalence of the state and publicness is articulated through the following discursive chain:

$$Public = public\ sector = State$$

The association – in Britain and elsewhere - between public and state (in the form of public policy delivered through state institutions and a state-centred public sector) brought enormous benefits, but also had its costs. These were not only the financial costs linked to charges of 'waste' and 'inefficiency' but also social costs represented in charges of paternalism, discrimination, oppression and unresponsiveness. The institutionalisation of the public in the state had particular consequences in terms of its association with bureaucracy, hierarchy and professional power, making it vulnerable to challenges from both the political left and right, as well as from a range of social movements. The mobilisation of such challenges in the political projects of the New Right in the 1980s and 1990s led to the rise of the New Public Management, the introduction of market mechanisms and contracts, the privatisation of some public bodies and services, and the incursion of business values into public management, all of which, we have argued, constituted a 'managerial state' (Clarke and Newman, 1997). The subsequent extension and enlargement of such processes, with a particular emphasis on promoting hybrid arrangements (such as public/private partnerships) have reworked forms of public and private authority in a multiplicity of ways, making it more difficult to trace their 'public' character. Is it a question of links to the state, to public finance, to publicly trained professionals, or of being subject to public accountability or regulation?

We examine such questions in Chapters 4 and 5. Underpinning our analysis is a concern with the proliferation of sites in which forms of public and private authority are entangled. With Foucault's work in mind, we can, perhaps, theorise this not as a decline but an expansion of governmental power: the power to constitute individuals, households, communities, social entrepreneurs, NGOs, public organisations, businesses, voluntary organisations as active partners in addressing many of the critical policy agendas that confront governments in the twenty-first century.

The entanglements between public, state and nation do not, however, exhaust the terrains of publicness that engage us. The dismantling of the public in the nation and in the state is also associated with the conceptions of liberalism that were inscribed in ideas of a public sphere. This takes us to a third discursive chain:

Public = legal and democratic values = Public Sphere

This discursive chain offers a view of the public sphere of modern Western nations as a secular domain that can be clearly differentiated from private beliefs and interests and from the commercialised relationships of the market (see, for example, Gamble, 2004; Taylor, 2004; and the critique in Brown, 2006). The public sphere is associated with values and norms that shape the possibility of democracy. Values such as openness, rationality, transparency, tolerance, equality and justice were inscribed in legal and democratic institutions and bureaucratic forms of rule that, in principle at least, insulated public bodies from private interests and that guaranteed formal equality. Such values underpin the idea that public actors – including politicians – will behave impartially, defend the public from corruption and promote the public interest. Although these values are well established as normative principles, much political conflict has been associated with contesting their failures in practice (corruption, discrimination, collusion, maladministration) and challenging their inherent limitations (e.g., the limitations of formal equality in delivering substantive social justice; or the cultural inscriptions of who counts as members of the public).

Much recent concern about the transformations of public services invokes such questions of value. For example, how can a public ethos based on principles such as impartiality, fairness and equality survive when the bureaucratic norms and rules that sustained it has become subordinated to business logics? Or how will a common public sphere of citizenship and democratic participation be maintained in the face of deepening social differentiation and inequality, and the increasingly embattled antagonisms around culture, faith and identity? Underpinning such questions of value is a challenge to liberal notions of progress, posing the problem of redefining the 'good society' to which public policy is directed.

Such issues are the focus of Chapters 6, 7 and 8 of this book. Chapter 6 traces attempts to re-inscribe publicness in public services through new norms of professional or management practice, and through concepts of public governance, public leadership and public value. Chapter 7 explores the turn to more participatory forms of governance and raises questions about the politics of public engagement. Finally, Chapter 8 addresses struggles over citizenship and its reconfiguration, and how these bear the marks of diverse and divergent political and governmental projects. In each, we pay particular attention to the dilemmas and conflicts produced by these transformations for those working for the public and for citizens engaging in struggles to bring about change.

These three discursive chains fixed notions of publics and publicness into particular assemblages and institutional formations. They are heavily sedimented, such that publicness has become lodged deep in the institutions and norms of liberal democracies. They were constructed in the face of complex social and political conflicts and have subsequently been the focus of other challenges: about exclusions and subordinations; about failures of principle and practice; and about the forms of power that they support and enable. These formations of publicness were, then, deeply contested long before the current dislocations, suggesting their unreliability as a philosophical, normative or political reference point. Nostalgia for the 'good old days' when publicness meant something – a national public, sustained by a nation state delivering services according to liberal democratic principles – is not a reliable vantage point from which to judge current changes. On the contrary, liberal principles were problematic; states could be oppressive and divisive; and in Britain at least the national public sphere was inextricably interwoven with colonialism and racialised thinking.

For us, then, the problem of publicness is always a double one – the vicissitudes, inequalities and conflicts associated with the old formations of publicness are being both overlaid with, and transformed by, new inequalities and conflicts. They are complexly interwoven and create problems of publicness that cannot be resolved by a sort of restorationist nostalgia. For example, the rise, in some European countries, of 'faith' in policy discourse as a means of rearticulating diversity – an issue we discuss in Chapter 2 – demonstrates a means of further dislocating the idea of a universal public bounded by the nation-state. It opens up new lines of antagonism as well as signalling the continuing presence – partly hidden in secular societies – of older lines of division within and beyond the nation. But the new categorisations of publics around 'faith' are also aligned with the transformations of states. In the UK, an increasing number of faith-based schools, care and welfare organisations have taken their place in the newly opened-up marketplace of public service provision, offering consumer choice but also challenging the boundaries of state regulation and control. This is significant, not least since faith based provision may challenge the secular norms of the liberal public sphere. The recognition of faith based publics, then, is neither a story of the gradual success of social movements and groups claiming recognition, nor of the growing acceptance of diversity as a core value of liberal, progressive societies. However, nor is it a story of neo-liberal triumph in which notions of faith are smoothly incorporated into market dynamics, with diverse claims being settled through a choice of providers. The different ways in which faith is framed – and its capacity to be enrolled into multiple and divergent strategies – suggests something of the tensions, contradictions and ambivalences at stake in this particular remaking of publicness; and why we need to look across the three discursive framings of the public we have addressed here rather than settling for simple binaries between states and markets or public and private.

Assembling new formations of the public

Our argument in the previous section was that the disruptions to publics and publicness are played out around a number of different struggles. There is not one logic driving such changes, but a plurality of potentially conflicting logics that produce strange confluences, alliances, antagonisms and paradoxes. Making sense of these is problematic, in part because this landscape is already extensively surveyed, discussed and accounted for. Too often, however, these surveys tend to provide epochal, mono-causal and uni-directional accounts of change – accounts that identify the dominant tendency and marginalise others. So, for example, we might consider the more or less triumphalist accounts of the 'liberation' of individuals, organisations and markets from the shackles of state control, the dead hand of bureaucratic regulation, or the narrow interests of 'producer power'. Such accounts are dominated by the global imperatives for the reform of public services that point to the inexorable force of market logics, understood as the triumph of market society over state socialism; as the globalising dynamic of individualism against collectivism; or as the cultural logic of the 'consumer revolution' (see, for example, Bobbitt, 2003; Le Grand, 2007). In such views, the process is an unfolding one. Countries may be positioned in more or less advanced locations on this path, but all are moving steadily in the same direction – and there can be no going back. This is an epochal shift, sometimes described as the rise of market society, as post-welfarism, as the emergence of the market-state or the competition-state (see Chapter 4). Paradoxes, tensions and contradictions tend to be treated as historical lags – the residues of earlier formations that will eventually be swept away on the tide of historical change, or are a consequence of the project of change not being prosecuted fiercely enough by tentative politicians and governments.

Such celebratory epochal accounts are mirrored in more critical analyses of the global 'roll back' of publicness under pressure from political and economic forces committed to expanding the scope of the market and the power of corporate capital. Recently, this has been predominantly theorised as the spread of neo-liberalism. However, this simple term has been the focus of intense development and it may be worth distinguishing three different approaches to the term (for more extended discussions, see Barnett, 2007a; Clarke, 2008; Larner, 2000). The first of these centres on political economy and treats neo-liberalism as the political and ideological project of a capitalist class seeking to break constraints on its power and creating new conditions of capital accumulation (see, for example, Harvey, 2005). The second takes a more regulationist view of the forms of capitalism and emphasises the role of states in creating the societal conditions of capital accumulation (e.g., Peck, 2001; Peck and Tickell, 2002). Where the first has tended to stress the anti-statism of neo-liberalism, the second distinguishes more between the 'roll back' rhetoric and early politics of neo-liberalism and its later 'roll out phase' in which states are re-tooled as means of extending possibilities for capital accumulation (Peck and Tickell, 2002; see also Hartmann, 2005).

The third approach to neo-liberalism derives from Foucault's work on governmentality rather than from Marxist political economy, and points to the processes of economising social and political realms, subjecting them to economic logics and constructing people as economic subjects – buyers, sellers, consumers, entrepreneurs and so on. Such processes form part of liberal governmentality's construction of 'governing at a distance' in which subjects are invited to regulate themselves rather than being directed, forced or coerced (see, for example, Brown, 2005; Rose, 1999). This is a perspective that we have found helpful in thinking about the de-centring of the state (e.g., Cooper, 1998; Dean, 1999, 2007; Petersen et al., 1999; McDonald and Marston, 2006). It has helped shape our approach to the remaking of publics and publicness, enabling us to highlight multiple reworkings of power rather than focusing exclusively on the dynamic intersections of states and market; and bringing gender and other lines of social differentiation into view.

For the moment, though, we need to establish a degree of sceptical distance between ourselves and these diverse accounts of the present as neo-liberal. Despite their many differences, they share two features that trouble us. First, they tend to have an overly integrated or coherent account of neo-liberalism as a project, ideology or governmentality. Everything in the present – or at least everything that matters – turns out to be an effect of neo-liberalism, making neo-liberalism seem both omnipresent and omnipotent (Clarke, 2008). As we have indicated, we see the present as formed by more heterogeneous currents, forces, tendencies and possibilities than can be accounted for by a singular motive force. Secondly, we fear that the attention to grand designs – whether class project or new governmentality – tends to presume that such designs are effective. On the contrary, we think it may be important to look at how grand designs get translated into politics, policies and practices. In such processes we may begin to see the contradictory and antagonistic effects of different social forces, different problems to be overcome or accommodated, different national or local contexts that bend strategies into new forms – and even divergent projects that steal ideas, images, languages and techniques and put them to other uses.

In this book we use several concepts to analyse the multiplicity of forces, projects, discourses and possibilities associated with remarking publicness. We have already indicated the importance of *articulation* as a central feature of political work – the hard labour of assembling a political project, creating both its direction, its relationship to the field of discourses and its ability to mobilise social groups in support of it (while marginalising or de-mobilising other discourses and other groups). We have also found the concept of *assemblage* helpful in thinking about these ambiguous spaces in which diverse elements may be mobilised, combined and made effective – or not (Latour, 2005; Li, 2007a; Ong, 2006; Ong and Collier, 2005). For us this points to the practices that bring together multiple sets of ideas, apparatuses, personnel and practices into apparently coherent entities that function as ways of governing. Sharma, writing about empowerment as a vital assemblage in the attempted reconfiguration of relations between government and people in India, defines assemblage as 'an evolving formation and flexible technology of government that potentially encompasses different meanings and methods, rather than a singularly coherent discourse and method' (2008 ms: 35). She argues that dominant ideas and hierarchies are contested; maintaining them requires work, and such work entails assembling features of hegemonic and counter hegemonic ideas and practices into new ensembles:

> The story I tell is not so much about hegemonic development but one about counter hegemonic moves and ruptures; it underscores the point that the process of maintaining the hegemony of dominant development ideas and hierarchies is bitterly contested and so requires an enormous amount of work. My point is not to replace a critical narrative ... with a celebratory one, but to tease out ethnographically the tensions, contradictions, the suppressions and indeed the enabling possibilities that ideas and practices of development engender on the ground. (Sharma ms: 12)

We share this orientation to the incomplete and contested character of dominant or hegemonic projects and practices. Assemblage offers some conceptual leverage by pointing to both the work of assembling (the building of assemblages) and their vulnerability to coming apart (under the strain of maintaining their internal connectedness and under pressure from counter-movements).

We want to suggest how emergent sites and spaces may themselves constitute new spaces of public action, producing contradictions, tensions and ambiguities. There is a growing literature about the ambiguities of new governing technologies. Some highlights the processes of constitution and incorporation associated with strategies directed towards the 'empowerment' of civil society actors, citizens and service users (Cruikshank, 1999; Elyachar, 2002, 2005; Sharma, 2008). Other literature highlights the ambiguities and instabilities associated with 'partnerships' (Andersen, 2008; Balloch and Taylor, 2001; Glendinning et al., 2002; Sullivan and Skelcher, 2002) or with the expansion of 'public participation' in the design and delivery of services or the governance of communities (Barnes et al., 2007; Cornwall and Coehlo, 2007; McKee and Cooper, 2007). Researchers examining the micro-politics of such encounters have tried to make visible the double dynamics of such spaces, bringing counter hegemonic perspectives to voice and action alongside their capacity for incorporation, deflection and silencing.

Such ambiguities bring to attention the work of social actors – publics, professionals, social entrepreneurs, managers, policy-makers, civil society organisations and many others – as mediators and translators of change. Processes of translation denote the creative and dynamic ways in which actors seek out, interpret and enrol ideas in new settings. Even where changes are experienced as imposed 'from above', actors have to find ways of translating them that are more or less congruent with 'local' contexts. Translation, then, forms a valuable counter to notions of the diffusion of ideas, usually assumed to be outward from a single source of Anglo-American New Public Management or neo-liberalism (see also Ong, 2006, who uses the term 'assemblage' to discuss such processes in relation to the mobility and flexibility of neo-liberal governmentality). Attention shifts to the local settings in which ideas are received, translated, mediated and adapted into new practices (e.g., Czarniawska-Jeorges and Sevón, 1996; Czarniawska and Sevón, 2005a; Hansen and Salskov-Iversen, 2005, 2007; Lendvai, 2005; Lendvai and Stubbs, 2007; Sahlin-Andersson and Engwall, 2002; Salskov-Iversen et al., 2000).

But as well as translating ideas across cultural, linguistic and national boundaries, translation also helps us to think about the active work of construction that goes on in what is usually described as the movement from policy-making to implementation. Rather than policy descending from its strategic conception to its execution by 'front line practitioners', the idea of translation requires us to consider how it is multiply re-interpreted, re-inflected and re-assembled in specific settings as it moves from central government to local governments or provider organisations, or from the realm of senior managers to the offices, wards and stations where it is practised. Each of these is shaped by the 'text' from the preceding stage, but that text comes to be worked upon, brought to life, suffused with meaning in specific local conditions. Lendvai and Stubbs' work on policy as translation links these questions of place and level. They argue

> The multiplicity of languages, representations, claims, and norms in the transnational social policy space raises important questions around translation practices. ... . We have argued that policy transfers are complex cultural, political and social practices, and as such, are far from mechanistic, top-down, and exclusively formal processes. Instead critical issues of distortions, displacement, negotiations and as a result transformation need to be addressed. Translation practices are always plural and multiple, and since our vignettes are as much about puzzling as about domination and resistance, we contest the complete closure that grand narratives of neo-liberal hegemony often seems to suggest. The trope of translation is to emphasise the alternatives, and processes of re-transcription, which produces very

diverse stories and voices in policy processes. Translation is also a dynamic framework to capture the fluidity of policy processes, with an emphasis on the constantly (re)-construction of issues, discourses, and actor networks, as a part of real human agency. (2007: 188–9)

Translation, then, is a critical term for helping us to explore what happens as actors engage in the processes of working with the ambiguities associated with new and emerging assemblages. We make extensive use of it in the work that follows, not least because, as Lendvai and Stubbs indicate, attention to translation can return us to central concerns with politics and power.

Politics and power

Politics and power are both critically important terms, but neither of them is exactly simple. If we turn first to the question of politics, there are at least five aspects that we need to distinguish in thinking about the significance of politics for changing publicness. The first is the view that 'everything is political'. This is a basis tenet of much critical social science and it is one that we share. The claim that everything is political establishes an orientation to contestation and conflict: all issues and aspects of social life are political in the sense that they are open to contestation, to divergent or conflicting perspectives. It is also a claim that everything is political in terms of being consequential for how people live together – involving arrangements of power, material and symbolic and inequalities, and forms of social relationship (affinities and antagonisms).

The second, by contrast, takes a narrower view of politics, treating it as what we might call 'institutional politics': the apparatuses and practices of representation, rule and government. Although there are clearly different forms of politics in this sense – from dictators or one party states through to different forms of multi-party electoral system – this is a view of politics as a limited set of activities associated with processes of governing and with state institutions. Politics in this sense involve politicians and their diverse means of relating to their populations.

The third aspect is closely and perversely linked to this narrower sense of politics as the process of government. This is a view of politics as fundamentally 'dirty': a set of unpleasant processes and people. This view of politics constructs a degree of sceptical distance from these processes and ordinary people, often based on a cynical view that 'They would do anything to stay in power'. Politics is 'dirty' because it involves cynical calculation, instrumental manipulation, spin and corruption. Given many of the practices of actually existing politics, such cynicism or scepticism is hardly surprising. However, this view often exists in tension with desires or aspirations that politics should 'make a difference' – either in the claim that 'they should do something' or that 'things could be different'.

Fourthly, we need to consider what takes place between aspects 1 and 2 above: the relationship between the view that everything is political and the confines of institutional politics. In this book, we will be suggesting that the two are linked – or mediated – by *political projects* (Dagnino, 2007). These are more than political parties, involving more or less coherent efforts to bring ideas, interests, people and power together. Such projects seek to remake the world (or part of it) in a different way: to give power to the people; to concentrate it in the hands of a deserving elite; to create social justice or to spread market efficiency. Political projects may involve parties, changing them to make them carriers of the vision or mission (e.g., the Thatcherite transformation of the Conservative Party in the 1970s) or even creating new ones to build new alliances or engage new political subjects. But political projects may also transcend party allegiances: for example, the project of turning unemployed citizens into active labour market participants is not confined to one party, nor indeed to one country. Finally, political projects do not just involve politicians: they are elaborated in and carried through by groupings of policy actors that transcend the administrative/political boundary, and that enrol the energies and resources of public service managers, civil society groups, non-governmental organisations (NGOs), local authorities, think tanks, academics, private sector stakeholders and many others.

Fifthly, and finally, we need to address the question of how things become seen or recognised as political. This is itself the result of political struggles. To insist that something – the decision to close a hospital, for example – is political is to make it contestable and to insist that it is open to different points of view, or to arguments about value. This perspective is reflected in its obverse: there are many strategies for trying to 'take things out of politics', or to take the 'politics out of things'. This is the process of de-politicisation which

> involves construing inequality, subordination, marginalization and social conflict, which all require political analysis and political solutions, as personal and individual, on the one hand, or as natural, religious or cultural on the other ... . Although depoliticisation sometimes personalizes, sometimes culturalizes, and sometimes naturalizes conflict, these tactical variations are tethered to a common mechanics, which is what makes it possible to speak of depoliticisation as a coherent phenomenon. Depoliticisation involves removing a political phenomenon from comprehension of its *historical* emergence and from a recognition of the *powers* that produce and contour it. No matter its particular form and mechanics, depoliticisation always eschews power and history in the representation of its subject. (Brown, 2006: 15; emphasis in original)

Power here refers to two interrelated aspects of social relations and political processes. The first involves the 'powers that produce and contour' a phenomenon of inequality, subordination, marginalisation or social conflict. The second involves the power to shape the meaning of representation of this phenomenon: the power to depoliticise it, to insist on its individual, natural, religious or cultural character. These are critical issues for this book because we will come across diverse attempts to depoliticise public issues, publics and publicness. We will also encounter many attempts to reassert their political character – to politicise or repoliticise issues. In the process we will be attentive to how power is at work in remaking publicness – what sorts of power, producing what sorts of effects, enabling what sorts of agents?

In doing so, we have to consider power and 'its disguises' (Gledhill, 2000) in very different forms. Let us take as an example the current enthusiasm for empowerment. Reformers constantly seek to empower people in many roles: as 'front line staff' in public services or as their consumers, as 'expert patients' or self-directing service users, as communities invited to take charge of their regeneration or safety, as would-be workers acquiring new skills and capacities or as participants in public planning processes. Such views see power as an easily transferable object; giving 'power to the people' (rather than states or their agents) is a principle that might unite many different political orientations. Others might view this enthusiasm for empowerment in different ways. Those oriented to a more political economic view of power as rooted in the exploitative relations between labour and capital might well take a more sceptical view of empowerment, treating it as merely rhetorical or as an ideological smokescreen that conceals real power-plays. Empowerment – especially through choice or consumerist innovations – conceals real movements of economic and political power to capital, not least through the process of accumulation by dispossession involved in the privatisation of public resources (Harvey, 2005). But it might also conceal the greater role of business or the 'business community' in the processes and networks of social and public policy (Farnsworth, 2004; Ball, 2007).

Alternatively, govermentality scholars might view such empowering moves as part of the process of constructing self-regulating subjects who are part of the move to 'governing at a distance' characteristic of neo-liberal or advanced liberal governmentality (Rose, 1999; Cruikshank, 1999; Maasen and Sutter, 2007). Here power is embedded in the field of relations between authorities and subjects with subjects being 'empowered' to govern themselves (in approved ways). Such subjects may be calculating (the prudential selves who manage risks, insurance and investments); entrepreneurial (producing value through putting resources – including themselves – to work); participative (reflecting on the public good and how it might be achieved); competitive (learning the 'skills' and 'rules' of many different life games) or self managing (acquiring the skills and confidence necessary to care for oneself and others). In all these ways, people are both 'set free' and 'empowered' to act on their own behalf (rather than being 'dependent'). Such empowerment is both more governmental and more conditional than its enthusiasts could contemplate.

Our own orientation to articulation and assemblage directs us to three other aspects of empowerment. One addresses the different ideas, projects and commitments that might be captured or enrolled into the politics of empowerment: to whom does it speak? More accurately, who finds that it 'speaks their language' in translating them into a governmental project? As we hinted above, empowerment is a strategy that calls on diverse histories and politics (Sharma, 2008). A second aspect suggests that 'empowerment' might take significantly different forms in different sites – as specific sets of forces, orientations and demands mobilise, coalesce and contest. Empowerment, in our view, cannot have any single pre-given political character or birthmark because the conditions of its enactment vary. Thirdly, we think it may be difficult to read off the consequences of empowerment from its dominant political tendency. Strategies are not the same as results and programmes of empowerment may fail to produce their intended effects. People may listen beyond rhetoric or see through smokescreens; they may be doubtful or sceptical about the blessings being offered in the act of empowerment; or they may take power all too seriously and begin to act in ways that go beyond the polite constraints of empowerment. Taken together, these define the problems and possibilities of looking for politics and power in the remaking of publicness.

This points us back to the question of assemblage. Empowerment – as rhetorical device, as governmental strategy, as principled commitment – moves from the abstract to the concrete by being enacted in specific assemblages: from community regeneration to parental choice of schools; from being co-producers of services to participating in citizens' juries. Assemblages bring together people (as specific sorts of agents), policies, discourses, texts, technologies and techniques, sites or locations, forms of power or authority, as if they form an integrated and coherent whole that will deliver the imagined or desired outcomes. Li argues that assemblage involves six distinctive practices:

- *Forging alignments*: the work of linking together the objectives of the various parties to an assemblage, both those who aspire to govern conduct and those whose conduct is to be conducted.
- *Rendering technical*: extracting from the messiness of the social world, with all the processes that run through it, a set of relations that can be formulated as a diagram in which problem (a) plus intervention (b) will produce (c), a beneficial result.
- *Authorizing knowledge*: specifying the requisite body of knowledge; confirming enabling assumptions; containing critiques.
- *Managing failures and contradictions*: presenting failure as the outcome of rectifiable deficiencies; smoothing out contradictions so that they seem superficial rather than fundamental; devising compromises.
- *Anti-politics*: reposing political questions as matters of technique; closing down debate about how and what to govern and the distributive effects

  of particular arrangements by reference to expertise; encouraging citizens to engage in debate while limiting the agenda.
- *Reassembling*: grafting on new elements and reworking old ones; deploying existing discourses to new ends; transposing the meanings of key terms. (Li, 2007a: 265)

 Each of these involves work that is clearly political: changing meanings, containing (managing) critiques, legitimising certain forms of knowledge and so on. Each is implicated in the production of some forms of power and the de-legitimisation of others; and the empowerment of some actors and the marginalisation of others in the process of forging new alignments. As we argued earlier, even the work of making some things technical rather than political is political work. We might add 'technical' to Brown's list of individual, natural and cultural as a device that de-politicises by obscuring the historical routes and powers at stake in forming the present issue. One recent example is the prevalence of 'what works' as an assemblage of forms of expertise, authority and policy technologies (standards, targets, funding mechanisms and many others). Such assemblages may be incomplete – there may be professional disagreements about what works, organisations may interpret policy guidance in terms of local understandings of context, technologies may fail and produce unintended – and unfortunate – consequences, and so on. But the rationality of what works is one that takes the politics out of public policy issues by rendering them not the site of contestation over competing values, or between different interests, but making them instead the focus of technical judgements about the efficiency or efficacy of different solutions. Not only does this render them non-political, it also detaches them from the contexts in which particular solutions were developed (a precondition for the 'policy transfer' model of translation). And it privileges a particular form of authority – the technical or scientific expert. Increasingly, such forms of authority are being challenged by perspectives which claim that ordinary people should be entitled to voices and views. In some public services, users operate as 'experts' – being either 'experts of their own condition' (as disabled peoples movements insisted) or bringing to bear the experience of being a user of the service, inhabitant of the locality, or member of a community. There are multiple forms of authority involved in the world of public services, and we will encounter many of them (and the conflicts between them) in the course of the book.

Conclusion: Decline and proliferation?

We end this chapter by returning to the puzzle with which we began: how to account for concurrent processes of the decline and proliferation of publics and forms of publicness. Narratives of both decline and proliferation tend to be based on a series of binary distinctions – states and markets, state and civil

society, citizens and consumers, public and private, empowerment and incorporation, care and control, expert and 'lay' actors, and many more. Each of these,
we think, tends to occlude, rather than illuminate, the dynamics of change with
which we are concerned in this book. Not only do we want to transcend these
binaries, but we also want to avoid recent attempts to collapse them in rather
unstable new formations – the public–private partnership, the citizen-consumer,
the partnership between state and civil society, the process of 'co-production'
and so on. In subsequent chapters we will be trying to show how the three key
concepts – articulation, assemblage and ambiguity – can be put to work in
addressing these new formations of publicness, showing not only the multiplicity of places and sites in which its meanings and practices are being reworked,
but also the different forms of power, authority and agency that are assembled,
and their potentially ambiguous outcomes.

   This attention to the process of assembly suggests the incompleteness of political projects. Such projects may be based on technologies, practices, agents and
forms of authority that may not be coherent – or that may fail to cohere because
of contradictions within the political project itself. But even it they are coherent
in intention, they have to be mediated, interpreted and translated. The spaces of
assembly, then, tend to be ambiguous spaces where the outcomes cannot necessarily be anticipated in advance. This does not, of course, dissolve questions
of power – as we will see in later chapters, elements of a particular assemblage
are likely be structured in dominance – but it does highlight the need to transcend grand narratives of decline (the story of neo-liberal triumph) or the proliferation of emergent spaces of publicness and public action (the 'progressive'
story). Our aim is to highlight the range of political debates and struggles with
which the remaking of publics and publicness is being conducted, and to argue
for a positive – and public – engagement with them.

2 Re-assembling the nation: difference, diversity and 'the people'

In this chapter we turn to the first of the discursive chains of connection in which publicness was institutionalised – the articulation of public, people and nation. This chain of connection once located publics as national publics, sharing a common territory, culture and polity. Nations, however, have been the focus for profoundly unsettling dynamics that have called into question their unity and capacities. As a result, nations are 'not what they used to be' – though, as we shall see, there are doubts about whether they ever were.

We highlight several dynamics associated with the changing fortunes of the nation, all intimately related to questions of national publicness. We begin by assessing the work of public institutions in building – and recomposing – the idea of nationhood and national unity. We then explore the unsettling of 'multi-culturalism' as a way of reconciling and accommodating difference. As societies begin to ponder the question of 'multi' populations (multi-ethnic, multi-cultural, multi-faith, etc.), so questions of how to produce accommodation, integration or cohesion have risen up the agenda of public and political anxiety. In exploring these issues we turn a sceptical eye on 'old' assumptions about unified and solidaristic publics, remembering that these were themselves differentiated and differentiating – and that those differences were the focus of social and political conflicts. We then turn our attention to the changing spaces and scales through which nations are being governed, with a particular interest in how new 'spaces of publicness' are being invented and assembled: regions, localities, communities and neighbourhoods, for example. These changing spaces and scales produce shifts through which the public is being enrolled into governing and form a critical part of how nations are being decomposed and reassembled.

Not what they used to be? Recomposing national publics

The model of the nation-state that dominated academic and popular thought during the twentieth century treated nations as territorially bounded spaces in which people share a common identity, culture and institutions (Gupta and Ferguson, 1992; Clarke, 2004a; Clarke and Fink, 2008). As Calhoun notes,

> It is only as nationalist discourse becomes institutionalised in a public sphere that 'nation' or 'people' are constituted as such. Thus nationalist rhetoric

> shapes the internal discourse of nearly every state … it operates to constitute the nation (the public, the people) as a putative actor – the claimant to ultimate sovereignty – in relation to the state (Calhoun 1997: 91).

Often, this identity has been racialised, mobilising ideas of a common stock, shared lineage or nation-as-race. Such ideas have dominated European thinking about nations and, through the relations of colonial governance, have circulated well beyond the European region. Images of national identities as a matter of racial/ethnic homogeneity have shaped approaches to nation building, from attempts to build a common language and culture to processes of forced expulsion and murder of specific minorities. Heterogeneous cultural, linguistic and religious populations have been brought together, usually involving efforts to suppress or accommodate difference. From this viewpoint, hardly anywhere in what is usually taken to be the core of Europe looks like a stable and unified 'nation' – whether we consider linguistically fractured Belgium; the persistence of linguistic and cultural difference (and separateness) along the borders between France and Spain; the continuing presence of nomadic indigenous people in Northern Scandinavia; or the intermediary German speaking spaces at the edges of Eastern France and Northern Italy. If we turn to the 'United' Kingdom, its unification required wars and internal colonialism; separatist political, linguistic and cultural movements have persisted in insisting on its internal differentiation; and its borders – like most other nations – have long been traversed by flows of migrants, itinerants, refugees and colonial subjects. The imagined 'homogeneity' of nations has demanded varieties of repression: military, political, cultural and psychic. The repression of the knowledge of difference remains a powerful and disturbing force in contemporary debates about diversity and solidarity (Gilroy, 2005).

Treating the conception of national unity as the outcome of political and governing processes points directly to the work that public institutions have done in creating national publics. Mass education systems, investment in health care to develop healthier populations, family policies to manage generational reproduction and expansion, national systems of law and policing, all contributed to the development of distinctive and unifying national public institutions and public cultures. In many European nations, the rise of such institutions was interwoven with their colonial relations. Colonial rule both contributed substantially to the costs of nation-building and shaped the character of national identities (and their visions of superiority/dominance). For example, 'Britishness' was forged out of internal and external relations of domination that contributed to conceptions of public governance and produced cultural objects and practices that came to embody a 'British way of life' (see, *inter alia*, Hall, 2002; MacPhee and Poddar, 2007; Morley and Robins, 2001; Ware, 2007).

However such processes of nation formation tend to be omitted or forgotten in current concerns about nationhood and cohesion in a globalising world.

The globalisation thesis has been the focus of sustained critiques that have prob-lematised the idea that globalisation is something that happens 'outside' the nation-state; the argument that it is something that is 'rolled out' from a single geographical centre; and the claim that states are relatively powerless to resist its imperatives (e.g., Clarke, 2003; Deacon, 2007; Hay, 1998; Jordan, 2006a; Sharma and Gupta, 2006; Yeates, 2001). Although the concept is now much discredited in academic terms, it retains a vigorous presence in governmental discourse as a way of framing and explaining state initiated restructuring pro-grammes; and as a means of encouraging public services – and publics – to transform themselves to succeed in the new global order. The following vignette (boxed text) provides one example of this process of re-assembling the nation.

Vignette: re-assembling the nation

In 2006 the Danish Government produced, after extended deliberation and con-sultation led by a Globalisation Council, a position paper titled *Progress, Innovation and Cohesion: Strategy for Denmark in the Global Economy*. The sum-mary paper (Danish Globalisation Council, 2006) begins with the challenges to the nation produced by globalisation, but does so not in the language of threat and potential decline but in terms of pride in Danish competitiveness, Danish prosperity and Danish social values and social cohesion. There is a clear sense of the Danish people as a cohesive unity with strong solidarities. The message is that it is necessary to transform the nation in order to retain these strengths: to change in order to stay the same. The report contains 350 proposals directed towards a series of objectives:

- Denmark must have strong competitiveness power, in order to be among the wealthiest countries in the world.
- Denmark must have strong cohesion, in order to continue to have an inclusive society without major divisions.
- Denmark must aspire to world class education.
- Denmark must be a top performing knowledge society.
- Denmark must be a top performing entrepreneurial society.
- Denmark must be a top performing innovative society.

Three features of this document are particularly significant in the context of this chapter. First, it has two primary objectives – competitiveness and cohesion – rather than one. Denmark is a 'small society' in which strong cohesion has tended to be taken for granted. But this is viewed as being under threat from recent patterns of inward migration, producing a new awareness of race, ethnic-ity and religion as dividing forces. This, in turn, has led to the rise of political parties of the right, challenging norms of openness, tolerance and inclusion that previously characterised Danish perceptions of their 'national culture'. Second, public services – and the state itself – are not necessarily residualised in the search for global competitiveness: indeed the document sets out plans for the growth of public research and education facilities in order to build the 'knowledge economy'. The strategy itself was produced by – and is to be delivered by – a partnership of public and private sector bodies developed and led by government; and the public sector is to play a key role in delivering change. However, alongside this expansion of public finance and public investment, there is to be more emphasis on competition within the public sector, with 'all suitable functions and services' being put out to competitive tender and more emphasis on the development of public/private partnerships (p. 28). Third, it is not only institutions that have to change – the public itself becomes the object of strategies of transformation:

> The Globalisation Strategy is complemented by a comprehensive reform programme aiming at more active years through faster completion of education, later retirement and a strengthened labour market policy, and better integration of immigrants... . The task of preparing Denmark for the future cannot be carried out by the Government and Folketinget (Danish Parliament) alone. *Everyone should assume their share of responsibility and be ready to innovate* (2006: 7; our emphasis).

This vignette suggests how projects to reassemble the nation are elaborated in the face of multiple dynamics and condense multiple strategies. They include not only economic repositioning but also a celebration of national character (what it means to be Danish); or attempts to restore 'traditional' national values that have been undermined by forces beyond – and within – the nation. For example, in the 2007 French elections, a local leaflet from the winning UMP announced their commitment to *'travail et mérite, sécurité et respect, justice et équité, famille, responsabilité et confiance'*. This list produces an image of a national future that is to be gained through a liberation of traditional French virtues. Meanwhile the future President Nikolas Sarkozy promised *'La France pour les Francais'* and a clamp down on illegal migration, producing a characteristic articulation of racialised and national identities. Since France does not officially recognise racialised or ethnicised differences, 'France for the French' is an uncontroversial announcement, but it simultaneously speaks to an understanding of the social distinction between the (real) French and their others, a distinction that fuels and fosters profoundly racialised inequalities within France. Within months of taking office, the new French Parliament had passed a law creating the possibility of DNA testing for migrants seeking to enter France under family reunion rules (24 October, 2007).

Similar national restorationist imagery can be found in many other places. Attempts to recompose or re-assemble the national public – what it means to be British or Danish, French or Australian – often combine multiple strategies that may (or may not) sit easily with each other. One might speculate, for example, whether the strategies addressing social cohesion – requiring the fostering of

new lines of solidarity across difference, or a sense of being part of a national community – are compatible with the individualising effects of a more neo-liberal
approach to achieving economic success and the pressures towards creating
more 'open economies' (see the discussion of Finland in Castells and Himenan,
2002). Our argument here is twofold: first, the idea of a national public is being
unsettled by multiple forces rather than a singular process that can be neatly
encapsulated under the title of 'globalisation'; and second, national publics are
being asked to undergo change 'in order to stay the same' – that is, to retain a
sense of national identity, values or international standing.

Our aim here is not to single out France and Denmark; rather it is to point to how
all societies of the global North are engaged by the project of renewing and securing the nation in the face of new transnational flows, and new global possibilities
and threats. All of these take place in the context of politics that are both transnational and national. For example, EU rules on discrimination are increasingly at
issue in national struggles around sexuality as national and/or local
governments (especially those of a Christian conservative character) attempt to
outlaw or repress homosexuality or the 'promotion of homosexuality' (e.g., events
in Lithuania, Poland and Italy in October 2007); while local gay activists strive to
use EU legislation to combat local and national governments' renewal of discrimination. More paradoxically still, some of the Christian conservative political
projects within Europe coincide uncomfortably with core elements of Islamic social
ideology – not least around questions of the family, sexuality and morality (what
Buss and Hermann (2003) describe as an alliance around 'global family values').

The crisis of the nation, then, arises from very diverse processes. Some
are economic – the dynamics of openness and competitiveness associated with
moves towards what is variously described as a new global economy, neo-liberal
globalisation or post-fordist processes of capitalist accumulation (Friedman, 2005;
Harvey, 2005; Jessop, 2002). Others are political, most notably global institutions
such as the World Trade Organisation, World Bank or International Monetary
Fund; supra-national regional bodies like the European Union, the South
American trading bloc, MERCOSUR, or ASEAN, the Association of Southeast
Asian Nations; and sub-national regional or local levels of governance (Brenner,
2004). Finally, some of these dynamics are concerned with the processes of
increased mobility – of industry, capital, commodities, cultures and, of course,
people (Appadurai, 2001; Jameson and Miyoshi, 1998; Castles 2004). But it is
the movement of people that generates the most potent imagery of a crisis of the
nation. This has led to a range of strategies for reconciling difference, not least
through notions of multi-culturalism.

Multi-culturalism and the accommodation of difference

While migration has been the focus of restrictive and exclusive policies in societies of the global North since the 1960s, such policies have been elaborated

alongside attempts to integrate 'minorities' within the national public. Multi-culturalism did not become a universal policy framework (e.g., France's insistence that all citizens of the Republic had no separate or distinct cultural identity), but many countries adopted and adapted variations around the multi-cultural theme (Bennett, 1998; Hage, 2003; Hesse, 2001; Modood, 2005; Triandafyllidou et al., 2006). In many nations it was promoted as a way of accommodating difference, producing new ways of conceptualising the public sphere and public culture (Parekh, 2000a, 2000b), and enabling new voices to be heard and new claims to be made. It challenged mainstream public service practice – based on norms of universalism – but was also supported by many public service professionals concerned to make services more 'relevant' to the diverse needs and experiences of their users or communities. Multi-culturalism, however, attracted a number of critiques. Anti-racist politics challenged the sidelining of 'race' and racial discrimination and the weak, celebratory view of cultural difference (Donald and Rattansi, 1992; Lewis, 2000a). Left and feminist critiques drew attention to the inherent assumption of homogeneity within a particular group:

> such constructions do not allow for internal power conflicts and interest differences within the minority collectivity: conflicts along the lines of class and gender, as well as, for instance, politics and culture. Moreover, they tend to assume collective boundaries which are fixed, static, ahistorical and essentialist, with no space for growth or change (Yuval-Davis, 1999: 118).

Multi-culturalism, then, both acknowledged and flattened difference. It acknowledged it by recognising – and often celebrating – certain sorts of difference (culture as religious traditions and cultural festivals, patterns of dress and comportment, and forms of food and music). But it flattened difference by separating 'cultural difference' from the varieties of economic, political and social inequality that have been organised and distributed through racialised or ethnicised differences. These problems were in large part a result of the attempt to accommodate racialised and ethnicised differences through the concept of culture (Brown, 2006).

Vignette: Australian multiculturalism and 'paranoid nationalism'

Ghassan Hage, writing about multi-culturalism in Australia, draws attention to the multiplicity of its meanings. For example he distinguishes between multi-culturalism as a mode of governing ethnic cultures and multi-culturalism as a national identity. While the former regards ethnic cultures as containable and manageable, having little impact on what was a 'European Australian' mainstream culture, the latter holds out the prospect of 'a new multi-cultural mainstream' (2003: 59). This opened up political cleavages between parts of the population enmeshed in 'White paranoia' and a middle class, cosmopolitan segment who 'wanted to shed the image of Australia as a racist colonial backwater and appear in a more symbolically competitive light in the eyes of nationals of other places' (2003: 61).

Hage also distinguishes between multi-culturalism as social policy and as cultural policy. The former, he argues, only ever had a fragile beginning in the Whitlam government of 1972-5, to be displaced by successive conservative governments 'in order to promote a culturalist version of Australian society ahead of a class one' (2003: 60). He continues:

> Along with the rise of Asian immigration, the greatest taboo of the White Australia policy, it is the movement – within a period of less than ten years – from a descriptive multiculturalism perceived primarily as a form of welfare and of cultural government to a multiculturalism that is more prescriptive and perceived to be primarily about national identity. [This] signalled the re-entering of White Paranoia in both its cultural and racial garbs into the sphere of public debate (2003: 60).

Many processes contributed to what Hage terms the rise of 'paranoid nationalism': worsening economic conditions during the 1980s, the rise of Asian inward migration, the creation of an Australian republic that detached Australian from Britain, and the granting of limited land rights to Indigenous peoples. 'It was this climate of economic uncertainty and reinvigorated internal and external traditional threats that sent White paranoia into external overdrive and laid the foundations for the long era of "debating multiculturalism" that then began' (2003: 62).

In Australia, the UK and elsewhere, multi-culturalism proved to be a rather fragile strategy, even as it was inscribed into official policy and practice. It was rarely endorsed by those who were tolerated within it, and was never accepted by those committed to regressive political orientations. But it was eventually undermined by a combination of social and political transformations that challenged the multi-cultural model of tolerant accommodation. Since the late twentieth century, migration has become an increasingly central political and governmental obsession in the global north. It has been articulated around questions of security; issues of movement control and border management; dilemmas of 'integration'; and in terms of pressure on – or 'swamping' of – public services. Such obsessions resonate with the rise of racially inflected nationalist politics across much of Europe in the late twentieth and early twenty-first centuries to create troubling challenges to both anti-racist and multi-cultural policy and practice (see, for example, West, 2005, in *The Poverty of Multi-Culturalism*, published by the UK right-leaning think tank Civitas). Such challenges centre on the need to bolster national identity (sometimes scaled up to be 'European identity' and 'Western civilisation') by curbing inward migration and rejecting multi-culturalism.

Instead, policies have re-emphasised the assimilation or integration of minorities into the 'mainstream' culture. Triandafyllidou et al. argue that:

> After the relative prominence of multicultural citizenship theoretical debates and multicultural policy developments in the 1990s, we witness today a change of direction. This crisis of multiculturalism comes at a time of heightened security awareness as a result of the events of New York (9/11, 2001), Madrid (14/3, 2004) and most recently in London (7/7 and 21/7, 2005). European citizenship is disorientated, increasingly linking a religion (Islam) with violence and anti-Western values. The upsurge of international terrorism has led to the increasing securitization of migration agendas. Even though suspected terrorists are apparently to be found among the educated, middle-class, legal immigrants – the 'good' kind of immigrants for whom Western societies and economies have been competing for the past decade – the argument of terrorism is now used in the policy debate to justify tougher controls of migration in general. In this context of high security awareness, existing models and policies of immigrant integration and the accommodation of (Muslim) minority claims are questioned. (2006: 1)

They go on to argue that 'receiving' societies are increasingly combining such tougher migration policies with a return to 'assimilationist' policies in place of multi-culturalist approaches to migrant/ethnic minority populations (see also Gingrich and Banks, 2006, on 'neo-nationalism').

Questions about the nation and national security are, then, complexly interwoven with the retreat from multi-culturalism. In 2008 a UK military centred think-tank, the Royal United Services Institute, published an article in its journal claiming that multiculturalism and social fragmentation had weakened national coherence and thus the UK's capacity to defend itself, making it a target for terrorism. It talked of Britain becoming a 'soft touch for terrorism, because it was now a 'fragmenting, post-christian society' with a 'misplaced, deference to multi-culturalism' that undermined the fight against extremists (*The Guardian*, 15. 02. 2008, p 4). Anxieties about terrorism are partly centred on 'homegrown terrorists' – radicalised young Muslims born in the West. Meanwhile, other forms of disturbance have been used to claim that multi-culturalism has failed as a policy for managing difference. Persistent disadvantage for some minority ethnic groups, forms of social and educational *de facto* segregation, growing antagonisms between poor white and minority ethnic groups over increasingly scarce resources (ranging from jobs to social housing) and, not least, the outbreaks of violence ('race riots') in northern English towns in 2002 led a number of liberal commentators to announce the 'death of multi-culturalism' in the UK, while right-wing commentators merely celebrated the fact that they had been right all along. The Cantle Report on the urban 'riots' (2006) argued that multi-culturalism had produced separate communities (each marked by their own culture) which did not mix or integrate, and that what was needed was a new integrative approach to social and community cohesion.

The assault on multi-culturalism heralded the emergence of a new politics of assimilation – expressed in initiatives on community cohesion, citizenship education, language tests for migrants and so on. Assimilationist approaches assume the integrity and coherence of the 'national' culture and demand that migrants make the effort to integrate themselves. Such arguments are supported by a growing literature that poses the problem of whether 'too much diversity' undermines the collective identities and sense of solidarity associated with publicness, and challenges the survival of welfare states. For example, Alesina and Glaeser's work (2004) develops the claim that ethnic (and/or racial) fragmentation undermines public support for the institutions of social welfare; while Putnam (2007) argues that ethnic differentiation produces forms of social retreatism or privatism, such that people withdraw from social life, public space and communal action. Trust – the core of Putnam's view of social capital – is thus undercut by ethnic difference. These arguments have been widely contested, and the applicability of US analysis to European contexts disputed (Banting, 2005; Clarke, 2004b, 2007c; Taylor-Gooby, 2005). We might do better to turn the claims of Putnam and Alesina and Glaeser on their head and argue that 'ethnic diversity' is the metaphor though which the crisis of the national public is being represented – and its power as a metaphor obscures other significant dynamics of change.

Reconciling difference? Faith, diversity and community

The process of reassembling a national public, as we have seen, operates on a tension between unity and diversity – or more accurately, between the persistence of unifying national imaginaries and ways of imagining diversity as a manageable field of difference. The question of difference has recently been reworked around ideas of Faith, such that the diverse 'communities' of the UK become indexed as 'different faith communities'. This shift is shaped by two different social tendencies. The first is the revitalisation of religion as a social forces, both transnationally (patterns of thought and attachment that work across national boundaries) and nationally (forms of social organisation). The second is the process of re-identifying sets of migrant populations previously identified by geographical, cultural and ethnic registers in terms of a faith identity. So people previously marked as Asian, Pakistani, Yemeni, Somali, Turkish and so on have been increasingly 'badged' as Muslims after the Al-Qaeda attacks on the USA and UK. The 'clash of civilizations' forecast by Samuel Huntington (1997) is thus brought to life as the faith binary Christian/Muslim comes to override and obscure other differences and identifications (including other religions).

This tendency is particularly disconcerting in societies of the global north for whom modernisation had been equated with secularisation. The decline of religious affiliation, while resisted by evangelists and fundamentalists of various kinds, was central to the narratives of modernisation and to the spread of liberal public values. For publicness in particular, secularisation has been a critical force. The image of the liberal public realm (and its values of openness, tolerance and equality) assume either the tendential disappearance of religion or its containment within the realm of the private – an individual attachment that is 'left behind' when people engage in the public realm (Brown, 2006). In practice the nations and public realms of the North reveal a more partial, hybrid or compromised set of accommodations between liberal secularism and religion. Varieties of Christianity are more or less explicitly sewn into public life and institutions – from marking religious events as public holidays through to church involvement in public and social policy-making, especially, though not only, around questions of family policy. Religious institutions have also been central to the organisation and provision of public services – particularly as 'provider organisations' in social and health care. US President George W. Bush's (2000) call for the greater involvement of 'faith organisations' in promoting social welfare aimed to extend such entanglements, even while limiting the sorts of 'faiths' that might be recognised as suitable partners.

The emergence of 'faith' as a way of acknowledging diversity, then, raises challenges that echo older problems associated with multi-culturalism – for example the assumption of homogeneity within particular faith communities. But 'faith' also amplifies them where such communities become part of the new landscape of service provision. This reminds us that the notion of 'faith communities', like that of 'minority ethnic groups', does not resolve the problem of diversity but suggests different possible accommodations and attempted reconciliations. Harzig and Juteau (2003) have argued that 'diversity' has emerged as the new 'master narrative' of industrial nations, such that 'diversity' works as a major social, political and cultural motif. Even where multi-culturalism may be 'in retreat', governments and other organisations continue to grapple with the issue – recruiting personnel from 'minority' backgrounds; making organisations 'diversity friendly'; and being subjected to pressures to be 'representative' (especially in the provision of public services such as policing or social work; Lewis, 2000b). Commercial as well as public organisations address the 'business case' for diversity as a route to maximising their 'human capital' and enhancing their public legitimacy. But this suggests that diversity itself has no fixed or permanent meaning – it too may be enrolled in very different political and organisational projects (Cooper, 2004).

In the UK, questions of diversity and difference are also being accommodated – and subordinated – within policies on social inclusion and community cohesion. A report from the Commission on Integration and Cohesion (2007) inspired government action to promote 'cohesive communities'. 'Community' signals an increasingly important set of strategies for managing difference in a post multi-cultural context. Community is both a normative concept (a source of solidarity and belonging, including being part of a national public); a territorial concept (a locality); and a concept that designates a group assumed to share particular characteristics (the 'minority ethnic' community or the 'gay and lesbian' community). This elasticity means that the idea of community has played a central role in the remaking of the nation in the UK. Although the term has a long history (in both colonial and domestic settings), under New Labour it was mobilised as a keyword in strategies for governing the social (Mooney and Neal, 2009). We will examine some of the virtues and problems of community as a site of governing in the following chapter, but here we need to note how its shifting meanings make community a critical link between strategies for managing difference and the rescaling of the nation. Community's place in colonial governance enabled its distinctive role with multi-culturalist and diversity discourses: communities can be formed from racial, ethnic, tribal, cultural or religious identities and attachments. From communal differences in colonial India (Pandey, 2005, 2006) to the 'two communities' of Northern Ireland, such communities of identity are to be governed (tolerated, regulated, directed) by the ruling power. Both multi-culturalist and some diversity discourses mobilise this sense of community. At the same time, the 'new localism' in public governance has made communities as places central to the reworking of the relations between people, nation and state. Devolution and decentralisation have aimed to make local communities more active, more responsible and more self-governing.

Vignette: Community cohesion, social difference and equality struggles

In the UK, the imagery of community cohesion has come to occupy a central role in government discourse and practice. Responding to the Commission on Integration and Cohesion's report, the then Home Secretary announced a major investment in strategies and projects for promoting cohesion, with responsibility devolved to regional and local government. She located the concern with community cohesion in the context of economic, social and cultural challenges associated with globalisation and 'new patterns of migration':

> Britain has a proud tradition of tolerance and different communities living side by side. In addition, migration has always made a tremendous cultural and economic contribution to the country. But whilst this remains the case, we cannot be complacent and must tackle the future challenges head-on...
>
> Our plan includes a comprehensive set of measures to tackle the new issues we face and promote integration and develop strong, resilient communities. It will promote our shared British values like respect for the rule of law, tolerance and fairness. New investment will help spread a stronger sense of civic pride and shared heritage. It also raises to a new level our work direct with local authorities and communities, ensuring they have greater support at a local level in building united communities. (06/09/2007; http://www.communities.gov.uk/news/corporate/500395; accessed 09/08/2008)

As with multi-culturalism, questions of racialised divisions haunt this concern with cohesive communities, not least because the Commission itself was established in the wake of what were defined as 'race riots' in Northern English towns in 2002. Such divisions mutate here into 'different communities living side by side', but as Britain 'grows more diverse' so there is a need to 'develop strong, resilient communities'. Imagining difference in the UK has moved through a sort of sequence – from race relations to black and minority ethnic groups to multi-cultures to communities and to diversity. The current governmental response stresses inclusion, integration and cohesion, to be accomplished through lower levels of government, closer to the places where 'communities' live. For example, the following view of community cohesion is offered by a tier of regional government – the Government Office of the North East:

> A cohesive community is one where:
>
> • there is a common vision and a sense of belonging for all communities;
> • the diversity of people's different backgrounds and circumstances are appreciated and positively valued;
> • those from different backgrounds have similar life opportunities;
> • strong and positive relationships are being developed between people from different backgrounds in the workplace, in schools and within neighbourhoods.
>
> The main purpose of the Community Cohesion agenda is to identify problems within a neighbourhood, to tackle barriers that exist between different groups living in the community, and thus avoid conflict and tension. Community Cohesion aims to promote greater knowledge, respect and contact between various cultures, thus promoting a greater sense of citizenship. ?Cohesion is influenced and affected by local demographic factors such as the ethnic, religious, or geographical make-up of the community. It is important to remember that community cohesion is not simply a race issue. Other factors such as age, disability, religion, gender, equality of opportunities and the distribution of wealth in a community should also be considered as part of the cohesion agenda. (http://www.gos.gov.uk/gone/peopleandsustcomms/community_cohesion/ accessed 14 Nov 2007)

We can see here how the landscape of governing is populated with different sorts of communities and how community is expected to both express and contain difference. 'Cohesive communities' may contain other social groups (marked by different backgrounds, various cultures, etc) who should all have a 'sense of belonging'. But we can also catch what Gail Lewis calls the 'now you see it, now you don't' quality of race in British governmental discourse (Lewis, 2000b).

The rise of community cohesion as a policy objective led to changes in how many local authorities funded community and other 'third sector' organisations. Organisations deemed to be providing 'specialist services' – that is, those offering services for women, for specific black and ethnic minority groups, for lesbian and gay groups and so on – saw their funding withdrawn in favour of organisations offering services to the 'whole community'. This led to a legal challenge by Southall Black Sisters, a group offering services and support to vulnerable women subject to domestic violence, often compounded by immigration and asylum difficulties. Ealing Borough Council, which had previously funded some of the group's work, withdrew its funding in favour of a 'borough wide' domestic violence service. Finding in favour of Southall Black Sisters, the judge hearing the case concluded that 'There is no dichotomy between funding specialist services and cohesion; equality is necessary for cohesion to be achieved' (*The Guardian*, 30.07.2008, p 3; see also www.southallblacksisters.org.uk).

This decision had significant implications for public bodies translating government policies and statements into practice. Many such bodies had followed the government view that separate funding for black-led organisations would undermine cohesion, instead favouring groups open to the 'whole community'. But this meant that they failed, in the eyes of the court in this case, to comply with existing race equality legislation. How diversity, difference and inequalities are imagined and addressed in governmental discourse and policy remains, then, a contested issue.

Community plays many other roles in contemporary policy and practice, from community development projects to images of the nation as a 'community of communities' (Gordon Brown, then Chancellor of the Exchequer, 2000: 5). This growing salience of the idea(l) of community involves the simultaneous identification of community as the normal mode of living (for a civil society); as the object of government enthusiasm (enabling and empowering communities); and as the focus of anxious recognition that some places fail to be communities (or cohesive) and thus need extra help to become normal (see Cochrane and Newman, 2009; and Craig, 2007 on community capacity building).

New sites of publicness? Rescaling the nation

The growing significance of 'community' suggests one way in which spaces of the public within the national territory are being reformed (though often with transnational conditions). In the UK, we have seen the partial devolution of political and administrative powers to the 'nation regions', Scotland, Wales and (Northern) Ireland, producing a multi-national nation (Mooney and Williams, 2007). Transnational institutions (from global capital to the EU) undermine the coherence and closure of national institutions (Jessop, 2002). Supranational governmental institutions and practices, together with transnational flows of people, goods and communication, have disrupted the imagined unity of national publics and their public spaces (Larner and Walters, 2004; Hansen and Salskov-Iversen, 2007). The spaces of public discourse are no longer only national forums, but public opinion circulates across more 'globalised' landscapes (though not without regional and national formations). Different and dispersed publics both traverse and contest national boundaries, formed through attachments to different places, cultures, religions or politics. International and supranational institutions make publicness flow across national boundaries – whether through the transnational corporations providing 'national' public services in health care or transport; or the greater role for both governmental and nongovernmental organisations in shaping publicness beyond the nation (from the European Court of Human Rights to Amnesty International). At the same time, levels of government below the level of the nation state have taken on greater significance in constituting publicness: global or world cities; new forms of regional government; or the politics of decentralisation and revalorisation of the 'local' – the city, community or neighbourhood (Allen et al., 1998, Allen and Cochrane, 2007; Cochrane, 2006; Mooney and Neal, 2009; Sassen, 1998, 2006). As a result, public services from broadcasting to health care have been dislocated by dynamics that simultaneously seem to internationalise or globalise and to localise their institutional formations.

These dynamics led some commentators to talk about the 'hollowing out' of the nation-state (Rhodes, 1994, 1997); however we want to draw attention to the role of the state – and other actors – in bringing into being new spaces and relationships. These spaces are, at least in part, public, but they are organised through new processes and mechanisms (networks, partnerships, or participatory planning). Of course, the national public space always had its internal spatial architecture – its regions, its localities, its cities and towns. In the present, though, we see a proliferation of scales, levels and spaces built around innovative or hybrid forms of connection and governance.

As a result these changing formations of space and scale – often carried through the organisational forms of public services and local government – have been the focus of different accounts. For some, these changes are best understood as a politics of scale, with economic, social and political forces committed to reshaping the organisation of power and governing (Brenner, 2004; Brenner et al., 2003). Such arguments have centred on core political economic transitions – towards post-Fordism or neo-liberalism (Jessop, 2002; Peck, 2001) – and have stressed the double dynamic of scales above and below the nation. In political science, it has become commonplace to refer to the rise of 'multi-level governance', indicating the multiplicity of levels, scales, or tiers of governance bodies or processes that may be nested together and involve differentiated but overlapping (and possibly even integrated) authority over, and claims on, particular governance issues and governable places (Bache and Flinders, 2004; Hooghe and Marks, 2003). There are problems about the concept of levels here – and the view that they are tidily nested within successively larger spatial containers (see, for example, Allen, 2003; Clarke, 2009;

Stubbs, 2005; Ferguson and Gupta, 2002). They are better compared to a Kandinsky painting, with uneven shapes and uncomfortable alignments held in tenuous balance, rather than to a set of Russian dolls, with each scale neatly nested inside a larger one (Newman, 2008).

Rather than focussing on the multi-level character of public governance, we might want to think about the ways in which its multi-ness brings new spaces into being, or makes new framings of space visible. In spatial and social terms, the object of governance (whether a locality or set of economic practices, interests and relationships) is constructed in the process of governing. And through governance arrangements, claims about who has the authority to govern, the foundations of such authority, and the means by which it may be exercised, are also established.

Such a perspective stresses the processes by which entities such as localities, regions and even 'Europe' are assembled through political processes, rather than being a pre-existing site that becomes the focus of new mechanisms of governing (see, for example, Aloreo, 2007; Stubbs, 2005; and Walters, 2004). Allen and Cochrane's work on the constitution of regional tiers of governance in the UK suggests that:

> The sense in which these are 'regional' assemblages, rather than geographically tiered hierarchies of decision-making, lies with the tangle of interactions and capabilities within which power is negotiated and played out ... . There is ... an *interplay* of forces where a range of actors mobilize, enrol, translate, channel, broker and bridge in ways that make different kinds of government possible (2007: 1171; emphasis in original)

We think that this view of the assemblage of regions as spaces to be governed has a strong fit with our orientation to the remaking of publicness in this book. The emphasis on sites as constructed outcomes, rather than having a pre-given character (whether this is their scale, territorial reach, or institutional type), allows a more productive engagement with both the current paradoxical and multiple dynamics of change, and the problems of thinking about their political effects. We can trace some of the complex dynamics involved in the assemblage of new sites of governing in the following vignette:

Vignette: The local control of policing?

In 2008 Sir Ronnie Flanagan (former Chief Constable of the Royal Ulster Constabulary) produced a review of policing in England and Wales for the UK government. One critical objective was to enable a more effective form of 'neighbourhood policing', freed from 'unnecessary bureaucracy' (2008: 2), while attending to the shifting challenges, demands and expectations that

characterise policing as a national service. Refusing a highly specified bureaucratic or managerial conception of how to face such new challenges, the Report
argues instead for 'a flexible, effective way of delivering public protection in the
twenty-first century' and highlights the key reforms that are required to achieve
the simplest – but best – test of success: 'the right people in the right places at
the right times, doing the right things, in partnership, for the public'. (2008: 5)

Questions of local accountability are identified as crucial, both for the neighbourhood policing strategy but also as a foundation of trust and engagement
between public and police. They are further connected to police involvement in
community safety and community cohesion strategies. The Report notes that
'people are most interested in issues at the very local (their own street) level and
in how they are treated. They are not actually so concerned to participate in more
formal accountability mechanisms and structures, although feel that they should
have the opportunity to do so' (2008: 83). However, existing structures of local
accountability are seen as failing to deliver either effective public engagement
(at the very local level) or transparent processes of accountability. The relationship between the public and the police encounters two difficulties as a result:
one involves establishing the right level(s) of engagement and the other concerns the relationship between policing and politics. The Report anguishes about
several proposals, identifying possible benefits and drawbacks. Meanwhile
the possibility of having locally elected chairs of police boards operating below
the current force-wide level of police authorities reveals how the local might be
too local:

> However, as with all solutions that operate below the force-wide area, the
> main danger is fragmentation of policing … . The increased focus at dis-
> trict level may impede police action on issues that require the co-ordina-
> tion across a force (or several forces). (2008: 90)

Alternatively, making policing the business of local authorities would generate
the problem of non-matching boundaries between local authorities and police
forces and raises anxiety about control of resources: would it be necessary to
'ring-fence' policing or community safety money to prevent its diversion to
other purposes (2008: 92)? Finally designing local ('bespoke') systems carries
both organisational and political risks:

> The chief drawback is this introduces yet another structure in a compli-
> cated landscape and one that may not be skilled to deliver what is
> required of it. Such localised arrangements may be captured by specific
> interests and conflict then build with the local police and the police
> authority. It is important that very localised initiatives are more than a
> plethora of meetings that simply sap energy and divert police officers.
> (2008: 94)

The Report comes to no definitive conclusion – except for insisting on the
importance of local engagement, responsiveness and accountability. But these
have to be articulated with the other forms of organisational governance that are
presented as ways of shaping the new model of policing. These include

'customer focused policing', 'citizen focused policing', and, of course, better management and leadership: a performance system (APACS) that focuses much more on key outcomes such as trust and confidence, so to create the space for entrepreneurial and innovative solutions from the leaders of the police service at all levels (2008: 6).

We will return to several of the issues identified in this report – accountability, leadership, governance, for example – in later chapters. Here our focus is on how it exemplifies the complex remaking of both the scales and politics of public services. One effect is, as Newman (2001, 2005b) has argued, that the processes of power, authority and control have become more difficult to track (both politically and analytically). While some point to the 'anti-democratic' tendencies of the decomposition of the nation into new tiers and spheres of governance, others suggest that institutional experimentation also creates new possibilities of political engagement and participation: popular planning, customer consultation, neighbourhood activism, and the mobilisation of different sorts of 'communities' (Holland et al., 2007).

Conclusion: reassembling national publics

Ideas and institutions of publicness have been deeply entwined with nations in at least three vital ways. First, publics have been national publics because the work of nation-building has often involved constructing the imagery of a united people who share a territory, a history, a culture, and an ethnic or racial identity – and who act together as a public (with collective will and a common interest in public goods). Second, the constitution of a *national* public provided both the conditions of democratic political participation and the foundation for collective models of public services. Third, the emphasis on national cohesion and solidarity produced a problematic relationship to questions of difference and diversity. The tension between the construction of a unified national public on the one hand and the recognition of social difference on the other has re-emerged at the core of contemporary debates about the nation and publicness.

In this chapter we have used terms such as 'unsettling', 'decomposition' and 'reassembly' to mark how the nation was always a composed, rather than a natural or pre-given, entity. National boundaries are contested, and only ever temporarily fixed, while images of cultural unity have to be constructed and are easily fractured. That is, national formations of peoples and places are the product of political-cultural work; and their unsettling produces antagonisms and anxieties that are currently the focus of considerable governmental activity. The current unsettling and reassembling of nations is, therefore, one phase in a longer process of national building, dismantling and re-building – involving dynamics of both culture and territory.

The challenges to nation-states as the primary locus of governance have produced not a neat series of 'levels' within and beyond the nation but the construction of new assemblages of power and authority that bring other spaces into view. But this territorial unsettling of the nation takes place alongside, and interwoven with, the political-cultural disruption of the idea of a national public united in a shared lineage, ethnicity or identity. Such ideas of unity were always imagined, produced in the work of nation building and the construction of national settlements that resolved – temporarily and conditionally – potentially conflicting interests and identities. The unsettling of these imaginary unities of nationhood brings questions of difference back into view – especially, but not only, differences of culture, race, ethnicity and faith. Many of the more problematic challenges to notions of publics and publicness derive from this double process of unsettling previous territorial and cultural formations:

- concerns about national security that challenge liberal norms of tolerance and openness, leading to questions about what might be the norms and principles around which a public domain might be sustained;
- concerns about how diversity can be expressed and accommodated 'after' the multi-cultural settlement;
- concerns about how social and community cohesion can be reconciled with the recognition and management of difference.

'Community' has been implicated in the re-mappings of the public that are produced in governmental response to these concerns. It provides a new way of imagining living together that invokes much older – and nostalgic – ways of life based on neighbourliness and local solidarities. It is central to the processes of rescaling we have addressed in this final part of the chapter, part of the re-imagining of places, practices and identities within – and beyond – the nation. But it is also a way of reframing diversity, with 'minority ethnic communities' taking their place alongside other supposed communities, fracturing and displacing the idea of wider public solidarity. The turn to 'community' as a governing strategy both seeks to accommodate diversity while at the same time separating it from the politics that shaped it. Similarly the idea of the nation as a 'community of communities' provides a way of governing difference while at the same time erasing the kinds of difference that might challenge the current politic-cultural project. Community, then, works across the twin dynamics of territorial and political-cultural reshaping of the idea of a national public. This is perhaps why it has taken on such a significant place in new strategies of 'recruiting' the public – a theme explored in the next chapter.

3 Displacing the public: recruiting 'ordinary people'

As we indicated in Chapter 2, the public, nation and state have been closely articulated: publics were constructed as national entities, and were interwoven with the nation-building processes of states. In the development of new forms of governing, however, these connections have been disrupted. In this chapter we focus on three formations that populate new assemblages of the public: community, civil society and the 'third sector' of voluntary, not-for-profit and non-governmental organisations. We stress 'populate' because each of them involves the recruitment of 'ordinary people' to processes, relationships and practices of governing. The three sites overlap in important ways, not least because they are all, in part, defined by their non-stateness. Indeed, we argue that these formations serve to displace the public from past territorial, institutional, and cultural associations with the nation-state. However, the question of their relationships with the state remains a critical issue.

The involvement of these three sites in new processes of governing can be read as evidence of the retreat or decline of the state. For example, they can be seen as part of the shift towards *governance*, in which governing takes place through markets, networks or processes of collaboration among a plurality of agents and agencies (see, for example, Kooiman, 1993; Rhodes, 1997; Pierre, 2000 and the discussions in Daly, 2002; Newman, 2001 and 2005; Walters, 2004). Alternately, the growing interset in *governmentality* also points to a displacement or decentring of the state, making visible the proliferation of sites and practices of governing, and linking the micropolitics of such practices to the larger mentalities or conceptions of rule (see, for instance, Dean, 1999 and 2007; Petersen et al, 1999; Rose, 1999; Stenson 2008). But both of these developments still leave open some questions about the state – about its role in meta-governance (e.g., Jessop, 2000); about the relationship between states and NGOs (Sharma, 2006; Sharma and Gupta, 2006); and about the relationship between political projects and governmental practices (e.g., Brown, 2005; Kingfisher, 2002; Larner, 2000). Elsewhere we have argued for using the more agnostic idea of 'governing' – and the conception of 'governing the social' – as a way of approaching these questions raised by the decentring of the state (and the dislocation of the nation: e.g., Clarke, 2004a, 2007a; Cooper, 1998; Newman, 2001). These questions will be a focus of continuing concern for the book.

Here, though, we focus on these three specific sites, exploring the growing enthusiasm for governing though community, civil society and the third sector or NGOs. These three sites all have specific genealogies, but what links them now is the way in which they have been inscribed in new assemblages of power. As we saw in Chapter 2, community is a concept that bridges spatial and political-cultural processes of reassembling the nation; it also encompasses a variety of material and symbolic resources on which political and governmental projects attempt to draw in recomposing the public. Civil society condenses multiple political projects and brings into view different conceptions of what it might mean to act publicly beyond the state. The 'third sector' includes a plurality of organisational types and forms, from the community group to the large voluntary sector organisation, charity or non-governmental agency, all seen as repositories of social, moral or cultural resources. Each has become valued as a site where people can govern, provision and manage themselves beyond the structures of state systems. As a result we will be paying rather more attention to how these sites are identified, valorised and recruited in the process of governing than to their diverse political and historical roots. Each is an object of desire, representing important moral, social or civic virtues that are assumed to be valuable or productive. Each is deeply implicated in strategies for state reform: viewed as alternatives to state services, as ways of mediating state projects, and as ways of drawing on resources beyond the state. They are all assumed to contain subjects – 'ordinary people' – who can be summoned as partners or participants in new assemblages of power.

However, each has been associated with forms of politics of the public that make them ambiguous and potentially difficult 'partners' of government. All three formations are sites of counterpublic mobilisation. Nancy Fraser defined 'subaltern counterpublics' as 'parallel discursive arenas where members of subordinated social groups invent and circulate counter discourses to formulate oppositional interpretations of their identities, interests and needs' (1997: 81). These are, then, not the 'general public' – indeed they are signficant precisely because a single, comprehensive, overarching public arena fails to accommodate different identities, interests and needs, leading to the formation of oppositional forms of identity and practice. Fraser's analysis drew on diverse examples of 'subordinated social groups': the women's movement, anti-racist struggles, gay and lesbian movements and others. In different contexts, such counterpublics have appeared as civil society based movements (challenging forms of state power); as communities of identity and interest; and as self-organising voluntary or non-governmental organisations (providing for distinctive health or care needs, for example).

As a result, all three sites have been characterised by highly diverse social, political and cultural projects. Anti-racist or anti-colonial struggles operate in the same domains as regressive nationalisms or the nostalgia for mono-cultural communities. Social movement challenges to oppression share the terrain of civil society with religious/faith-based movements, including those re-asserting family values, heteronormativity and the subordination of women. Organisations seeking transformative politics (around inequalities and oppressions) encounter 'restorationist' movements trying to turn back the perceived victories of earlier struggles (e.g., of gender, racial or sexual 'equality'), as well as emergent publics reacting against perceived liberal-cosmopolitan elites who, in the UK at least, are viewed as having captured public institutions from the BBC to the civil service.

So, why do these three sites – with their turbulent political inheritances – now appear as the desired and desirable partners in new approaches to governing? In part, answering this puzzle means paying attention to the ambivalent relationship between each of the sites and politics. Civil society is both the site of association and mobilisation against the state; and a domain of free association that is understood as different – and separate – from the state, politics and government. Community is both a way of claiming collective identity as the basis of mobilisation and action and a domain of imagined organic, harmonious, social (not political) relationships. Finally, voluntary organisations may be either collective mobilisations by counterpublics or philanthropic, charitable provisions. In the recruitment of each of these sites to new assemblages of governing, it is their second aspect – the organic, harmonious, non-political qualities – that is emphasised. They represent ways in which ordinary people are expected to do good things.

These ordinary people are, however, gendered, classed and racialised. Fraser argues that the nineteenth century formation of the bourgeois public sphere in France, England and Germany was nourished by a 'civil society' of voluntary associations: 'But this network of clubs and associations – philanthropic, civic, professional and cultural – was anything but accessible to everyone. On the contrary, it was the arena, the training ground, and eventually the power base of a stratum of bourgeois men, who were coming to see themselves as a 'universal class' and preparing to assert their fitness to govern' (1997: 73). In contrast it tends to be women who are targeted in contemporary 'empowerment' initiatives that view civil society as the locus of development (Sharma, 2008). Women have traditionally formed the primary source of informal labour and volunteer work, though they may be less strongly represented in the new managerial cadres produced by the professionalisation of the voluntary sector. And voluntary work, community engagement and civil society association are implicated in the gendered formation of the 'social capital' much sought after by governments and development agencies (O'Neill and Gidengil, 2005). There are tensions between the gender dynamics of community and civil society formed through mundane acts of neighbourliness, informal care and attention to the building and nurturing of relationships, and other forms of 'active citizenship' based on labour market participation (Newman, 2005c). Similarly there are tensions in the UK between the focus on recruiting black and minority ethnic groups to government projects and the increased scapegoating of 'Muslim' communities in political speeches and popular media. The emerging forms of governing that we address in this chapter are, then, traversed by the complex – and contradictory – dynamics of difference highlighted in Chapter 2.

Finally, these three formations connect developments in the North and the South, or in the developed and developing world. They certainly take different forms: community governance in the UK may not be the same as micro-credit schemes for enterprising nations in the South. Civil society has a very different place in the South, where it is understood as a resource for 'development', from the 'transition' countries of central and eastern Europe, where a discourse of civil society came to frame and direct the action of the democratic opposition to the former communist regime (Mastnak, 2005). But the threads that connect them are worth exploring, not least because studies of community, social enterprise, and the 'third sector' in the North are rarely cross-referenced to critical studies of NGOs, development and empowerment in the South. In part, such exchanges do not take place because of their location (the North being understood as modern; the South as 'developing'); in part because of how they are framed (governance innovation versus empowerment); and partly because the terms are often different: are things called non-governmental organisations the same as voluntary or third sector organisations? Is empowerment the same process in Indian social development as in community development in the UK? We do not wish to erode the differences of place or organisational forms in this discussion, yet it is important to draw out some shared tendencies as well as posing some puzzling questions that emerge if we look across these differences. They make visible the difficulties of engaging people into new projects of development – economic, social or governmental. They also reveal the paradoxes, tensions and contradictions that such processes bring into play.

Becoming partners: governing with, by and in communities

We begin with the very British recruitment of community. Community has a long lineage as an object of desire in very different political formations: Craig and Mayo (1995) trace its roots in Britain through Fabianism, colonialism and the community development projects of the 1980s; while Driver and Martell (1998; 2002) identify its re-inflection through the communitarian strands of New Labour politics. These different roots enable the elasticity of the concept, allowing its enrolment to projects of community care, community governance, community development, community capacity building, community policing, community safety, community enterprise, community schools, community cohesion and many others. This proliferation of policy concepts suggests how far community has become implicated in the business of reforming government, especially, but not only, in the UK (see, for example, Creed, 2006; Craig, 2007; Mooney and Neal, 2009).

As we saw in Chapter 2, community has become one means of mapping – and managing – difference. Here our focus is on ways in which community is mobilised as a resource in new processes of governing the social (Clarke, 2009; Rose, 1999). It is simultaneously the object of governance (governing agencies seek to act on communities), the desired outcome of governance (dysfunctional areas/people need to become communities) and the subject of governance (communities who govern themselves). Communities are invested with authority and capacity, and are conceived as moral agents. They require the attention, respect, and engagement of (local) government apparatuses and personnel through consultation, participation and 'co-governing'. At the same time, communities are the storehouses of values, commitments, resources, and capacities that may be 'activated' in the process of co-governing. Once activated, such desirable qualities may reduce the costs of public provisioning by providing resources that substitute for public expenditure (HM Treasury, 2002, 2005).

Strategies of 'governing through community' construct new relationships, new agents, new agencies and new spaces that are authorised, directed and 'empowered' by the state, even as states shrink, become fragmented or are re-invented. As we argued in *The Managerial State* (Clarke and Newman, 1997), the result of processes of 're-inventing government' are dispersed state forms – embodied, often uncomfortably, in new decentralised, devolved, and fragmented sites. The previous chapter traced some elements of the territorial decomposition of the state through decentralisation and devolution. These processes combine scalar and spatial realignment, creating a new imagined topography of governing. In this topography, the nation is understood as a series of places in which people, politics and progress are embedded. Some are inhabited by individuals, families and places who are 'excluded' from mainstream social life (Levitas, 1998; Lister, 2004), existing alongside normal society and requiring strategies of regeneration, renewal and reintegration (Cochrane and Newman, 2009). Other communities can be trusted with the business of localised co-governance or self-governance. Indeed, communities can be empowered to take on the challenge of directing and developing themselves, rather than being directed by a central authority that has limited ability to adapt general solutions and strategies to distinctive local needs and wishes. Community's status as an object of governmental desire is exemplified in the UK's approach to community safety:

Vignette: communities and government in partnership against crime

In the UK Community Safety became a key focus for new policies, practices and apparatuses of governing. Every locality had a community safety partnership (dominated by the police) that constructed and consulted upon local community safety strategies, and worked through new types of personnel – community safety

officers (Gilling and Hughes, 2002). In this part of the community vision, communities were vulnerable, insecure and at risk – and needed to find ways of protect-
ing themselves against the 'anti-social' (see Hughes, 2007; Hughes and Edwards,
2002; Crawford, 2006). It has been argued that this nexus of community, security and policing has emerged as the dominant mode of 'governing the social'
(e.g., Garland, 2001; Stenson, 2000). It is certainly the case that 'community
safety' condenses many significant governance developments in the UK, but it is
only one of many moves to localise processes of urban governing that include
processes of economic regeneration, the development of 'social capital', the
embedding of new forms of welfare and 'activation' in community settings and
spaces, and forms of localised participation, consultation and decision-making
(see Cochrane, 2006, chapter 4).

The construction of 'community safety' as a new field and form of governmental
practice involves processes of localisation (see, for example, Burney, 2005;
Hughes et al., 2001; Squires, 2006; Stenson, 2008). It requires the construction
of partnerships between agencies, including the police, and between agencies
and communities. It is both the object of national (and some international)
policy-making, and the subject to be created in practice 'at arm's length' from
central government (since each locality must construct its own strategy and put it
into practice). It is also the effect and the focus of 'evaluative' agencies (such as the
Audit Commission in England and Wales). Indeed, such evaluative scrutiny is an
essential part of constraining the autonomy of 'community safety partnerships':
compliance with the objectives, priorities and modalities of the national specifi-
cations and guidelines (and their performance targets).

This form and site of governing produces several ambiguities. What harms
do communities need to be kept safe from? Should the partnership centre on
the crime–policing nexus? What 'communities' are to be included and excluded
(for example, does community safety include protection of minorities from 'hate
crime')? Such questions reveal something of the 'dark side' of publics and publicness mentioned in the Introduction to this volume. Community based publics
tend to be formed in relation to, or against, minoritised or excluded others. The
'ordinary people' that constitute them are not people in general: they may be
more parochial than cosmopolitan in their orientation, more conservative than
progressive in their politics (Clarke, 2009).

We return to these arguments in Chapter 7; here we focus on how community
safety partnerships are linked to the rescaling of the public discussed in the previous chapter. In the UK, the reform of existing systems of local government
intersected with the construction of new local apparatuses from crime prevention
and community safety partnerships to local health economies (Hughes and
Gilling, 2002; Stenson, 2008; Aldred, 2007). Such localities then become the
focus of further governance innovations, such as the creation of 'local strategic

partnerships', part of whose purpose is to integrate different governmental agencies and communities in the production of (locally) 'joined up government' (Allen and Cochrane, 2007; Cochrane and Etherington, 2007). These approaches to the social have led some to talk in terms of 'governing at arms length' or 'governing at a distance' – that is, the exercise of indirect forms of state power through the constitution of new forms of governable subject. Our conception of these sites as assemblages of different strategies, agents, technologies and forms of authority renders them more ambiguous, however. Writing about the governance of anti-social behaviour in the UK (a key goal of community safety partnerships) Painter argues that:

> it is impossible to draw a line between 'state' and '(civil) society'. A range of partnerships, community organisations and voluntary bodies are enrolled not only as the objects of policy, but as the agents of policy too. This is not a classic case of Foucauldian governmentality in which individual members of the population come to be implicated in their own subjectification. Rather, the picture is one of a diverse set of assemblages that effectuate (or sometimes fail to effectuate) particular kinds of state effects. These assemblages are necessarily hybrids of nominally state and nominally non-state institutions, practices and actors. Each assemblage comprises numerous prosaic relationships and activities … .The production of the state effect – fighting anti-social behaviour – thus depends not only on myriad mundane and prosaic practices, but also on those practices successfully combining in the particular time-space configuration that will enable the magistrate to make the order, that will allow the anti-ASB machine to *work*. And of course sometimes it doesn't. The approach advocated in this paper stresses that stateness is failure prone, partial and never completely fulfilled (Painter, 2006: 767–8).

Painter reminds us that new governing projects may be unstable and/or unsuccessful. Such instabilities may result from contested views of the definition of the field of action; conflicting political, policy and business agendas; and ambiguities around the forms of power and professional/lay/business expertise that are to be viewed as legitimate. But communities themselves represent a second source of instability. They are 'weakly bounded' systems: permeable and leaky. People, ideas and resources move in and out (either spatially, or in terms of affinity and attachment). One aspect of this is the membership question: who counts as a 'member of the community' and, indeed, who counts themselves as members? Governing implies a degree of calculability – but communities often threaten to spill over the categories of calculation. A variety of real and imaginary relationships and identities traverse the boundaries of the local and the particular. In postcolonial spaces, for example, 'minority ethnic communities' are typically located in transnational or diasporic relations of connection, obligation, and identification (e.g., Brah, 1996; Ghorashi, Salemink and Spierenberg, 2006; Ong, 1999). Such communities may, perhaps, be particular, but are rarely just 'local'. Nevertheless, community can occupy this central role in new governing assemblages because it is such a potent object of desire. As Creed notes:

> Political and economic projects, from rain forest conservation to urban improvement zones, focus on 'the community' as the appropriate vehicle and target of change. Social movements to resist these very efforts often constitute themselves around the same concept, as do others trying to assert a claim on the resources that community recognition promises (Creed, 2006: 3).

Very diverse political and governmental projects, then, seek to speak in the name of community, use it as a mobilising identification, and claim its aura of value.

Non-governmental? Volunteering for the public good

One effect of the many varieties of anti-statism has been a search for new means of 'delivery' for development and aid, for welfare and empowerment and for public services. National governments and international organisations have been enthusiastic in the search for new organisational forms:

> The voluntary and community sector has a vital role in society as the nation's 'third sector', working alongside the state and the market. Through its engagement of volunteers, the services it provides and the support it gives to individuals and groups, its contribution to community and civil life is immense, invaluable and irreplaceable. (Home Office, 1998: 5, foreword)

Organisations variously described as non-governmental, not-for-profit, civil society, community-based, voluntary, third sector and, more recently, social enterprise, occupy larger and more significant places in the reconfigurations of the public realm (Fyfe and Milligan, 2003; Fyfe, 2005; Holland et al., 2007; Stubbs, 2006). This shifting and multiple terminology hints at the contested conceptualisations of such organisations and their place in social, political and governmental landscapes. But they, like communities, have become central to emergent ways of producing and distributing the public good, even as what counts as the public good is being redefined. Their virtue lies in their associations with the popular dimensions of social life, non-political, and non-state. They tend to be viewed as the expression of organic social relations and their associated sentiments – solidarity, trust, compassion and engagement. They have also been the sites of activism, forming the organisational bases of counterpublics that were constructed in opposition to exclusion, marginalisation and oppression.

This points to a certain political ambivalence about NGOs and 'third sector' organisations: are they the extension of the state by other means, the agents of neo-liberalisation, or the bulwarks of the poor? We want to emphasise the necessity of thinking about their multi-faceted character, rather than treating them as the simple embodiment of an overarching project. Even as NGOs have become identified as the 'transmission belt' for neo-liberal and neo-colonial development in Africa, Asia and parts of South America, they have also been means of counter-hegemonic mobilisations (Townsend et al., 2002; see also Hickey, 2002; Hickey and Mohan, 2004; Sharma, 2008; Stubbs, 2006). Ong, for example, argues that NGOs have been centrally involved in articulating the claims of non-citizens:

> By mapping a biocartography of the politically excluded, NGOs negotiate with various governments and cultural authorities for a transnational sense of moral responsibility to migrant workers and trafficked individuals. In short emergent geographies of claims are mapped by novel political systems that are neither state nor market, but that articulate with both. (Ong, 2006: 21)

Non-governmental organisations, then, occupy ambivalent places in the re-invention of the public. They are located outside the state, among the people, or in civil society. Their virtue and their value derive from this social location, being part of what we might call an 'economy of moral value'. In some settings – micro-credit schemes that make the poor into enterprising selves, or schemes for local economic development – moral value is assumed to be convertible into economic value. But this is only one example of an emergent approach to valuing popular resourcefulness: the knowledges, skills, capacities, cultures, relationships and practices that may make things happen. This has been formalised (after Putnam et al., 1994; and Putnam 2000) as 'social capital' that may be exploited, developed, enhanced and enrolled in the business of social and economic development (Elyachar, 2005). But its role is wider than just economic development. Chapter 2 identified the significance of 'faith communities' in new mappings of diversity. The Home Office document *Working Together: Cooperation between Government and Faith Groups* identifies the value of faith communities (with faith mapped onto current anxieties about migration and ethnicity) in such terms:

> Faith community organisations are gateways to access the tremendous reserves of energy and commitment of their members, which can be of great importance to the development of civil society. In the case of some of the newer communities who include among their members many

recent arrivals to the UK, these organisations are perhaps the principal gateway since these new arrivals frequently relate to the wider community mostly through trusted organisations serving their religious or ethnic group. (Home Office, 2004c: 7).

Such communities are viewed as the repository of valued resources – morality, property, energy and networks – that might be put to work in the service of the public good (Dinham, 2008). Similarly, voluntary organisations typically aim to mobilise – and enhance – sets of capacities, competences, orientations and relationships as elements of individual or collective 'self-help'. The objective may be economic independence, but in the field of social welfare, for example, may involve other forms of self-sufficiency or independence. In recent years, states and international organisations have come to see such organisations as more effective, economical and productive than state agencies. Whether in the work of economic development, peace building, empowerment or delivering care services to vulnerable groups, such organisations are value-bearing and valued.

Social enterprise is clearly another in the line of hybrid forms generated in the remaking of the public realm. For example, one British minister argued that:

> Buoyed by public support, driven by a can-do attitude and egalitarian values, and appropriately supported by government, social enterprise can be another channel for our idealism. It can be a force for dynamism, pros-perity – and social justice.
> (Miliband, E. 'A force for prosperity – and social justice', *Guardian Society*, Social Business special, 07.02.2007; p. 7: Edward Miliband was then a junior minister in the Labour government.)

Social enterprise organisations, as we will see in Chapter 4, are one of a range of 'hybrid' organisations that populate public service provision. But it is not clear whether the 'social' in social enterprise relates to its social objectives (like the 'social' in social policy); to its social values (a commitment to social justice or ethical standards); or to its organisational goals and character (not-for-profit status). Such definitions deal explicitly in mixing, blending, combining – the work of assembling or hybridisation, we might say. But they mark the conver-sion of moral value (ethics, values, social justice) into a tradable value, either as reputation or in the capacity to raise funds. The specific mix being claimed for social enterprise also valorises enterprise: the 'can-do attitude' and the 'dynamism and flexibility of the private sector'.

The moral value of voluntary/non-governmental organisations is complex: it derives, in part, from being 'not the state'. It represents or mobilises types of popular resource: networks, relationships, commitments and sets of energies and knowledges. And, like community, this both produces – and possibly

contains – forms of instability. Such organisations need to prove themselves efficient and effective, even where that might run counter to other orientations (such
as advocacy or mobilising work). In the UK, they are subject to regulation, bench-
marking and monitoring by funders, as well as being expected to form – or
manage – partnerships. They are subject to competitive processes of tendering
and contracting which impose major demands of 'market entry' (that is the competences and capacities that organisations must demonstrate before they can be
'successful' bidders).

At the same time, volunteer workers are proving harder to recruit and retain –
a problem in the context of the imperative towards expanding role for the 'third
sector'. This resistance to expanding demands and intensifying disciplines at
work make 'volunteering' a fragile element of the envisaged new 'mix'. To some
extent, the limits of volunteering have been compensated for by the expansion of
paid work within the sector – but such workers are typically paid below equivalent public service rates and are more part-time and short-term (often subject to
the contingencies of contract income or time limited projects). Finally, the
processes of contractualisation and projectisation produce organisations with
short lives or, at least, short attention spans – whose attention is re-directed
towards the next big thing (and its associated funding) that features in increasingly hyperactive governing (Stubbs, 2006).

Organisations are expected to absorb and mange such tensions (so that they can
be viewed as reliable partners for funding, contracting, etc). Nevertheless, their
legitimacy may rest on the effective involvement and/or representation of specific
social groups (Hudson, 2000). The engagement of new subjects can be measured,
evaluated, and be the subject of 'field visits' by sponsoring or donor organisations
(see Elyachar, 2002 and Sharma, 2008 on the performative character of such
visits). But 'the people' have to be present or voluntary/non-governmental organisations risk losing their value. In the process, unstable negotiations aimed at
enrolling, recruiting and representing 'ordinary people' are established.

Above and below politics: the place of civil society

Civil society occupies a central place in the 'modern social imaginary' (Taylor,
2004) yet its contours are indistinct; it tends to be defined by both its 'otherness'
from, and relationships to, both state and market. Gupta (2006) suggests that this
makes it a less than helpful concept, but we suspect that its political and governmental value derives precisely from this mobile and contested character. In some
contexts, civil society forms the domain in which public and private realms
are articulated, rather than being institutionally separated. Civil society is the
public domain in which private individuals associate, yet it stands apart from the
state. It is imagined as social, rather than political: an organic, rather than artifi-
cial, entity that is inhabited by people (rather than political subjects). For example,
Michael Walzer argues that: 'The words "civil society" name the space of

uncoerced human association and also the set of relational networks – formed for the sake of family, faith, interest and ideology – that fill this space' (Walzer, 1995: 7).

Here we can see the emphasis on 'uncoerced association' that often underpins the contrast between civil society and the state (understood as institutionalised power exercised over people). Organicist conceptions of civil society thus have strong overlaps with communitarian views of social order, while radical democratic conceptions point to civil society as an alternative base for political development and mobilisation (Keane, 1998; Kessl, 2007). In recent decades, a variety of political forces and movements have come together in the rediscovery and celebration of civil society. These range from the anti-statism of dissident movements in the former Soviet bloc to the discovery of social capital as a resource for both economic and social development (Stubbs, 2006; Putnam, 2000). In the former Soviet bloc, the overwhelming power and penetration of the state produced social and political movements that located sources of resistance and hope within civil society – beyond and outside the state and its apparatuses. Janine Wedel's work (2001) on aid to the East and the former Soviet Union points to how 'civil society' organisations were identified as the only legitimate channel for development funds and partnerships with Western agencies, because 'government' or state agencies were so profoundly discredited. Meanwhile critiques of aid to the South, and to Africa in particular, pointed to the institutionalisation of corruption within states (and political parties) as a primary mechanism that prevented the 'poor' or 'ordinary people' benefiting from aid and its promise of development. International organisations involved in the transactions of aid and development began to look for alternative footholds in 'receiving' societies. Civil society – in its many facets – offered a possible alternative location for development (Elyachar, 2005; Li, 2007b).

At the same time, states became identified as the agency and the machinery of ethnic domination, turning ethnic and national identities and their imagined 'ownership' of places into what Gregory, writing about Palestine and Israel, calls the 'facts on the ground' (2005). Such developments – the return of repressed national dreams and the invention of new nationalities – supercharged 'ethnicity' as a social and political force and led to a renewed interest in civil society organisations as the site of potential peaceful, integrated or harmonious co-existence, from the North of Ireland to post-Yugoslav countries. If politics, governmental apparatuses and the forces of states were tied up in the ruthless or murderous business of ethno-nationalism, then 'ordinary people', outside of politics, were the bearers of hope (Stubbs, 2006). Such anxieties about the power and effects of states also connect with longer political traditions of anarchism and libertarianism. Whether this is European anarcho-syndicalism that saw the state as the repository of power over people, or Gandhian conceptions of popular tradition and self-sufficiency (Sharma, 2008), anti-statism has been a powerful mobilising political philosophy that brings civil society to the fore.

These philosophical and political movements coalesce in more tenuous – though effective – ways with two other current tendencies. One is the tendency to 'anti-politics' (Rosanvallon, 2006; Taguieff, 2007): the denigration of everyday institutional politics as 'dirty', tarnished by large or small corruptions, evasions, lying and forms of political manipulation. As we saw in Chapter 1, politics and politicians have become the objects of increasing scepticism and cynicism. Some of this derives from long running popular scepticism about politics and politicians. Some is produced by the complex and unstable relationships between mass media, economic interests and political parties, in which collusive alliances and scandal-revealing pressures produce media that lurch between 'lap dog' and 'mad dog' roles, even as they try to represent themselves as public interest 'watch dogs' (Hackett, 2001). As Taguieff suggests, the expansion of forms of populist politics may be one result of such 'anti-political' tendencies, in which politicians attempt to position themselves 'outside' of political elites or the political club – as ordinary people, as everyman/woman and so on (see also Andrews, 2006, on Berlusconi's impact on Italian politics). In the process, civil society becomes a pole of opposition to the state. For example, Dagnino argues that in Latin America, it is important to

> recognize that in some interpretations, the distinction between State and civil society, based on structural determinants, is not only frequently taken as an irreducible given of reality, but also ends up being converted into a relationship of "natural" opposition, into a premise, a starting point, that exempts us from understanding the political processes that constitute and explain it. Such an understanding is behind the well known and widely disseminated vision of civil society as a 'pole of virtue' and of the State as the 'incarnation of evil' (2007: 4)

As we have tried to show, there are many routes to arriving at the distinction between the state and civil society. We think it is important to be attentive to these multiple flows of ideas, people and projects since they reveal civil society as something other than simply the creature of global/neo-liberal forces. Rather, civil society looks like a keyword that is suffused with multiple possible meanings and values, but which has been given a strong contemporary inflection towards anti-statist and anti-politics movements that valorise and celebrate the strengths of 'ordinary people' – whether as the bearers of social capital; the resources for peaceful co-existence; or the members of communities that can be empowered and self-governing. Civil society is where 'real people' are to be found (Elyachar, 2002). Such everyday lives and ordinary folk are represented as being simultaneously above and below politics: above because they have ethical characters that disdain the corruptions and manipulations of 'dirty' politics; and 'below' politics because their concerns are centred on the everyday matters of getting a living, getting by, and getting along. Paradoxically, then, civil society is thus both the organic condition of society that provides the springboard for economic and social development and the domain that needs to be constructed and tutored (by governments and international organisations) as the site for future development.

Displacing the public

In the remainder of this chapter we look across these three governmental 'objects of desire' and tease out some of their consequences for enrolling, engaging and displacing the public. As we have suggested, the shift towards voluntary/non-governmental/community-based forms of organising marks not exactly the retreat of the state, but the remaking of the state and state power – in part through its 'dispersal' (Clarke and Newman, 1997). In the process, the delicate balances that marked state–society, state–market, state–people relations have been reworked in search of a new equilibrium, a new settlement. At stake are a variety of grand claims about the new arrangements of autonomy, authority, and responsibility of 'ordinary people'. But as Elyachar, Sharma and others indicate, such arrangements always seek to encourage particular sorts of people to act 'autonomously' in certain delimited ways (Maasen and Sutter, 2007). Empowerment seeks to develop certain sorts of power – producing appropriately active (but not activist) citizens.

The harnessing of voluntary/non-governmental organisations and civil society projects is both 'big business' (in the sense of funding flows) and contradictory in its effects. For example Andersen notes how

> (I)n their partnership with the public sector, voluntary organisations have to expect that the public sector may see them as merely another set of institutions to be governed, which is something that could potentially jeopardise the relationship between the voluntary organisation and the voluntary base (2008: 6).

Governmental and development projects seek to engage such organisations for their distinctiveness – what the UK government calls their 'value-driven' character – but, as we have seen, attempt to govern them by turning them into recognisable types of organisation: being 'business-like' and 'well-managed' (Eikenberry and Kluwer, 2004 on the US context). This contradictory relationship produces a number of organisational and social consequences. For example, Harrow (2007), writing about the 'third sector' in the UK, argues that it is simultaneously *underpaid* (relying on volunteer or low-waged labour, because of the value-or ethos-driven character); *overworked* (both in terms of stretched organisations and individual workers); and *overvalued* (with unrealistic expectations about the scale and quality of third sector contributions). Both of the first two problems are associated with the governance arrangements in which third sector organisations are located, and the demands that they make on organisations to work in specific ways.

Vignette: becoming 'businesslike'

One of the claims for, and pressures on, voluntary/non-governmental organisations has been the expectation that they will be 'economical' (a service at lower cost than a public equivalent) and demonstrate that they can be well-managed or businesslike in their conduct (Charlesworth et al., 1996; Clarke and Newman, 1997: 89). The Home Office argued that third sector organisations 'have to concern themselves with strategic planning and budgeting, staff recruitment and development, quality management, statutory reporting requirements, public relations, membership systems, more formal management of relationships with stakeholders' (Home Office, 2004: 19). Similarly, the modernisation of charitable governance in the UK involved advice about the six 'hallmarks of an effective charity'(Charity Commissioners, 2004: 4). These are:

- Focus on impact and outcome
- Fit for purpose
- Sound governance
- Maximises potential
- Accountable and transparent
- Flexible

(Charity Commissioners, 2004: 5–11)

This looks remarkably like the New Public Management. Writing about NGO work in the post-Yugoslav countries, Stubbs points to a similar set of dynamics around good management and a 'success culture' that shapes organisational forms, priorities and dynamics:

> In particular, the imposition of the rules of the 'new public management' with its emphasis on particular organisational structures, including a US style management hierarchy, as well as on structures of efficiency, effectiveness and measurable results, has distorted and inhibited grassroots innovative practices.
>
> In this way, there is a real danger of the 'projectisation' or 'technocratisation' of community development, in terms of a 'toolkit' or 'transplanting' approach, and a race to show results, which often involves cutting corners, not learning lessons, and utilising informal networks of influence, which ironically contributes to a lack of transparency in projects which were, in fact, set up to challenge this. An alternative approach, emphasising processes, feedback loops, mutual learning, and a recognition of problems and failures, runs counter to the 'success culture' of external assistance programmes. (Stubbs, 2006: 171)

This managerialisation of organisational forms, relationships and practices is one of the means through which voluntary organisations are articulated with states and markets in ways that displace their publicness. Others include the changing relationships induced by governmental priorities, contracting and scrutiny. There are also critical issues of scale – can such organisations reproduce the national scale of provision and the (more or less) universal patterns of access offered by national state systems?

Reluctant partners and mediating practices

As we have seen, community, civil society and the third sector provide sites for recruiting 'ordinary people' into social, economic and political projects by drawing on anti-statist and anti-political sentiments. They nevertheless remain peculiar places to govern, in part because people consistently refuse to 'know their place'. The different strategies though which people are recruited may not be coherent. But even if they were, the intentions of government – or development – actors may not be delivered in practice: they have to be mediated and translated by a range of practitioners, and summon partners who may be reluctant to take up the roles that are envisaged.

As the community safety vignette illustrated, partnership working is at the centre of these new assemblages. Not surprisingly, the idea of partnership conceals several critical issues. First, partnerships have become increasingly compulsory: central government requires agents and agencies to 'do partnership'. Second, the cooperative ethos of partnership working means bracketing social, political and organisational inequalities, pretending that they don't exist (e.g., Craig, 2007; Whitehead, 2007). The language of egalitarian cooperation that saturates partnership is almost as 'warm' as the idea of community. But the bracketing of inequality tends to work to the advantage of dominant groups and larger organisations, and to privilege certain forms of expertise, language and claims to legitimacy (see Chapters 5 and 7). Third, 'partners' in the new governance may be ranked according to their attributes and attractions as potential partners. Responsible and already active communities are preferable to the inactive (or the activist). Communities with clearly established 'leaders' are preferable to the amorphous or unstructured variety. Communities with clear boundaries (spatial or social) are preferable to 'leaky' entities. Stable communities are preferable to mobile or transient ones. We could go on, but it may be more important to note that one other distinction overshadows most of these. There is one type of community that is more avidly sought than any other as a partner in the business of governing: the 'business community' (Ball, 2007; Farnsworth, 2004; Holland et al., 2007). From the large scale of the Private Finance Initiative (PFI) and Public Private Partnerships (PPP) down to the micro-management of local agencies, projects and partnerships, the participation of the 'business community' has been avidly sought for its investment capital and business 'knowhow' (Clarke and Newman, 1997; du Gay, 2000).

However, people, organisations, communities and businesses of different kinds may be reluctant partners. Business may be occupied elsewhere, and may only turn up to the partnership table in very specific circumstances. Communities are often reluctant to materialise when summoned, leaving the agents of government anxiously scanning the locality in search of the community and its usable representatives. When communities do materialise, they often do so as plural, contradictory and contentious entities. Localised communities are contested by different interests and identities that seek to be recognised as representing the character and needs of the community. Communities of identity are equally prone to be divided or contested since differences (of class, gender, age, etc.) exist in tension with essentialised identities and their representation by, or embodiment in, community leaders. For the purposes of governing, communities are both difficult to form and difficult to hold stable, rather than being entities waiting to be discovered and put to work.

There is a further difficulty: people inhabit these sites in ways that are often very different from the imaginings of their designers. A study of NGOs and development in Cairo by Julia Elyachar points to the contradictory dynamics involved in the processes of micro-credit and micro-enterprise as a vehicle for development. In what she calls the neoliberal 'market mirage', people were encouraged to take on debt ('credit') to become enterprising:

> Those who were empowered by this form of debt did not passively receive the lessons they were taught in training sessions and NGO meetings. They turned the tools of empowerment to their own ends through weapons of the weak: they used loans that would get them into hopeless debt to buy apartments and get married; they forged order forms from public sector stores to get their loans released from the bank; they made their microenterprises into shells for wealthy businessmen seeking new ways to escape government taxes. Since empowerment debt reconfigured relations of power, apparently technical fights over business arrangements and the flow of loans were simultaneously a struggle over power. (Elyachar, 2005: 216)

Other studies (e.g., Li, 2007b; Sharma, 2008) point to outcomes that are different from the governmental objectives. This is more than just the 'implementation gap' as understood in policy studies. Rather it points to a generic form of instability since such projects rely on soliciting, inciting, enrolling and recruiting 'ordinary people'. Subjects may prove sceptical, doubtful, calculatingly compliant or even – as Elyachar's examples suggest – irritatingly innovative. And policies seeking to enrol new kinds of actor are mediated by government practitioners in 'contact zones' (Pratt, 1992) that may produce difficult encounters and unexpected outcomes. In the case of post-Yugoslav countries Stubbs argues that:

> In the 'contact zone' of course, encounters are rarely, or rarely only, about words and their meaning but are, almost always, more or less explicitly, about claims-making, opportunities, strategic choices and goals, interests, and resource maximisation. In the 'contact zones', all kinds of complex negotiated interactions occur, on multiple stages, as well as off-stage, in which, in fact, multiple belongings and flexible identities are, in and of themselves, extremely useful devices. The philosophical question about whether the actor or activist in civil society who has become skilled in presenting different faces to different audiences is, somehow, less authentic or honest than the activist who remains consistent to a single idea or ideal is, in my view, less important sociologically than to root both of these strategies in their social context. (Stubbs, 2006: 3)

The 'contact zones' where government and community/civil society meet are, then, profoundly unstable places – rather than sites for the smooth roll out of neo-liberal, neo-colonial or other projects. This points towards the problem of governmental practitioners, especially those who are newly located within the field of the dispersed state. Governing through community, civil society and the 'third sector' restates what Terence Johnson (1973) once defined as the problem of the 'mediating professions'. He argued that these were vulnerable to different senses of obligation: to the state (as employer, as policy definer and as collective will of society), and to the client/s (as embodied public, as need-bearing individuals, as the objects of ethical/professional purpose). The shift towards governing with or through community multiplies new categories of occupation that may be differently classed, raced and gendered from the 'traditional' professions: the community safety officer, the community development worker, the partnership broker, organisers of micro-credit schemes, managers and fieldworkers of NGOs, coordinators of community or voluntary groups, and the commissioners of new functions or services. Located in new sites, working 'interstitially' between both organisational and professional forms of authority and discipline, these agents typically have mediating roles – doing the work of brokering, negotiating, translating, and assembling the people and practices involved in governing (see, for example, Larner and Craig, 2005; Lendvai and Stubbs, 2007). They have to manage themselves in an overlapping series of (potentially) contentious relationships – between the local and the national; between agencies; between conflicting policy objectives; and between different representations of the community or civil society (Gilling and Hughes, 2002). These are new settings in which the 'liberal professional' imaginary of serving the people, improving the quality of life, making progress and working with people may be re-invented. Such workers are enrolled into specific projects; and may become, from, the point of view of their employers, 'over-identified' with particular communities (the colonial image of 'going native'). But as the risk of loyalties being pulled away from the organisation towards 'the people' reappears, then new managerial strategies for disciplining such a workforce may also have to be invented.

These 'contact zones' also produce problems of disappointment, exhaustion, disillusion and failure. While this may be true for both parties in the partnership, it could be argued that non-state actors tend to suffer more. There are specific nodal points for the dynamic of attachment, investment, disillusion and withdrawal. The most obvious, and most recurrent, issues centre on the pleasures and problems of 'incorporation' (Craig and Taylor, 2002). How closely 'leaders' become involved in the machinery of governing is a matter of complex, and continuing, political calculation: weighing influence gained against loss of local credibility; reasonableness against radicalism; reputation against effectiveness; popular support against insider power, and so on. Such issues are usually framed in terms of the choices that non-state actors and their leaders or representatives confront. But they also exist for the agencies of government: where, and how do you find the right sorts of leaders? How do you sustain them in the tension between the 'business of governing' and the 'needs of the community' when these may be disjunctured? And how do you make them into responsible agents of governance without disconnecting them from their roots?

It is here that 'training' and 'capacity building' have emerged as key strategies for incorporating communities into governance (see, for example, McKee and Cooper on the role of training in 'tenant empowerment' in housing associations in Glasgow: 2007; and Craig, 2007, on community capacity building). Such processes tend to remove the 'real people' whom governments seek from the contexts and reationships that produced them. Susan Hyatt's study of 'self-government' in public housing projects in the US dramatises these dilemmas. Women from the projects were recognised by local level agencies as 'natural leaders' and invited to become community managers, taking responsibility for the community/housing system. In some cases the women were then sacked for failing to behave 'properly':

> The community caretaking work that has long been carried out by poor women ... has been aptly named by Naples (1998) "activist mothering".... . Yet when it was co-opted by the state for the purpose of getting women to participate in local-level bureaucracies and when, as a result of this move there was friction between communities and government agencies, many of these same acts of activist mothering were reinterpreted by the state as evidence of nepotism and as proof of the inability of poor people to become self-governing. (Hyatt, 2001: 223)

This, too, has colonial echoes – mothers as the 'natives' who cannot govern themselves despite the best efforts and good intentions of their masters. It is, however, important to see it as highlighting a distinction between the aims or objectives that we identify in governmental projects and strategies, and the ways in which such projects play out in practice. It is too easy – and too risky – to read off results from intentions (Li, 2007b). This is not to say that such failures are inherently 'progressive' – all sorts of possibilities are in play, not just optimistic ones. But it remains vital to recognise the contested passage from strategy to effect. When strategies move from the minds of the strategists (or their textual representations) into the complex of contentious relationships, other things become possible. Alongside the practices of responsibilisation, privatisation, managerialisation and the production of self-governing subjects (as individuals, families, communities), we ought also to notice the refusals, the resistances, the alternative imaginaries and solidarities that get in the way (Clarke et al., 2007c).

We illustrate this with the final vignette in this chapter: one based on a project focusing on the empowerment of women in India. This not only illustrates some of the ambiguities and difficulties associated with the term 'empowerment'; it also suggests ways in which people may act on new governmental strategies to inflect, bend and translate them to different purposes and to new possibilities.

Vignette: the ambiguities of 'empowerment'

Aradhana Sharma has written about how Mahila Samakhya (MS) – a government organised non-governmental organisation (GONGO) in India – worked uncomfortably in the space between government and the people (2006; 2008). MS, she suggests, drew on resources and relationships that government agents could and would not (resources developed by feminist politics in India that fed a particular view of empowerment) while being confined by the demands of government funding and direction (avoiding 'politics', for example). Sharma explores some of the complex routes and calculations that fed into this GONGO status and some of its effects:

> When the opportunity of designing MS presented itself in the late-1980s, some activists saw it as a chance to take their feminist ideas of gender equality and social change to scale — that is, to reach out to large groups of marginalized women, to use state resources for social transformation, and to "mainstream" gender within state institutions ... . This decision did not, however, preclude debates about reformist versus radical activism. Many questions were raised about the why and how of feminist collaboration with state agencies ... .
>
> The activists and bureaucrats who designed MS desired a partially non-governmental program structure that would mitigate the problems with state development models and bring in added benefits. NGO advantages,

as described by my informants, included grassroots-level accountability and legitimacy, bottom-up approaches, decentralized planning, participatory and democratic ways of working, flexibility, and a motivated workforce. (2006: 66–67)

Sharma reveals how MS was assembled from different political and governmental currents, including different conceptions of empowerment. Its form and practices were articulated with the state in critical ways (even as it formed part of the process by which the Indian state was itself changing). The assemblage of MS was contradictory – the site of many compressed ambiguities and the political and practical ambivalences flowing from them. For the state, MS provided an example of a 'modern' approach to social development among the poor, one that was able to draw on ethically and politically committed workers (and pay them at much lower levels than equivalent government salaries). While drawing on their ethical and political commitments as a resource for the programme, the government also imposed civil service rules about being 'non-political' on MS workers (in particular not challenging other government agencies). Women workers of MS proved creative in dealing with such constraints, while also using the ambiguous status of MS as a flexible resource – at times emphasising its governmental character (to add authority), at others, stressing their non-governmental status (to distance themselves from government policies and practices).

Sharma stresses how this mix of political currents, the ambivalent and multiple character of MS as an assemblage, and the political-organisational initiatives of women working within the programme make it impossible to predict what its outcomes would be. Although it was dominated by a neo-liberal conception of empowerment, the 'delivery' of this model could not be guaranteed because the space of MS both created and required the agency of women workers and the women recruited to its programmes. The shift towards voluntary/non-governmental forms of public provision extends these possibilities, in part by extending the problems of governing across organisational boundaries, and in part by the reliance on popular commitments and resourcefulness. This means other values, ethics and political orientations are required to energise the process – and always threaten to unsettle the articulation of such organisations with the dominant tendencies.

Let us restate the point: we do not mean that this form of indeterminacy – these spaces of possibility – are inherently progressive. On the contrary, the voluntary/non-governmental has long been the site of values, ethics and politics that reproduce or institutionalise patterns of social difference, inequality and authority – for example, in models of philanthropy addressed to the poor or 'less fortunate'; or in religious/faith based approaches to public services that enact exclusionary principles (rather than principles of universalism). However their current engagement in new assemblages of governance makes them the site of the intended displacement of their public character into smaller sites: communities, civil society or voluntary organisations.

Conclusion: Displacing politics?

Both ordinary people – and the good things they do – are apolitical: civil society, community and voluntary organisations are recruited because they are understood as non-political sites to which the tensions, antagonisms and political conflicts of publicness may be safely displaced. Of course, the desire for non-political sites and forms of governing does not guarantee that politics can be so easily dispelled (Ferguson, 1994). But while the displacement of the public from its national or state-centred forms may bring new possible publics into view, it may also render a wider public imaginary – and the democratic processes that it sustains – less possible. To take this argument further we want to return to Tanya Li's identification of six crucial practices linked to the concept of assemblage in the work of governing (cited in Chapter 1): *forging alignments; rendering technical; authorising knowledge; managing failures and contradictions; de-politicising; and re-assembling*. Each of these is implicated in the processes of governing examined in this chapter. The enrolment of community-based actors or not for profit organisations serves to forge new alignments between government and non-governmental agents. Such alignments may be fraught, but the resolution of areas of difficulty brings the chosen 'representatives' of civil society, community and voluntary bodies into direct relationship with governmental practitioners, producing new alliances and forging compromise solutions (see Schofield, 2002, on the discursive work of 'regenerating community' in local partnerships). Such solutions may privilege the interests of some players – perhaps large not-for-profits organisations that already consider themselves to be 'in business', seeking to move into territory vacated by the state, or the NGO involved in development projects in which funding comes with strings attached – at the expense of others who wish to retain a more adversarial relationship with government (see also Stubbs on the 'meta-NGO', 2006).

The problems faced by organisations and agencies working in the new landscapes of economic and social development or service delivery, with all the messy dilemmas around role and purpose, staffing and management, values and principles, are apparently made technical in the contracting or commissioning process. Anything that does not fit within the specification or contract is bracketed away. And many such organisations find themselves moving from long term development work into shorter term projects, in which the problem to be addressed has, for funding purposes, to be rendered into a form in which specific interventions can be linked directly to measurable outcomes. This in turn authorises particular forms of knowledge, in particular, managerial forms of knowledge. As we have seen, these non-governmental organisations are valued by government precisely because they enable it to access and recruit a variety of forms of knowledge and experience that are likely to 'add value' to governmental initiatives. They are closer to the 'real people' of communities and civil society and so better able to bring their knowledge and expertise to bear on intractable problems. But the process of forging new alignments and rendering complex, messy problems into technical ones means that 'everyday' forms of knowledge and experience are subordinated to other forms of expertise – a theme we develop in Chapter 5. Failures tend to be explained as technical or procedural failures, or as the result of the lack of capacity (or commitment or determination) of ordinary people themselves. Meanwhile, contradictions are smoothed away by rendering areas of conflict and ambiguity into manageable problems; by making them seem superficial rather than fundamental; and/or by displacing them away from government itself.

The fifth of Li's processes explicitly focuses on de-politicisation: restating political questions as matters of technique; closing down debate about how and what to govern and the distributive effects of particular arrangements by reference to expertise; and encouraging citizens to engage in debate while limiting the agenda. Many non-governmental actors are implicated here as they become 'partners' of government, both participating in debates themselves and acting as brokers who elicit and mediate citizen participation in a range of public participation initiatives. This cannot be read as a straightforward process of incorporation; but the dominant tendency is towards rendering participation as a technical and procedural matter, delivering it within particular deadlines and ensuring that governmental criteria of legitimacy are met.

Finally, Li highlights the potential depoliticizing effects of re-assembling: grafting on new elements and reworking old ones; deploying existing discourses to new ends; and transposing the meanings of key terms. We have seen in this chapter numerous ways in which the discourse of publics and publicness is being displaced to notions of community, civil society and the 'third sector'. This produces newly empowered actors – and possible activists. But each is marked by a conception of places and publics that are inhabited and animated by people who are in some way 'real', 'ordinary' or 'authentic' (Elyachar, 2002). The problems of finding such 'real people' and enrolling them into processes of governing emerge as characteristic tensions across these different sites. The processes of reassembling combine old elements (the voluntary organisation, the community resource, the women's group) with new ones (notions of partnership, social enterprise, self-governance, community self help) that narrow the possibilities of political engagement. But, as we have seen, such strategic ambitions do not turn simply into achieved outcomes – people may also bend, inflect and enrol such developments into other purposes and possibilities. They may also, of course, ignore their invitations to 'engage' or be 'empowered', or may engage in ways that are calculated and exploitative. Our point here is that despite such strategies being 'structured in dominance' – attempting to organise people, power and resources in value-producing ways – their translation into practice creates unstable fields of action.

Furthermore these new formations cannot be collapsed into a singular trend: each has its own situated genealogy that means that new governance spaces are occupied by actors and organisations who bring their own histories, and who have the capacity to introduce alternate rationalities or perspectives into the assemblages to which they are summoned. New formations of community and civil society may invoke forms of translocal, national, regional and global connection. These may include imagined collectivities of people connected and united in resistance to forms of power and domination, whether anti-globalisation protests, mobilisations around AIDS activism in Africa, protests and movements against the Iraq war or environmental campaigns. Creed argues that 'some global mobilisations and movements appear to be creating effective communities of interest that supercede states and influence state and international policies' (2006: 10). Even 'localised' communities may persist with demands and desires for connections that stretch beyond the locality. This includes mobilising understandings of the nation-state as collective resource, collective provisioner, and site of power and authority. As Hansen and Stepputat (2002) argue the 'persistence of the imagination of the state as an embodiment of sovereignty' is essential to understanding the paradox that

> while the authority of the state is constantly questioned and functionally undermined, there are growing pressures on states to confer full-fledged rights and entitlements on ever more citizens, to confer recognition and rights on ever more institutions, movements, or organisations, and a growing demand on states from the so-called international community to address development problems effectively and to promote a 'human rights culture', as the latest buzz-word goes (2002: 2).

There are tensions here between the strategies of state dispersal and displacement and the ways in which people continue to imagine governments and states as integral and authoritative. The move to new modes of governing may resolve problems, contradictions or instabilities associated with earlier state formations. But they create new dynamics, new loci of contention, new potential antagonisms and new instabilities of their own. The attempted displacement of publicness away from the state into new 'non-political' configurations – communities, civil society, voluntary/non-governmental organisations – cannot be guaranteed: people persistently and unpredictably refuse to know their place.

4 Making (up) markets: discourses, devices and agents

As we saw in Chapter 3, new forms of governing involve the creation of new kinds of agent: communities, non-governmental organisations, voluntary associations, all constituted as 'ordinary people'. These are being enrolled into new articulations with nations and states as 'subjects of value': the bearers of economic value in the struggle for individual and national success in the global marketplace. In this chapter, we highlight the marketising strategies, discourses and devices that produce this proliferation of economic agents. But we also attempt to challenge the idea of the market as a singular entity:

> The notion of the market is so familiar that we tend to take it for granted. But like so many things that we take for granted, we don't really know what it is. 'The market' functions as a folk concept more than a scientific term . . . Rather than the market, we need to think about a multiplicity of markets that are the outcomes of specific forms of labor, culture, techno-logical mixes, and modes of organisation specific to time and place. (Elyachar: 2005: 15, 24)

Our aim is to consider the multiple dynamics involved in assembling new alignments of states and markets. The idea of 'making up markets' highlights the political work that goes in to creating and managing market-mimicking devices, market imagery and economic agents in the remaking of public services.

States and markets

The dominant narrative about the reform of public services treats markets as having replaced – or displaced – states. There are variants of this narrative offering slightly different views of the relationship between states and markets:

- That states have become subservient to markets;
- That states have reduced in scope as markets have grown;
- That international markets (especially financial markets) have made nation-states more vulnerable, and less in control of their own destiny;
- That states have contracted out core public functions to markets (changing the 'delivery' of public services);
- That states have privatised public goods and resources.

This list indicates the rather diverse phenomena that are bound up in arguments about the 'rise of the market'. Nevertheless, market mechanisms and market imagery have come to dominate the landscape of public service reform (Le Grand, 2007). This may be a tribute to the power of claims that markets are more efficient, dynamic and responsive than states in delivering services and better attuned to the needs and desires of people living in 'consumer cultures'. Markets, then, have come to take on different roles in the remaking of publicness, leading some to claim that we are now witnessing a fundamentally different kind of state.

Philip Bobbitt's idea of the 'market-state' (2003) as successor to the nation-state is one much-cited account of processes of change. It shares many features with similar accounts that stress the rise of markets, market forces and capital, identifying the undermining of the post-war model of welfare-nation-state, and the expanded reach and scope of market relationships: see, for example, Cerny's idea of the 'competition state' (1997); Jessop's model of the 'Schumpeterian workfare post-national regime' (2000, 2002); or Harvey's view of neo-liberalism (2005). Both enthusiasts and critics identify similar transitions, even if they attribute them to different forces. In Bobbitt's account, the focus is on the changed economic and political conditions that force a mutation in the institutional form of the state itself:

> What are the characteristics of the market-state? Such a state depends on the international capital markets and, to a lesser degree, on the modern multinational business network to create stability in the world economy. In preference to management by national or transnational political bodies, its political institutions are less representative (though in some ways more democratic) than those of the nation-state . . . Like the nation-state, the market-state assesses its economic success or failure by its society's ability to secure more and better goods and services, but in contrast to the nation-state it does not see the State as more than a minimal provider or redistributor. Whereas the nation-state justified itself as an instrument to serve the welfare of the people (the nation), the market-state exists to maximize the opportunities enjoyed by all members of society. ... [F]or the nation-state, full employment is an important and often paramount goal, whereas for the market-state, the actual number of persons employed is but one more variable in the production of economic opportunity and has no overriding intrinsic significance. If it is more efficient to have large numbers of people unemployed, because it would cost more to the society to train them and put them to work at tasks for which the market has little demand, then the society will simply have to accept large unemployment figures.(Bobbitt, 2003: 229)

This is a compelling story, partly because it is possible to see many empirical examples that illustrate its claims, and partly because we have heard it as a story in many forms over the last thirty years, not least in policy narratives. It marks the inexorable and inevitable rise of the market, market forces and market interests as the overwhelming determinants of social and political life. Globalisation, liberalisation (and neo-liberalisation), marketisation and privatisation are ways of naming the processes that point to this dislocation of the place of the (welfare/national) state and its associated ideas of public interests and public services. But it is, nevertheless, a story and one which strives to be compelling as it seeks our assent to this version of the future. Confronted by such inexorable forces, how can we do anything but accept (whether enthusiastically or grudgingly) the rise of the market-state? We want to tease out a few problems with this story, looking at what it conceals as well as what it announces. Even in the short extract above, we think it is possible to see a number of problems that demand more attention: the mixture of empirical and normative elements in the concept of the market-state; the disappearance of politics in the inevitabilist model; the 'standpoint' (in geo-political terms) from which the story is being told; and some small empirical troubles about whether it is true.

Let us begin from some of the small empirical problems. Contrary to what the Bobbitt thesis would suggest, the amount of public spending on forms of welfare/social protection among the OECD countries has stayed stable or increased during the last twenty years (Castles, 2004). There are important arguments about why such patterns of public spending have been sustained, and about whether they are directed to the same policy goals and objectives as before (Clarke, 2004a; Ellison, 2006; Hartman, 2005). At best, this issue of public spending points to an uncomfortable overlap between Bobbitt's 'market-state' and 'nation-state' models, in which public spending is partly being sustained through the claim that national competitiveness requires welfare investment. We can see this most clearly in the issue of un/employment. Bobbitt suggests that unemployment has become just a question of market-based 'efficiency' calculations, with high unemployment an inevitable – and acceptable – consequence of low market demand for particular skills. However, many societies (at least those of the global north) spend money and effort on policies of activation, welfare to work programmes and workfare schemes (Peck, 2001; van Berkel and Valkenburg, 2007; Hvinden and Johansson, 2007). Such programmes combine economic, social and political calculations in complicated ways. Few societies, even Bobbitt's USA, think they can be seen to do nothing about unemployment, even as they rewrite political scripts in order to attribute the problem to the unemployed themselves. In the USA, surplus populations (of different sorts) are maintained through publicly funded programmes, from Temporary Aid to Needy Families (TANF) and other forms of workfare, through philanthropic provision and, especially, the prison–industrial complex. Indeed, most societies of the global North are importing extra workers (as both legal and illegal migrants) to support economic growth. Entitlements and access to public services and goods have certainly become more fragmented, more conditional and certainly more grudging in some places, but this is rather different from Bobbitt's market logic.

Through this point, we might also appreciate the disappearance of politics from Bobbitt's story. Consider the market calculation of efficiency about large numbers of unemployed people. If the market has no use for them, 'then the society will simply have to accept large unemployment figures' (Bobbitt, 2003: 229). But we want to insist that politics in various forms intervenes in this process of calculation. National publics exert pressure on the political institutions of the state – demanding forms of welfare and social protection, or at least the maintenance of social order. Without this, large numbers of unemployed people have the capacity to be either a political threat or a social problem. The market calculation of efficient employment is only one element of the political calculation that needs to be performed by state actors. The costs of large numbers of unemployed people are not simply transferred out to 'society', but are borne in public as well as private ways: whether in the form of social programmes, increased policing, expanded prison systems or the costs of managing the anxieties of 'respectable', hard-working citizens.

Politics at this level – the processes by which popular desires, doubts, aspirations and anxieties are negotiated – is strangely absent from the market-state narrative (in part because of the way that Bobbitt attributes the nation to the past). But politics in a larger sense is also missing – the domain of politics as a field of contested and conflicted choices about the future. Bobbitt treats the market-state as a necessary future. But in places other than the USA, conflicts continue about whether this is a desirable model, whether there are alternative futures, or whether markets can be constrained or controlled in service of other possibilities. Even in the USA, the logic of the market-state is not universally accepted, even by its enthusiasts (who constantly seek to make exceptions to its logic in pursuit of other compelling political interests: Wedel, 2009). Only by taking politics seriously can we see how such an account of the new forms of states (and their interrelationships with markets) is itself a politicised narrative – politicised in the sense that it tries to make one possible future come true in practice. By making politics disappear, by emphasising the necessity of market logics, Bobbitt projects a fantasy of the future as though it is already true (or in process of becoming true). It is both a political narrative (attached to market-centric thinking) and a geographical narrative, projecting the USA as the model of the future and as the norm to which everyone else will aspire, or at least conform. It is one of the (more polite) versions of US imperialism, seeking to shape the world in its image, trying to create 'market democracies' everywhere that it can (and failing).

The UK has occupied a complicated relationship with this geo-political vision. It is one of the other exemplary reference points for the 'market-state', given the processes of state and public service reform since the 1980s. Many of the elements identified in Bobbitt's summary can be traced here: the openness of international capital markets; the internationalisation of production and consumption; the emphasis on opportunity rather than welfare; and the attempt to shrink the state are all familiar themes. Indeed the UK forms part of an (ill-named) 'Anglo-Saxon' project of marketising reforms that other European nations often view with alarm. But in place of such reifications of the market (and indeed the state), we may be better served by thinking about the proliferation of market-like processes, and of markets as made – rather than natural – phenomena.

Making markets

Rather than just seeing the rise of the market, we might consider a range of ways in which markets have been invented and installed in the processes of reform. This requires a more focused attention on the ways in which public services and states are being refashioned and new assemblages constructed. For example, Holland et al.'s study of the changing forms of local democracy in the US points to what they call 'market rule'. They argue that the Reagan/Bush/Gingrich revolution in government was associated with the 'privatisation and devolution of social services to state and local municipalities', prompting

> fairly dramatic changes in the way public monies have been allocated. For example, relatively less is spent on schools and more on speculative economic development projects, less on pollution control and more on prisons. The role of government has been radically questioned, as has the definition of public resources and, indeed, whether a public sector should exist at all. The institutional changes wrought by this 'revolution' and the economic transformations just mentioned have been joined by the rise of neoliberalism – briefly the idea that the market offers the best solutions to social problems and that governments' attempted solutions, in contrast, are inefficient and antithetical to the value of freedom. Together these processes – privatisation, devolution and neo-liberalism – have constituted what we call 'market rule'. Market rule is an experiment of grand proportions that has fundamentally shifted the meaning of America democracy in the late twentieth century . . . (Holland et al., 2007: xi–xii)

This is a more considered view than Bobbitt's idea of the market state. Holland et al. trace the multiple processes contributing to the rise to dominance of market rule. They also understand it as a specifically US phenomenon (with complicated variations from place to place within the USA). Even though many of its trends and tendencies might be visible elsewhere, it is important to not submerge differences of time and place in one 'globalising' story about markets. Certainly, the UK has shared in this emergence of market rule: the combination of privatisation, devolution and neo-liberalism is a familiar one. But the forms of market rule are not exactly the same, especially in terms of thinking about how markets have been made in the process of public service reform. The following list suggests some of the innovations that have taken place during the last three decades:

- the privatisation of public services, involving the sale or transfer of public assets to private ownership operating in market-like conditions;
- the construction of 'internal markets' within services by separating purchasers and providers;
- the delegation of commissioning functions to non-state actors, who then act as proxy principals for the state;
- the opening up of public services to tender from competing providers alongside public agencies;
- the involvement of private financing for capital projects through Private Finance Initiative (PFI) or Public Private Partnerships (PPP);
- other forms of partnership model designed to create resources and innovation in specific organisations through corporate investment in, or sponsorship of, schools or health care;
- government sponsorship or incentives for privately provided alternatives to public provision;
- government incentives for individuals to 'shop around' in the market place for privately provided financial services;
- the construction of some market-like relationships around or within specific public services, with funding formulae based on the capacity of the organisation to attract 'customers'.

These 'marketising' reforms have produced different sorts of market, and have reworked the relationships between states, markets and citizens around public services in diverse ways. They produce distinct social, organisational and economic arrangements. Nevertheless, we might draw out some connecting issues about the consequences of these processes of market-making.

First, each of them is the result of political agency – there is no natural or inexorable spread of the market. On the contrary, they emerge from political calculations, choices and the investment of public resources. Whether market-making involved the sale of council houses to tenants, or the invention and installation of a distinction between purchasers and providers within a particular service, these changes involved political, social and organisational work. Second, each of these specific changes was then recruited as part of the market narrative, supplying evidence of the inexorable spread of the Market and the diminution or decline of the State. Despite their differences, and despite their specific political construction, they are run together (by enthusiasts and critics alike) as evidence of the triumph of the market.

Third, each of them changes a particular field of practices, relationships and processes. The scale and scope of these particular sites does indeed vary – from multinational capital buying into public utilities such as water, gas or electricity provision, or global finance capital investing in building new hospitals or financing new employment services, to the division of the same departmental corridor into a dual world of purchasers and providers. But they produce different types of economic 'opportunity', establish new types of economic calculation, and produce new types of economic agents: people who are required to act *as if* they are consumers, purchasers, entrepreneurs, contractors and so on. Their specificity matters, in part because they produce particular consequences. Expanding the role (and sources of profit-taking) for corporate capital is different from creating a field of choices for consumers of a particular services (patients choosing hospitals, or parents choosing schools). Neither is the same as subjecting organisations to the rule of internal or quasi-markets as a substitute for market forces.

Fourth, each has consequences for those working for the public, whether in the public sector or in commercial or not-for-profit organisations to which services have been transferred, or who are contracted to provide services. For example, in the UK the introduction of PPP and PFI has produced worsening material conditions for workers transferred from public to private or not-for-profit enterprises (Hebson et al., 2004; Mooney and Law, 2007; Ruane, 2004; Sachdev, 2004). But the heightened demands for flexibility and an increase in job insecurity now operate across public services, producing a rise in temporary employment contracts and agency work – although, as Kirkpatrick and Hoque (2006) note, the latter may also be a result of workers attempting to regain some control of their work in the face of increased performance pressures within employing organisations. Shifts in working practices have taken place as organisations have turned to an increased reliance on IT, have disaggregated services to call centres, and introduced closer monitoring and control over the workforce. As Mooney and Law point out, these transformations have been accompanied by attacks on collective bargaining, constraints on trades union rights, and widespread redundancies, job cuts and processes of casualisation. Increased workplace regulation, through audit and inspection processes, has taken place alongside work intensification processes and 'a declining sense of job security and increasing levels of workplace stress and related illnesses' (Mooney and Law, 2007: 8). At the same time there has been increasing pressure for workers to 'self-manage' their own employability through engaging in re-skilling and/or the acquisition of additional qualifications.

Finally, each of these marketising innovations has been the subject of political, moral and organisational contestations. Trades unions, professional associations, political parties and other movements have contested the place of the market in the service of the public. Wherever markets are being made, there are other voices and other discourses that challenge the appropriateness of market relations – questioning their subjection to profit rather than need, pointing to the risks of corruption and collusion, demanding that values other than market value are relevant, or insisting on the superiority of morals, ethos and solidarity to individualism and self-interest (e.g., Elyachar, 2005; Hohnen, 2003). This returns us to the idea that it is through *political processes* that different market-like instruments are assembled with public resources, functions and policy instruments.

States, markets and the public–private divide

Earlier in this chapter we highlighted the ways in which market narratives elide or obscure the political choices that are made in the remaking of public services. Such choices are fundamental to the changing relationships between states and markets, or public and private sectors. Rather than a narrative of the inevitable opening up of more and more public functions to the market, the story tends to be one of oscillations and uncertainty about what is properly the function of the state. In the UK, the failure of rail infrastructure privatisation, the politically disputed privatisation of the London Underground, scandals about excessive profit taking in privatised public utilities, and the 'nationalisation' of a failed financial institution (Northern Rock) in 2008 all unsettled assumptions about the relationship between state and market, and drew attention to the oscillations between the privatisation and renationalisation of key services. Forms of public and private ownership prove to be less distinct than they appear. For example, Jenkins (2008) borrows a term from African political economy to describe the rise of 'para-statals' – enterprises whose business and balance sheets are dependent on government contracts. This hints at the development of complex relationships between – and within – public and private sectors.

The imperative towards opening up public services to markets and market-like principles remains strong, in part because of pressure from multi-national service industries to capture new markets, but also because of competition between states in the global marketplace of service industries. Jordan, for example suggests that the development of public–private partnerships

> is not simply a way of extending the scope for funding new hospitals, schools and care homes, or of making efficiency savings in how they are run. It is a far more concerted effort to tailor the long-term trajectory of domestic social policy to the strategies of those financial interests and service corporations on the world market. Because the General Agreement on Trade in Services (GATS) promises to open up all these for competition worldwide, to secure the benefits accruing from the growth of such industries, the cultivation of resources and experience in these sectors within the domestic economy puts the leaders in this field (the USA and the UK) in favourable positions in the global market. (Jordan, 2006a: 90)

The following vignette suggests ways in which attempts to stimulate new markets are associated with shifting social policy problems and priorities. In the process, those targeted by policy interventions are drawn into newly marketised relationships.

Vignette: Making a market of the unemployed

In 2006 the Secretary of State for Work and Pensions commissioned a review of the UK's Welfare to Work programme to make recommendations on how to 'reduce inactivity and in-work poverty, and meet the Government's 80% employment aspiration' (Freud, 2007: 1). The Review was undertaken by David Freud, who had previously worked as a Financial Times journalist and an investment banker at Warburg (later UBS). He described the resulting report, *Reducing Dependency, Increasing Opportunity: Options for the Future of Welfare to Work*, as

> a radical reform designed to reduce social dependency of the most disadvantaged. I am proposing a structure in which the private and voluntary sector would be prepared to invest substantial sums, with minimal risk to the state. In return, I am looking to people with more barriers to work to engage fully with the new support system. (quoted in Sandeman, 2007)

Comments on the Review have ranged from enthusiastic endorsement by government ministers to criticisms by anti-poverty campaigners, challenging its emphasis on responsibilities over rights, its support for intensified 'conditionality' for public benefits, and its proposal to contract out aspects of welfare to work provision (Sandeman, 2007). Here, though we want to draw attention to the process of translation – how the 'problem' addressed by the Review was redefined. The Review distinguishes between 'streamlined, mass market provision based on Jobcentre plus' which will focus on 'providing a professional, high-quality, work-focused service for all claimants in the first year of their claim' (Freud, 2007: 10) and the problem group of 'long term workless' or 'the hard to help' (seen as 'multiply disadvantaged' and/or 'benefit dependent') who require a system that 'treats people's individual needs' (Freud, 2007: 51). While Jobcentre plus can deal with the mass business, the more refined qualities of the private and voluntary sectors are to be recruited to deal with the 'hard to help':

> In my view there are good reasons for taking this involvement of the private and voluntary sectors further in the delivery of welfare to work.
>
> - Outcome focused contracts, properly managed, mean that the Government can pay by results, so that contractors rather than the Department bear a greater share of the risk.
> - Competition for contracts through bidding processes enables the Government to obtain better value for money, as well as driving up the quality of the service offered to the public.
> - With proper information sharing, a diversity of providers will engender innovation, leading to better results.
> - The use of more than one provider means that the claimant can be offered a choice.
>
> Dealing with high volume is what Jobcentre plus is good at. Moving towards a system of flexible, forward-looking, outcome-focused provision for people with more disadvantage would provide the opportunity to make effective use of the qualities that the public, private and voluntary sectors have to offer. (Freud, 2007: 51–2).

> The Report dramatically shifts the problem being addressed to a new discursive framing. It does so by examining the processes and problems of contracting for such services: how to shift 'risk' from government to providers; whether to have quasi-monopolistic 'prime contractors' or 'multiple providers'; how to stage payments by results; how to set incentives correctly, and how to manage contracts in the longer term. These are, it is assumed, technical and procedural issues. What begins as a social policy problem (how to move people from welfare to work) is translated into a technical problem (how to contract most effectively).

Contracting is a market-mimicking device that enables the 'principal' (the state or its proxy) to shape the actions of the 'agent' (the entity delivering services on the state's behalf). As the Freud Review indicates, there has been considerable innovation in contracting (or commissioning) for public services, much of it directed towards trying to overcome governance problems arising from the principal–agent model. How is risk to be distributed between states and business? What mechanisms exist for managing failures that disrupt services, often affecting vulnerable service users and producing potential media scandals? How will the search for economies of scale be reconciled with the current focus on engaging publics in deliberations about local needs and aspirations? How are outcomes to be evaluated and rewarded? All of these point to one overarching question: what means are available for managing the potential governance failures that arise from the difficulty of specifying complex, dynamic problems in contractable form?

New models of commissioning attempt to displace such questions, making them the concern of 'prime contractors' rather than the state, exemplified in the 'flexible New Deal' service that evolved from the Freud Review. The tender advertisement placed by the Department for Work and Pensions called this:

> A radical new approach to sourcing, procuring and managing employment provision . . . It is envisaged that successful contractors will need to engage with a wide range of private, public and third sector organisations to deliver the services. DWP will consider applications from organisations that will deliver part or none of the employment provision themselves. (advertisements in the UK press, April 2nd, 2008, e.g., *The Guardian*, p. 7)

Such new models appear to offer technical solutions to intractable problems, reducing the burden of 'public' risk in the process. But as Bredgaard and Larsen's (2007) study of the contracting out of employment services in Australia, Holland and Denmark suggests, the use of market models involves much more than technical issues – important policy content can emerge from institutional design factors. For example, the process of contracting employment services may speed the shift to a focus on 'work first' rather than a personal development or support-oriented approaches, since it is easier and cheaper. The result may be a depoliticisation, through processes of technicalisation and displacement, of the policy process itself.

Such displacements have been associated with 'governance failures' (Bovens et al., 2004) that derive – at least in part – from failures in the contracting process. In the UK these have included failures of government-commissioned IT systems (delivered late and massively over budget, and much criticised by those expected to use them); the loss of personal data held by contractors; the spread of MRSA infections in hospitals in which contracts for cleaning services have been financially squeezed, and many others. Governance failures are perhaps inevitable, though we might suggest that the reliance on contracts and competition makes them more difficult to prevent and to resolve. Contracting is one means of 'displacing' political dilemmas or problems away from states; but failures tend to rebound on governments, further exacerbating the decline in public trust and political legitimacy. One of the respondents in Catherine Needham's recent study claimed that for public services: 'It's about time we had a government that looks after these things rather than giving it to a bloomin' supermarket' (2007: 189). This echoes claims in our study of citizen-consumers that, for public service users, 'it's not like shopping' (Clarke, 2007b).

Competition and choice: the rise of market imagery

Competition and choice are conventionally seen as core elements of the New Public Management and they are understood as ways of installing market-like practices and disciplines within the realm of public services. Competition is often announced as the core dynamic of the Market: the mechanism by which efficiency, innovation and customer satisfaction can all be assured. In a range of public service reforms, competition has served as a proxy for marketization, especially in education and health care. Competition between providers has been promoted even where markets do not exist: it is seen as an improving discipline on provider organisations, driving the same sorts of outcomes that market-place competition is supposed to deliver. Non-market competition between providers has typically been organised through two devices – quasi-consumer choice mechanisms and performance evaluation.

Public services are often provided outside of the cash nexus exchange mechanisms of markets. Indeed, as Esping-Andersen (1990) and others have argued, that has been a key element of the *raison d'etre* of public services. They decommodify services and benefits in ways that insulate them from the impact of economic inequalities. Provision on the basis of right or need involves principles that are different from ability to pay. Consequently, enthusiasm for the disciplines and dynamics of the market has encountered problems when key market mechanisms (the cash-mediated exchange between buyer and seller) proved difficult to replicate in public service reform. Promoting the principle of user/ consumer choice among competing providers has been one alternative route to reform that has played a significant role in the UK (Clarke et al., 2005, 2006; Clarke et al., 2007a; Clarke and Newman, 2006; Jordan, 2006b; Taylor-Gooby, 1998; see also Le Grand, 2007).

Choice has been controversial as a policy mechanism. It has been attacked for its specific social effects (as in the field of parental choice in education, e.g., Ball, 2005; Gewirtz, 2001; Gewirtz et al., 1995). Critics have claimed that choice functions as a rhetorical device that conceals other political intentions. Choice both stands for and masks these other dynamics, acting as a proxy for deeper processes of privatisation or marketisation, and is the product of political calculation (Clarke et al., 2006). At the same time, choice as a device in policy and political discourse slides between at least three types of meaning:

1 the specificity of choice as a particular policy mechanism (e.g., choice meaning the expression of parental preference for the schools that their child may attend);
2 choice as a practice involving the exchange of resources for a desired object, service or outcome (the market principles of exchange through the cash nexus or its equivalent);
3 choice as a generic social and political value (the 'freedom to choose' as a liberal and libertarian value).

This slippage between meanings has proved to be a powerful discursive resource in the politics of choice, allowing its proponents a certain tactical mobility in relation to criticism of choice-based reform (Clarke et al., 2007b). The defence of choice has moved between policy pragmatics (choice works in this service for these objectives); market equivalences (choice works because it is how markets work); and abstract value or right ('choice for the many, not for the few': Blair, 2003). The critical hinge for this discursive work is, of course, the equation of choice with market exchange. Choice as an abstract liberal value does not centre on the market (though it may include it). Rather, choice is about the capacity for self-direction exercised by a self-possessed individual in personal, social, economic and political arrangements (from choice of partner to freedom of expression of political views). The collapse of these into a market model of exchange evacuates other domains and forms of 'choice' in favour of the freedom to spend one's own money. Through this hinge discursive equivalences can be constructed between specific policy mechanisms and the abstract value of choice. Choice is good; choice is exercised in the market through exchange; public services need market-mimicking mechanisms to promote choice. This mobile character of choice also enables it to act as a political and policy condensate – containing, combining and compressing multiple meanings (Ball, 2007; Clarke et al., 2006).

In practice, choice is carefully specified: 'the small print' of choice policies reveal crucial limitations on what can be chosen, by whom, and in what conditions. For example, in the Freud Review the commitment to choice (on the part of service users) becomes subordinated to the pressing problems of constructing a good commissioning model. Rather than choice of provider, '[t]he main aspects of choice for clients should surround the contract they agree with their provider. Here they will select and agree to the programmes which will become available to them, and agree activities with their provider' (Freud, 2007: 64). The idea of a contract thus plays two different roles. There is the business of contracting for services – the construction of a series of principal–agent relations (between government and the commissioner; between commissioners and providers). But the same word is also applied to the 'agreements' between service providers and clients. Contracts between the state (or its agents) and individual citizens who are dependent on, and required to consume, these services do not much resemble the economic and legal fictions of agreements between freely exchanging individuals. These are compulsory or coerced contracts, initiated and enforced through power differentials between users and state agents. More generally, though the attempt to use choice as a 'liberation' of the citizen from public monopolies is intended to act as a discipline on producer power, requiring producers to compete to attract (non-cash paying) customers). Being competitive and being successful are thus naturalised as dominant organisational imperatives for individual schools, trusts, and hospitals.

As we will see in the next chapter, choice (in this non-cash nexus form) is closely linked with the management of organisational performance through other competitive framings, notably evaluation, inspection and audit. The rise of evaluative systems has been justified by reference to providing information that will enable members of the public to act as well-informed consumers, as well as to the more general needs of government to stimulate (and simulate) competition as a driving force for service improvement. However, such systems also play a crucial role in coordinating or controlling public services. Responsibility for 'service delivery' has been simultaneously fragmented and devolved to multiple 'autonomous' provider organisations (such as schools and hospitals) each of which is (more or less) responsible for managing its own performance, and subjected to competitive performance evaluation (represented in 'league tables' or 'star ratings'). Even in the most generous interpretation, these institutional arrangements do not look like markets. Consumers do not purchase anything, producers do not sell anything, the product itself is difficult to define (do hospitals produce health?); and the price mechanism (to the extent that it exists) is established by formulae that fix the rate for the job (and are thus subject to governmental revaluation). These are market-mimicking devices that seek two different sorts of effect. The first is to institutionalise principles of coordination based on competition that challenges, disrupts or controls producer/professional power. The second is to encourage all sorts of agents (from individual users to groups of workers to organisations) to think of themselves as economic agents.

Inventing economic agents

Markets and market-mimicking devices require people to understand themselves as specific sorts of economic agents (motivated and powered by economic means). Anthropological work on markets, such as Elyachar's (2005), suggests that economic agents are not born, but have to be made. Our own study of citizen-consumers in England revealed people who were profoundly reluctant to identify themselves as 'consumers of public services', rejecting the impersonal and transactional model that such an identity implied (Clarke et al., 2007a). Getting people to think economically, and to think of themselves as economic agents, is a process of construction that requires intensive political and discursive work (and may not always succeed). Public service reform through market means involves the construction of array of economic agents, each invested with a specific form of power or authority; for example:

- *Provider organisations* are invited to imagine themselves as a business. Some, of course, are already businesses in a fully corporatised sense (major utility, construction, and medical corporations, for example). Some are 'small businesses' (e.g., some providers of residential or nursing care). What were organisations based in the public or voluntary sectors are subjected to pressures to be 'business-like' in the way they manage themselves. 'Thinking like a business' – identifying and improving the product; mapping competitors and collaborators; assessing the market; planning investment; capturing and satisfying customers – becomes a framing device for organisational decision-making (even when this model fits uncomfortably with what the organisation actually does).
- *Senior figures in organisations* are invited to understand themselves as chief executives, strategic managers or, most recently, leaders. Leadership has become a major reinvention of management, with many programmes attempting to institutionalise its development and practice in UK public services (e.g., the National College for School Leadership; the Leadership Foundation for Higher Education; the Leadership Centre for Local Government; the NHS National Leadership Network and so on: see O'Reilly et al., 2006; Wallace and Hoyle, 2007). Across the range of public services, this development of senior, strategic, innovative or even transformational management is one of the long-term and now deeply embedded effects of the 'new managerialism'. The proliferation of training and development programmes directed at senior organisational strata encourage two related phenomena: a self-consciousness of being a leader

(in the generic sense); and a sense of being the embodiment of the specific corporate entity (providing the vision that motivates others, being the bulwark against external dangers and threats, anticipating the opportunities to 'grow the business').

- *Clients, contractors and commissioners* are invited to see themselves as purchasers or providers of services. The distinction within or between organisations transforms formerly collaborative, and often professional, relationships into competitive or even antagonistic relationships that are contractually mediated. Both parties are expected to think of themselves as engaged in a struggle of value extraction – how much can each gain from the other in the contracting process? The question of gain may be short term (economic or other advantage) or it may be long term (guarantees of provision, continued business or profitability). But how to contract (and manage contracts when established) becomes part of a new organisational skill set, and leads to dynamics of mutual exploitation, uncertainty and adaptation.
- *Producers and consumers* are foundational economic identities and were always central to Public Choice theory and its critique of public service provision. This argued that public monopolies enabled producer interests to dominate consumer interests because, in the absence of market competition and choice, consumers had no countervailing power (Dunleavy, 1991; Finlayson, 2003). However, public services have an ambiguous relationship to consumers – needing to recruit and satisfy them, while trying to manage levels of collective and individual demand downwards (since use of a service often consumes budgets rather than generating income).
- *Workers in organisations* are invited to understand themselves as (more or less) valued human resources. In particular, they are expected to see themselves as corporate agents, grasping and executing the organisation's mission. This is a source of particular sorts of strain in public service organisations, given the centrality of bureau-professional roles in which identifications have historically been as much to the profession as to the specific employing organisation. The pressure to 'think like a business' increases demands for corporate identification from employees, since professional attachments risk being a deviation or distraction from the organisation's conception of its 'core business'.
- *Entrepreneurs* are summoned to help expand the market for public services. But entrepreneurship has a much wider resonance: as we noted earlier, one overarching image of economic agency is the invitation to almost everyone to think of themselves as entrepreneurs. The image of being entrepreneurial has been propagated across many sites – whether taking 'investment risks' with pension planning, being enterprising in the workplace (du Gay, 1996), or learning to be entrepreneurial (through education or training).

Vignette: being socially enterprising?

As we saw in Chapter 2, the concept of social enterprise has become increasingly significant, identifying a desirable merger of social objectives (or values) and businesslike efficiency and innovation. In the UK and elsewhere, ideas of social enterprise and social economy have begun to replace earlier terminology (such as voluntary and community sector). Defourny, for example, claims that 'we are witnessing today a remarkable growth in the "third sector", the new or renewed expression of civil society against a background of economic crisis, the weakening of social bonds and the difficulties of the welfare state'. (Defourny, 2001: 3)

'Social enterprise' tries to name and unify a heterogeneous field of organisational forms, practices and objectives, ranging from cooperatives to philanthropic organisations. Many are located in political and moral commitments and seek to differentiate themselves both from business and from the state. For example, Gibson-Graham (2006: xxi) points to the 'myriad projects of economic activism' through which post-capitalist politics are being imagined and which create 'a zone of cohabitation and contestation among multiple economic forms'. However, bringing this heterogeneous field together under the title social enterprise risks obscuring significant political, economic and organisational differences. Pearce insists that the 'primary purpose of a social enterprise is social: it aims to benefit the community or a specific beneficiary group. Commercial activity is secondary in the sense that it is the means to achieving the primary purpose' (Pearce, 2003: 33). This is, however, a rather thin conception of 'social' and much writing on the social enterprise tends to elide descriptive and normative claims.

The UK government has become an enthusiast, having established a social enterprise fund and unit, advising on how to create and manage social enterprises, and extolling the benefits of the model. In one document, the advantages are set out for different groups of beneficiaries:

For patients and service users
Social enterprises involve patients, staff and service users in designing the services they provide. This means that services are better tailored to meet patients' and service users' needs and are based on expert knowledge of a particular area. Social enterprises re-invest any surplus profits into the community or into service developments. This means that social enterprises very often benefit the whole community as well as the people who use their services. . .

For health and social care organisations
Social enterprise offers health and social care organisations the opportunity to deliver high quality services in ways that are flexible, non-bureaucratic and have the potential to deliver good value for money. It also allows health and social care organisations to deliver services that are tailored to their local population, and make a difference to the local community. Because staff have a stake in social enterprise organisations, experience has shown that they are very committed to the aims of the service, and that this delivers benefits for the organisation, for example, improved staff retention. . .

> **For the third sector**
> Third sector organisations have expertise in specific areas, and great under-standing of the groups they represent. They understand how services should be delivered to best meet people's needs. Social enterprise models offer the opportunity for a sound commercial relationship between public sector commissioners of health and social care services and third sector providers of those services.
>   (Department of Health, 2007)
> Social enterprise here bears the characteristic marks of a hybrid formation or assemblage. It is depicted as efficient (producing 'high quality services', deliver-ing 'good value for money') and offering a 'sound commercial relationship' between commissioners and providers. But it also speaks to ethical – and 'public' – considerations: benefiting the 'whole community', or 'making a difference to the local community'.

Social enterprise is seen as carrying particular virtues (ethical commitments, energy, dynamism), the capacity to mobilise enthusiasm and social capital, and an orientation to promoting social change and social justice. For example, Pearce claims that 'Social enterprises are not businesses like any other. They are funda-mentally different because of the values which underpin them and guide what they do and how they do it. Those values distinguish social enterprises, from first system businesses and from second system organisations' (Pearce, 2003:146). But we might note how these new articulations of 'business', 'enterprise', 'social' and 'justice' subtly change the meanings of each other. The idea of enterprise plays a key role here – combining ideas of innovation (being enterprising) and being busi-nesslike. The businesslike values and virtues are as important to the recruitment of social enterprise to processes of governing as their social purpose.

Social enterprise points us towards a more general conclusion about the impact of markets on public service reform. The results have rarely been a direct replacement of the state by the market as advocated by enthusiasts or as bemoaned by critics. Instead there are murky mixtures of privatisation, forms of marketisation, devices that mimic markets within the state, the promotion of reg-ulated forms of competition and non-cash nexus processes of consumer choice. In their US study, Holland et al. talk of 'neo-liberal hybrids' that bridge – and transform – previous public–private distinctions, creating partnerships that may both serve 'public interests' by drawing on private resources (financial capital, expertise, etc.) but may also put public resources (including political legitimacy) into the service of private interests.

We will return to the question of hybrid forms in Chapter 5. Here we want to note the strong resemblances between social enterprise and our discussion of community and civil society in the previous chapter. We can see both the governmentalisation of other sites and forms of social action and emergent ambiguities – for organisations enrolled into governing, for states trying to manage heterogeneous providers through contracting and evaluation systems, and for publics confronted by diverse, uneven and potentially unpredictable sets of providers. Social enterprise is marked by this characteristic double process of governmentalisation and displacement – enrolled into new assemblages for governing the social, and dispersing political and public concerns into fragmented, disconnected and localised forms.

Seeing like a market: the rise of market populism

In this final section we want to develop one other point from Holland et al.'s study about the character of market rule. This, they suggest, is not just a process of institutional reform, it also produces a reworking of political and popular discourse about the relationships between society, politics and economy (at least in Anglophone contexts):

> . . . we noted a subtle but powerful means of unequal influence on political decisions. Since the 1970s, neoliberal thinking has come to dominate local government, and is now a dominant language spoken by local elites – elected and appointed officials and the members of growth coalitions that influence them. It is this language that has most influence over local resource allocation and priority setting. This for-profit mentality assumes that market rule naturally makes for a good society. However, market rule privileges citizens with disposable income, and it focuses on the values of consumption, assuming that people are not first citizens with rights as well as responsibilities with respect to society but instead are individual consumers responsible for satisfying their own individual needs by making smart, economical choices in the market place. This orientation produces a highly individualistic vision of society, one that is blind to issues of social justice and equity. In such a society . . . politics is no longer a place for conversation and contest over conflicting ideas about goals for the community. Market-oriented, neoliberal, for-profit thinking puts forward instead the idea of society as a technocratic arrangement for individuals pursuing wealth and economic growth, even as it is clear that one, the so-called good market performers, will benefit significantly more than others . . .
>
> This neo-liberal blueprint sets the stage for a select minority being players while the rest exist off (or exit from) the map of the new political landscape. When community development and local political discourse are organised on such grounds, business people are cast as super-citizens while those without the means to contribute – that is, without business

know-how or capital to invest – emerge as de facto subcitizens. (Holland et al., 2007: 236)

Here we can see the significance of discourse – understood as ways of seeing and thinking that become institutionalised in politics, policies and popular culture. Market-centric discourse crafts a new understanding of how society, politics and the economy are to be ordered, what relationships between them should prevail, and how people are expected to behave (as citizens, as members of society, but – above all – as economic agents). Holland et al. point to two further consequences. First, political decision-making is shaped by market-centric discourse in new ways, partly though the criteria and frameworks of calculation in which decision-making takes place. Second, access to decision-making is re-shaped in terms of the differential valorization of sorts of people and sorts of knowledge. This points to a wider implication of thinking like a market: this way of framing the world attributes different value to particular individuals, groups, knowledges and behaviours. Some people have desirable qualities: they possess capital, or business knowhow, or are at least 'hard working families' or 'good consumers'. Others might be developed to become valued subjects through education, welfare to work schemes, empowerment programmes, or the cultivation of economic, cultural or social capital. There are others who have failed to be the right sorts of subjects – unproductive in employment, making the wrong sorts of consumption choices, lacking an 'entrepreneurial self', these devalued and denigrated subjects become problems of social management: the excluded, the 'hard to reach', the 'unwilling' (Baumann, 1998). They require other governing strategies and mechanisms: ones that are sterner, more punitive or disciplinary (Burney, 2005; Simon, 2007).

Market-centric discourse has proved a mobile and flexible way of thinking and seeing. Its global dissemination owes much to the double process of its association with the USA (in an era of economic, cultural and political expansion) and its adoption by international policy-making agencies (from the World Trade Organisation to the International Monetary Fund). The naturalisation of the market has been a powerful outcome: as Holland et al. (2007) note, market society is now understood as the natural (and desired) condition of human society, and the market is the first choice of means for fixing any social problems that persist. This holds true even for those areas of activity that either might be seen as resulting from market failure (unemployment, as in the Freud example above) or were aspects of social life that had previously been nationalised, taken into public ownership or subjected to state regulation because of market incapacities and failures (health provision, railways, education, etc.). Market-centric thinking has memory problems.

Perhaps the most significant feature of this discourse is the deep and pervasive role it has come to play in linking political, policy and popular thinking. Frank's analysis of market populism addresses the transformations of US politics and culture – and its appropriation of anti-elitism – but surely identifies a travelling discourse:

> Wherever one looked in the nineties entrepreneurs were occupying the ideological space once filled by the noble sons of toil. It was businessmen who were sounding off against the arrogance of elites, railing against the privilege of old money, protesting false expertise and waging relentless, idealistic war against the principle of hierarchy wherever it could be found. They were market populists, adherents of a powerful new political mythology that had arisen from the ruins of the thirty-year backlash. Their fundamental faith was a simple one. The market and the people – both understood as grand principles of social life rather than particulars – were essentially one and the same. By its very nature the market was democratic, perfectly expressing the popular will through the machinery of supply and demand, poll and focus group, superstore and Internet. In fact, the market was more democratic than any of the formal institutions of democracy – elections, legislatures, government. The market was a community. The market was infinitely diverse, permitting without prejudice the articulation of any and all tastes and preferences. Most importantly of all, the market was militant about its democracy. It had no place for snobs, for hierarchies, for elitism, for pretence, and it would fight these things by its very nature. (Frank, 2001: 29)

This market populism has been profoundly influential in remaking the imaginative landscape of society, economy and politics during the last thirty years. We would, however, want to offer some cautionary notes. This way of seeing and thinking like a market is distinctive, but it works on a longer history of ideas of the market and its proper role in social life. It is a process of redrawing boundaries, reconstructing relationships, and inventing new assemblages rather than a simple process of moving from state to market. Secondly, it is a naturalising discourse, trying to establish the naturalness – and necessity – of the market as a global phenomenon. However, it is not uniformly established: places continue to construct different arrangements of society, economy and politics (even if market-centric discourse is dominant). Thirdly, it is a universalising discourse, but it is not uniformly successful: people retain attachments to other principles of social life (intimacy, solidarity, publicness, politics) as alternatives to market coordination. They also develop emergent conceptions of alternatives in the face of the failures, costs and consequences of market coordination.

Conclusion: Making markets and remaking power

In the course of this chapter, we hope to have developed a more differentiated view of how relationships between states and markets have been remade in processes of public service reform. We have argued that states remain central to the new regimes of organising public services, even as their institutional forms, structures and relationships change dramatically. Images of decline or subordination are not adequate ways of describing the changing forms and roles of states. Although making markets and installing market-mimicking devices into the coordination of public services are certainly significant, the increase of market discourse has been at least as significant in terms of constructing people and organisations as economic agents, and as a way of circulating market imagery in political and popular discourse. In the process, we have seen that the binary distinction between state and market obscures the multiple ways in which markets, market-like mechanisms and market imagery have been deployed in reform programmes. Grasping this multiplicity (and its differential consequences) also means giving attention to the shifting intersection of multiple sectors, types of organisation and principles of coordination. Such processes of reform have produced strange new forms of organisation, regulation, coordination and governance – new assemblages – that we explore more extensively in the next chapter.

. Finally, Elyachar reminds us that the process of making markets (and, we might add, market-mimicking processes) is itself inherently political:

> The labor of making particular forms of markets is also the labor of politics. It is about power. Attempts to teach the poor of Cairo to budget their time and money with more streamlined methods resembling those of capitalist forms, and to learn accounting, 'the language of business' (Davidson, Schindler and Weil, 1982), are more than ethnographic anomalies. They are attempts to reshape the nature of power and subjectivity. (Elyachar, 2005: 24)

Different forms of power are produced and distributed in such processes. The decentralization of governmental authority to multiple service providers is one example – highly conditional and delimited authority is devolved by central government to such organisations. Their exercise of it is subject to double pressures: the demands and desires of service users and would-be service users on the one side; the apparatuses of inspection and evaluation on the other. Nevertheless, as Pollitt (1993) and others have shown, the managers of organisations 'liberated' from direct central or local government control have often relished the 'freedom to manage'. Similarly, citizens as service users are 'empowered' or authorised as consumers to exercise choice over services (in terms of patient or parent choice and in such policy developments as direct payments for social care). But there are also re-alignments of forms of political and economic power at stake in these processes (or what others have called forms of public and private authority; see Hansen and Salskov-Iversen, 2007). These re-alignments sometimes involve transfers of power and resources (from the state to corporate bodies); they sometimes involve creating fusions or hybrid forms of power (trusts, public private partnerships, social enterprise). But the creation of markets (in their different forms) certainly changes the landscape of power and its exercise – a theme we pursue in Chapter 5.

5 Blurring boundaries: private authority and public governance

In the previous chapter we argued that binary distinctions between state and market, or between public and private, are less than helpful, obscuring the multiple ways in which market-like mechanisms and market imagery have been deployed in state reform programmes. The remaking of public services has been much more complicated than this binary would allow, involving new scales and spaces of governing, new sectoral mixes, and innovative forms of organisation that have often been called 'hybrids' (e.g., Kickert, 2001). Direct privatisations exist alongside internal markets; public-private partnerships alongside social enterprises; large 'third sector' or voluntary organisations involved in major contracted service delivery operate alongside the service user managing their own individual budget to buy care. In some places the logics of contracting are giving way to a greater reliance on public–private partnerships and privately financed public services. The expansion of external oversight and regulation develops alongside the growth of management boards and corporate governance frameworks. All of these involve new dynamics that change the shape of the 'public' elements of public services, bringing some features of publicness into view but making others less visible.

But hybridity, we would argue, is not just a matter of new, complex organisational forms. It also involves assembling different forms of power – state power, corporate power, managerial power and, in some cases, power derived from 'civil society', communities and citizens – in uneasy alignments. As such it has implications for the possibility of democratic governance. The UK – particularly England and Wales – has formed the test bed for many of the developments we consider. This may be because it is at the forefront of a particular form of neo-liberal governance; or may be attributed to problems of translation of some of the key concepts (Osborne, 2000; Osborne and Brown, 2005). But while there are parallel developments in many countries, there has been a marked proliferation of new configurations of public and private authority in the UK, and rapid successive cycles of reform – what Pollitt (2007) has termed 'hypermodernisation' – whose effects might be described as 'disorganised governance' (Clarke, 2006a; Newman, 2006a).

Publics, markets and hybridity

We begin by exploring the new configurations of public and private authority in the development of 'hybrid' organisational forms. Such forms have multiplied: public–private partnerships, private finance initiatives, franchising, joint ventures, strategic partnering, the outsourcing of governmental functions to charitable or voluntary bodies but with some forms of public governance, social enterprises, trusts and so on. This proliferation of forms has taken place as governments have attempted to make greater use of commercial and not-for-profit actors to design, manage and deliver public policy; and as organisations have sought competitive advantage. Rather than a sector-based analysis, we want to emphasise how different forms of authority are assembled in a single entity. Hybridity suggests rather more than ideas of 'mixed economy' or 'partnership' in which sectors remain clearly bounded and organisations work 'across boundaries'. Kickert, for example, argues that

> Hybrid organisations are situated between the public and private spheres. On one hand, they are supposed to function like customer oriented and efficient firms. On the other hand, they carry out intrinsically public tasks. The nonprofits, the QUANGOS, and the independent social welfare agencies, as well as the quasi-autonomous executive agencies are all hybrid organisations. This hybrid third sector is important to the Netherlands and will remain so. (2001: 148)

For many organisations it is crucial that they are able to face both ways: that is, to be able to legitimise themselves both as profit-making enterprises and as public bodies; or as voluntary/not-for-profit enterprises and as businesses (Moe, 2001). This means acting, in Wedel's terms, as 'flex' organisations. These are adaptable, multi-purpose organisations, playing multiple and conflicting roles, and developing chameleon-like qualities in order to 'switch their status and identity as situations dictated' (Wedel, 2001: 152). Different forms of 'public', 'private' and 'ethical' legitimacy may be played off against each other. This creates sites of strain and tension:

> it may appear difficult to conceive an organisation with a strict and effective management style and operating in a competitive environment, while at the same time being situated at the margins of the public sector, and at the same time mirroring the more informal and trust based climate that one knows from 'community based' organisations (Schultz and von Stein, 2007: 6).

This study, based on empirical work in the former East Germany, highlights a number of different strategies and responses to such strains, including structural differentiation, 'muddling through', or adapting to the structures and logics of one sector and marginalising the rationalities of others. Such approaches to managing hybridity, they suggest, 'primarily call for sociological and psychological tools rather than [those] of business or public administration which were designed for single sector organisations' (Schultz and von Stein, 2007: 27).

This marks the importance of those actors who have to manage new boundaries and relationships. Wedel (2001, 2009) introduces the concept of 'transactors' to describe individuals or organisations that face in multiple ways when working across boundaries. They may formally belong to or represent a particular group of interests (a government, a public service organisation, a corporation, a charity) in a project that has additional goals that may, in some circumstances, subvert those interests. Wedel's work examines the intersection of public and private interests and organisational forms, but transactors may also carry public – or philanthropic – values into new settings. Some of these features are illustrated in the following vignette.

Vignette: the modernisation of schooling in the UK

Education reform was a key political priority under each of the Blair governments, leading to a rapid succession of initiatives 'freeing' schools from local authority control, introducing new categories of school and more parental choice. Many developments relied on new forms of cross sector collaboration between public and private sectors in joint ventures, sponsorships and profit sharing arrangements. Stephen Ball argues that such schools 'represent and contain all the uncertainties and tensions created by the unstable duality of empowerment and control and the diverse and competing elements of Labour's reform agenda . . . They drastically blur the welfare state demarcations between state and market, public and private, government and business, and they introduce new agents and new voices within policy itself' (Ball, 2007: 171). As such they bring schools much closer to the business agenda. Indeed in February 2008 the headteacher of one Academy school called for greater freedom from state control so that they could be run more like businesses, with incentive pay structures for staff and with an end of independent appeal panels for excluded pupils (*The Guardian*, 25 February 2008: 12).

However, Ball argues that this cannot be understood as 'rampant and enforced privatisation as an ideological state strategy'. Rather 'The private sector is one of several devices deployed to reorganise the local state and reform public sector organisations, sometimes replacing them, but also very often working as a partner. There is no simple, unidirectional move to privatise, although the scope of privatisation is expanding as the obvious 'solution' to public sector difficulties and the role of local authorities in moving more towards commissioning and monitoring rather than delivery. Both points need to be registered.' (Ball, 2007: 120–21).

Ball also maps the new policy communities that have developed in education – communities that are both 'routes of influence and access for business voices and at the same time new ways of realising, disseminating and enacting policy' (2007: 122). Such communities are ways of embedding a business approach and entrepreneurial calculus into the public sector. By tracing the membership of such networks and the complex flows of influence between different actors, Ball shows the depth of interlinking between business, philanthropy, quasi-governmental agencies and public and private sector entrepreneurs. This interlinking means that it is not possible to separate entrepreneurial from 'philanthropic' values. Indeed 'One of the interpretive problems involved in thinking about how these networks work is that of deciding, at least in the case of some of the participants, where business ends and philanthropy begins . . . Perhaps it is pointless to attempt to pin down the motives involved here or to try to separate out different elements, and it must be accepted that motives are mixed'. (Ball, 2007: 124).

We can trace a number of themes here. One is the proliferation of new organisational forms (such as Academy and Trust Schools) with a complex mix of autonomy and control, part-funded or sponsored by other organisations (businesses, universities), They are largely positioned outside of the control of local education authorities with considerable new managerial and educational freedoms. A second is the complexity of partnership arrangements, producing a complex overlaying of 'public' and 'private' interests. A third is the shadow presence of new policy communities that mix elements of business and philanthropy with 'public' policy concerns and values.

This example raises questions about 'hybridity' as a concept. Some view it in terms of the dissolution of any clear boundary between sectors. Schultz and von Stein (2007 argue that 'The intermediate area between state, market and community is seen as a contested field, constantly influenced by the logic of markets, the impact of various communities and conceptions of the private life and, finally, by state policies' (2007: 3). This creates organisational tensions: collaboration and competition, openness and boundary management, and notions of entrepreneurship and 'good governance' are brought into uneasy juxtapositions. But for us, such organisational forms might be better thought of as complex assemblages, combining and condensing different forms of power and authority. They are not two dimensional, linking public and private sectors; rather they are cross cut by multiple goals, forms of internal governance, and organisational practices and relationships. They also condense different political projects: governmental strategies to shift services from state to market; the turn to civil society as a resource for government; the pursuit of emerging public agendas that require the involvement – or 'empowerment' – of multiple agents (for example in responses to obesity, or climate change). They are also entangled in new governance strategies, for example enhancing public participation in the design and delivery of services. Some enrol multiple sources of authority into new projects; while others resemble virtual partnerships or shells for the pursuit of one set of interests (the recurrent criticism levelled at the Private Finance Initiative and Public Private Partnerships in the UK). Many appear as 'compulsory partnerships' where the power of the state is used to enforce partnership between agents and agencies. As a result, we think the idea of assemblage may illuminate rather more than hybridity, which tends towards seeing two origins merged into a third form (public + private = third sector, intermediate zone, etc). Assemblage points to the multiple sources, resources and combinations that appear to be at stake in these organizational innovations.

Digital dynamics, individualisation and personalisation

In these processes of remaking relationships between public services and the public, new technologies are often seen as critical forces, capable of blurring boundaries without necessarily requiring new organisational forms. For example, Dunleavy et al. (2006) talk of the capacity of 'Digital Era Governance' (DEG) to reintegrate dispersed functions and services, exploiting new technology to bring together many of the different elements that NPM separated out into discrete organisations or business units. They suggest such technologies enable a new configuration of the public into a series of persons around whom services are clustered in an image of needs based holism. This is in line with the current policy orthodoxy of personalisation in which public services are to be tailored to meet the needs and circumstances of individuals rather than delivered in a standardised way (Department of Health, 2008; see also Leadbeater, 2004; Leadbeater et al., 2008; and critical commentaries by Barnes, 2008; Cutler et al., 2008). This development is the site of some ambiguity. It potentially opens up new spaces and practices of citizenship; at the same time, however, the responsibility for integrating public services into usable packages may be 'devolved' to citizens. The use of DEG for public services further marginalises the publicness of those services, making it harder to see differences between the call centres of the bank, the insurance company, the tax office and the local authority. As in 'flex' organisations, differences between public services and business or commercial services are flattened out. However, new technologies may come to offer rather more than the potential for individually tailored services. Leadbeater and Cottam (2007) point to new business models that enlist users as participants and producers, suggesting that Web 2.0 opens out the possibility of parallel forms of user generated innovation in public services:

> For the past decade most of the debate about public service reform has focused on delivery, making the public sector value chain work more efficiently, to resemble reliable private sector delivery. But you cannot deliver complex public goods the way that Federal Express delivers a parcel. They need to be co-created. That is why these emerging models of mass user-generated content [such as MySpace, Wikipedia] are so intriguing. They point the way to the user-generated state (2007: 97).

This suggests ways of bringing the public itself into new assemblages of public and private authority through strategies of 'co-production', 'choice' and 'empowerment'. That is, boundary blurring and flexing are not just organisational dynamics, but take place at the interface between publics and public services. Social care services for disabled people, older adults and people with learning difficulties led the way in these developments, often responding to user challenges and demands (Leece and Bornat, 2006; Newman et al., 2008). These mostly do not rely on digital technologies (though there are interesting experiments in opening up access to ICT for older people: Loader et al., 2007). How do such innovations reshape our notions of public and private and shift the role of service organisations?

Vignette: Modernising adult social care

Services providing adult social care in England and Wales – and in many other European countries – have been going through profound changes. User groups and movements of disabled people have long campaigned for greater independence; that is, for a move away from professionally defined needs and state-provided services to a regime in which service users have greater choice and control over the forms of support they use. Developments such as Direct Payments and Individual Budgets now enable (some) service users to take control over public funds, purchasing and managing their own care. These developments are only partial (professional and organisational resistance has been strong), and are uneven across different groups (developments in relation to older people and mental health service users have been slower than those for disabled people and people with learning disabilities: Fernández et al., 2007). But they nevertheless can be viewed as a shift towards a more central place for the user in the design and delivery of services, as this recent Demos report suggests:

> This report advocates a simple yet transformational approach to public services – self-directed services – which allocate people budgets so they can shape, with the advice of professionals, the support and services they need. This participative approach delivers highly personalised, lasting solutions to people's needs for social care, education and health at lower cost than traditional, inflexible and top-down approaches. It could transform not just social care but many other public services, including maternity services, mental health provision, education and training – especially for those excluded from school, drug users, offenders seeking rehabilitation and much more.
>
> In a joint policy statement issued in December 2007 five government departments joined the Local Government Association and the Association of Directors of Adult Social Services and the NHS in committing to a more personalised approach to social care. Our research shows that the most effective way to deliver on this commitment is to introduce self-directed services based on personal budgets. When self-directed services are introduced with the right kind of support for people and their choices translate into how money is spent they deliver huge pay-offs: people get personalised solutions that give them a better quality of life, allow them to

> participate more in society and form strong relationships at lower cost than traditional service solutions that often isolate and leave them feeling dependent. (Leadbeater et al., 2008: 7)

There are important issues here about the 'public' role of public institutions. First, the shift to direct payments and individual budgets poses questions about the regulatory role of the state, exercised through an ever shifting array of regulatory, inspection and audit bodies. The key virtue of Direct Payments and Individual Budgets is that they enable service users to purchase and manage their own care. Even if the regulatory services had the capacity to scrutinise their efficiency or effectiveness, it is doubtful whether this role would be viewed as legitimate – should, for example, a neighbour or friend employed as a personal assistant be subject to criminal record checks?

Second, new models of care have implications for the boundary between public and private. Individuals, households and families are coming to take on responsibilities previously viewed as state functions: coordinating their own care (or that of others), managing budgets, supervising staff and so on. What, then, is the public role of public bodies in pursuing a 'duty of care' in the face of an increasingly consumerist approach to care services? And what might be the public duty towards the carers and family members who are increasingly assuming responsibility for managing such services on behalf of vulnerable service users? What are the obligations and responsibilities that individuals may take on in personalised arrangements, and how might these be enforced?

Finally, there are important questions about how personalised budgets can be reconciled with the public purposes and commitments of public services (Clarke et al., 2007a: chapter 6). Discussing the proposed extension of individual budgets to health care, Peter Beresford has argued that

> This raises the question of how we square the circle of a universalist NHS, still in many ways free at the point of delivery, with a model of cash payments or allowances borrowed from a selective social care system – a system whose funding and rationing are currently subjects of both raised public concern and government review (Beresford, 2008: 4).

Such developments involve 'reshaping' the publicness of public services and creating forms of 'flexing'. Here service organisations, and the professionals who work in them, have to reconcile – and mediate between – business rationales, inspection and audit bodies, professional norms of good practice, and public desires and expectations. We will return to the potential of new digital technologies and models of participation to foster democratic innovation in Chapter 7; but here our point is that such innovations offer both the potential to diminish the publicness of public services *and* to shape new relationships with the public itself.

The democratic implications of public–private partnerships are equally ambiguous. As Holland et al. comment: 'The public–private partnerships so common to the experiment in market rule pose deep challenges to democracy but, at the same time, the arrangement, ironically, creates an opening, albeit a small one, for democratic empowerment' (Holland et al., 2007: 9). This is because 'in cases where the neo-liberal priority of profit making is difficult to achieve, outsourcing to non profits is acceptable. As a result, governments also partner with non-profit organisations that are community oriented rather than market oriented' (2007: 10). As we saw in Chapter 3, this may well lead to the managerialisation and incorporation of such organisations as social movement and 'third sector' organisations negotiate their response to new governance requirements and managerial norms (Bodi and Laurie, 2005; Brown, 1997; Taylor, 2003; Fyfe, 2005). As 'flex' organisations themselves they become part of what Wolch (1990) terms 'the shadow state'. Where they take over service delivery obligations from the retreating welfare state they become subject to the requirements of managerial efficiency and good governance, such that their capacity for advocacy and activism may be squeezed. But public- and community-based principles and norms nevertheless become more visible, opening up points of leverage and sites of agency. Services may have to appear open, accessible and inclusive; public values may become explicit in publicity materials, job advertisements, tender documents, and other devices that help organisations flex their public muscles, even when controlled by private finance. Publicly oriented codes of practice become inscribed in new governance templates; and may be reassembled with business norms in strategic 'vision' statements. All of this means that publicness may become a strategic asset rather than an implicit – and devalued – resource. Such processes point to the growing centrality of governance processes; in particular, how such organisations go about securing legitimacy with both public stakeholders and private shareholders – as well as with the wider public.

In the name of the public: regulation and 'good governance'

The proliferation of new ways of organising the provision of public services has been matched by a proliferation of new forms of governance. We noted in Chapter 1 the salience of the concept 'governance'; our usage here denotes practices and technologies through which public authority may be exercised in the context of 'shape-shifting' organisations and 'boundary-blurring' practices described in the first part of this chapter. Institutions concerned with scrutiny, audit, evaluation, inspection and regulation have proliferated in what might be called a 'performance/evaluation nexus' (Clarke, 2004a). This can be viewed as a response to the problems of exercising state power once the direct levers of control (through bureaucratic hierarchies of the 'machinery of government') are replaced by a dispersed, fragmented system. It offers one way for governments to attempt to resolve the paradox of public doubt and desire. The creation of league tables, star ratings and other forms of ranking has been enabled by the rise of an elaborate regulatory apparatus in the UK, referred to variously as the

'Audit Explosion' or the 'Audit Society' (Power, 1993, 1997); 'the Waste Watchers' (Hood et al., 1999) and 'the New Bureaucracy' (Travers, 2007). Such competitive evaluation enables central government oversight of 'arm's length' and fragmented service provision; it provides incentives to organisations to improve perform-ance; it promises a deepened system of accountability for public resources and it claims to work through 'independent' systems of inspection, audit and evalu-ation (Clarke, 2005c). Whether all of these objectives can be delivered by the current apparatus of evaluation is another matter, as is the question of whether the burden of evaluation has distorted organisational priorities and purposes, as well as distracting organisations from their original purposes. As Paton (2003) argues, organisations may have become better at managing performance evalua-tion than managing performance.

These developments have been subject to a range of critiques (Clarke et al., 2000; Clarke, 2005b; Hood et al., 1999; Newman, 2001; Pollitt et al., 1999; Power, 1997; Strathern, 2000) that we cannot do justice to here. Rather, we wish to focus on the different forms of power at stake in these developments. We might distinguish between the overt extension of state power, exercised through audit and inspection bodies; the dispersal of state power through 'self-regulat-ing' managerial agents; and the emergence of templates of 'good governance'. These appear at first sight to be analytically distinct: audit and inspection bodies carry the direct authority of the state, even if the functions are discharged by quasi-autonomous organisations or even contracted out to private enterprise. They carry with them the power to impose state penalties and award state favours: the ranking in a competitive field, the award of new freedoms and flexibilities following a period of good performance, a change of funding regime, the 'naming and shaming' and possible closure of 'poorly performing' organisations, the imposition of penalties or the mandatory appointment of new executives charged with 'turning around' a failing organisation. Here the coer-cive – and 'prize-giving' – powers of the state, coupled with the use of hierarchi-cal, bureaucratic and sometimes professional authority, are tangible.

Yet such forms of authority are also exercised through less overt forms of power: the constitution of organisational actors as self-managing subjects and the rise of new technologies and practices associated with 'good governance'. In policy terms these different strategies are often functionally related: the possibility of self-management is offered to those who perform well against the state's performance criteria. For example, Hood et al. note how new modes of governance are less dependent on external directives than on a 'system of enforced regulation [that] involves the deployment of heavier regulatory tackle against the incompetent or recalcitrant, while lightening the regulatory yoke over good performers' (1999: 296). However good governance, with its conno-tations of transparency, accountability, participation and performance, has become a significant discourse that is not simply dependent on state power for its authority.

Good governance constitutes a 'regulatory space' (Hancher and Moran, 1989) that cuts across the boundaries of state legislators, inspection bodies and service delivery organisations. For example McDermont's study of housing association governance draws on the idea of the state, regulators and regulatees inhabiting a shared regulatory community. She argues that

> organisations that are subject to regulation always feel that regulation is a thing that is being done to them . . . They portray a process by which external bodies, usually the state, impose upon them systems of control: all they can do is work within such systems. Research tells a different story, however . . . Their position as being subject *to* the control of a regulator . . . is only part of the story; at the same time they make themselves subjects *of* a regulatory system through shaping their own identity, as well as the identity of others around them (McDermont, 2007: 374-5).

This regulatory space is occupied by actors who have a shared language and a shared expertise that brings with it a capacity for self-discipline and self-governance. This draws attention away from notions of power as hierarchically ordered, focusing instead on the flows and relations of authority, and on the forms of expertise that shape access to, and exclusion from, the regulatory space. We can trace here a discursive reframing of notions of regulation (with its links to government and its proxies as superordinate authorities) into notions of governance. Governance condenses a number of developments: the rise of private sector notions of corporate social responsibility and corporate governance; an increasing focus on problems of corruption and the framing of good governance as a global good by transnational bodies such as the World Bank. But it also stems from wider issues that have challenged traditional public service concepts such as accountability. The problems of assuring accountability in the context of a complex array of networks, partnerships and hybrid forms has led to a range of debates and developments (Bovens, 2004, 2007; Newman, 2004a; O'Neill, 2002; Sullivan, 2003). But the meaning of accountability has always been contested. As Bovens remarks, 'In contemporary political and scholarly discourse "accountability" often serves as a conceptual umbrella that covers various other distinct concepts, such as transparency, equity, democracy, efficiency, resourcefulness, responsibility and integrity' (2007: 449). He also notes that 'Accountability is one of those golden concepts that no one is against. It is increasingly used in political discourse and policy documents because it conveys an image of transparency and trustworthiness' (Bovens, 2007: 448).

But how might transparency and trustworthiness be conveyed in the context of the 'boundary blurring' and 'flexing' we discussed earlier in this chapter? While financial accountability and accountability for delivery of particular service or organisation specific targets remain significant, the complexity of the contemporary forms of coordination and control have problematised traditional based models of accountability that ran 'upwards' to superior agencies. Given the weakening of the role of elected governments as arbitrators of substantive knowledge and judgement, the dominant discourse in the global template of good governance has shifted towards notions of *transparency* (Blomgren and Sahlin, 2007; Clarke, 2005c). This discourse is articulated by international agencies (such as the World Bank, International Monetary Fund and the Organisation for Economic Cooperation and Development) and enacted in regional, national and local systems of governance. The demand for transparency is a demand for a visible, or at least, traceable, decision-making path. It rests on a view that organisations (should) be able to account for themselves and their actions – the awarding of contracts or professional judgements; the allocation or rationing of services; or their employment practices. The quest for transparency, however, may become stalled in the face of the shape-shifting and boundary-blurring processes traced earlier in this chapter. As a result governance arrangements may, in practice, give primacy to some aspects of transparency (often fiscal or financial measures) over other, looser, or more difficult to specify, social, political or professional criteria.

The discourse of transparency is combined, in uneven ways, with notions of *performance* that have come to dominate the governance and management of public services as well as private corporations. Performance marks a discursive shift from earlier dominant discourses which framed public services in terms of narrow economic calculations of spending levels (too high), financial efficiency (too low) or financial management (too weak). Performance is more directed to issues of 'outputs', or even 'outcomes', although this should not be taken to mean that concerns with spending levels, narrow concepts of efficiency or improving financial management have gone away. Rather the discourse of performance – and the practices of performance measurement and management – enhance and extend the power of managerial forms of governance.

Transparency and performance are articulated with a third strand in the performance/evaluation nexus – *participation*. The detachment of public services from an integrated public sector, and the development of complex, hybrid forms, mean that what Sorenson and Torfing (2006) have called the 'democratic anchorage' of public services is being loosened and reassembled with more fluid conceptions of public participation and stakeholder involvement. Participation, like transparency and performance, has come to resemble a 'global good' in normative templates of reform. Publics – of various kinds – are being invited to participate in the design, management and governance of services. This raises difficult questions – whose voice should be heard, through what means, and based on what models of representation – that are difficult to resolve within standardised templates of good governance. And the intersections between public participation and managerial rationalities are, at best, uneasy – an issue to which we return in Chapter 7.

These themes – transparency, performance and participation – intersect, not always comfortably, in a global, or globalising, governmentality of governance ('good governance'). They establish norms, ways of seeing and thinking, ways of calculating and acting that both create the conditions for specific governance innovations and infuse the practices of governance that ensue. Good governance – whether on the part of public sector bodies, businesses, NGOs or many of the 'flex' organisations discussed earlier – is, then, both a normative discourse and a set of technologies. The latter renders areas of potential political conflict, or struggles over different kinds of 'public' interest, into more neutral decisional spaces, offering 'a technical fix that will insulate policy choices from the passions, dangers and seductions of politics' (Clarke, 2005b: 217). Political judgements and calculations are displaced away from the formal – and cumbersome – mechanisms of representative democracy to a plethora of governing bodies, boards, consultative committees and trustees. But this displacement of politics, its transformation into the decisional calculus of good governance, is vulnerable to destabilising processes.

> Politics tends to rear its ugly head recurrently (since governments are also political – as are the 'hard choices of policy) . . . the 'above the fray' technical fix is vulnerable to social, political and cultural challenges to its mode of authority – whether this be social scepticism about how trustworthy the 'experts' are, or the competence of managers. Claims to authority are always only claims and are intrinsically susceptible to challenge (Clarke, 2005b: 217).

One line of potential instability arises from the ways in which values associated with the public domain – openness, equality, justice, democracy – are translated into norms of good governance. It may well be that openness is successfully translated into the more problematic idea of transparency; equality into 'fair process'; justice into powers of redress for 'dissatisfied customers'; and democracy into a more amorphous concept of participation, with all of the dilemmas this raises. But these remain subject to challenge. For example, the kind of transparency that is compatible with norms of commercial confidentiality may not be able to withstand challenges made through the courts; while elected representatives may well reassert their power if injustices are brought to their attention (often by a more than willing media acting as 'watchdogs'). Such difficulties are compounded by ways in which states such as the UK seem to be moving away from inscribing norms of equality, justice, fairness and access to prescribing norms of governance. This is in line with the award of conditional freedoms to organisations in a dispersed field of power, with the role of the state as guarantor of standards or entitlements being residualised.

We began this section by highlighting different forms of power at stake in the new architecture of public governance. Some, we suggested, involved the explicit extension of state power through audit and inspection bodies and performance management regimes, to say nothing of the 'delivery units' inscribed at the centre of government in the UK. Others relied on the constitution of organisational actors as self disciplining subjects within norms of good governance. The relationship between these raises two issues:

- the role of the state in shaping and managing the new architecture of governance; and
- the forms of power on which 'empowered' actors draw in a dispersed system.

These two 'governance puzzles' are the focus of the next section.

Governance puzzles: states, power and authority

The emergence of flex organisations, public–private partnerships and the greater use of private capital for public projects raise significant governance challenges. How far can the performance–evaluation nexus discussed in the previous section moderate the power of corporate capital in public service delivery? Processes of audit and inspection may act as a brake on profit-seeking behaviour by requiring businesses to conform to particular standards of service delivery (for example in health or social care). Government targets may mean that businesses or partnership bodies have to take account of a wider public interest; for example, requiring schools to admit a certain percentage of 'special needs' pupils, or housing developments to include a proportion of low cost or 'social' housing. But the significance of 'good governance' as a global template is that it works across corporate and state institutions. Rather than the state having to act as a directive power, organisations from all sectors are constituted as responsible actors in a dispersed field of power. Business legitimacy and public legitimacy may become blurred rather than offering alternative criteria against which performance can be judged.

What, then, of state power? Governance theory of the late twentieth century was preoccupied with the 'hollowing out' of the state, such that the state was viewed as having ceded power to a range of subsidiary – and superordinate – bodies: regional or local tiers of governance, private sector companies, civil society organisations, regulatory bodies, the boards of individual schools, hospitals or housing authorities, transnational corporations, supranational governmental bodies and so on (Kooiman, 2003; Pierre, 2000; Pierre and Peters, 2000; Rhodes, 1994; 1997; see also critiques in Newman, 2001, 2005b; and Walters, 2004). Such narratives implied the displacement of the (nation) state as the sovereign authority, such that governance involves co-steering between different types of authority, rather than merely being (contingently) devolved authority from the state. Attention was drawn to the co-existence of, and possible collaboration between, different agents – combining the public power of the state and varieties of 'private authority' (corporations, communities, consumers: Hansen and Salskov-Iversen, 2007). Network-based modes of coordination were assumed to have, in part, displaced the exercise of hierarchical power on the part of the state, leading to the emergence of concepts such as the 'partnership state', and 'empowering' or 'participative' governance.

However, there has been renewed interest in the state's role in 'meta-governance', managing the sites and spaces in which other forms of governance were brought into existence and managing their relationships (Kooiman, 2003). For Jessop 'meta-governance' is one of the ways in which the state adopts a role in attempting to manage or orchestrate dispersed actors and agents. Rather than the power of the state disappearing, the state 'reserves to itself the right to open, close, juggle and re-articulate governance arrangements, not only terms of particular functions, but also from the viewpoint of partisan and overall political advantage' (Jessop, 2000: 19). This implies something rather different from epochal claims about the disappearance or even death of the state. Like Sharma and Gupta (2006) we want to insist that the state persists, albeit in new formations, relationships and assemblages. In particular we want to highlight the powers that the state retains to itself: especially the power to organise sites, scales, spaces and relationships, and to allocate forms of power to different agents. The first governance puzzle, then, concerns the changing character of – rather than the demise of – state power, expressed in concepts such as disaggregation (Slaughter, 2004), de-centring (McDonald and Marston, 2006) or dispersal (Clarke and Newman, 1997).

The second governance puzzle concerns the forms of power at stake in the 'empowerment' of actors involved in the new architectures of governance. This brings into view the discursive power of the state in constituting new forms of subject. In *The Managerial State* (Clarke and Newman, 1997) our focus was on the constitution of managerial actors charged with coordinating a fragmented array of organisations and services through a particular set of decision-making logics – logics that privileged economic over social criteria, that looked to business rather than the state for appropriate technologies, and that privileged performance in a competitive field rather than collaboration and integration. Here our focus is on how new governance arrangements may have to discover, or even create, the agents that they need to do the business of governing. Governors, stakeholders, trustees or representatives for particular interests have to be discovered, groomed and developed to take up their governance roles. At the same time, governance arrangements often need the subjects being governed to be 'represented' – embodied in persons who can 'speak for them'. Neighbourhoods, communities, service users, regions, or specified socio-demographic groups have to be 'brought to voice' in governance. Such representatives are one distinctive variety of stakeholders, bringing 'voices of experience' or the views of 'ordinary people' into governance (echoing the valorisation of ordinary people discussed in Chapter 3).

Such governance bodies become agents themselves, acquiring powers, capacities and interests. They enact governance, shaping the principles, models and schemas of good governance in practice. Freeman and Peck (2007b), for example, trace the symbolic and dramaturgical features of 'performing governance' on partnership boards. Alternatively we might consider the work of such boards in terms of processes of translation, with meanings of transparency, participation and performance being subject to inflection and interpretation by active agents in specific locations (Czarniawska and Sevón, 2005a and b). Practices of transacting, translating, mediating and brokering are central to these new forms of governance (Lendvai and Stubbs, 2006; Larner and Craig, 2005; Wedel, 2001, 2005). They also create the conditions in which new knowledges, skills and roles may flourish.

What does this attention to the new forms of agency associated with governance add to the second of the governance puzzles? On what powers do 'empowered' actors draw in a dispersed system of governance? We think it brings two critical things into visibility. It highlights an important question about the forms of knowledge and expertise that are valorised in governance (and the forms that are devalued or demobilised). Some of these valued forms of knowledge derive from the field of what Cutler and Waine (1997) call 'generic management' – the belief that all organisations share common characteristics, and thus can be directed using a set of universal principles, knowledge and skills. It also makes visible the structuring of who gets to enter into governance roles, with preference being given to those who are the bearers of such 'relevant knowledge and expertise': legal and financial knowledge, business experience and so on (Ball, 2007; Cowan and McDermont, 2006). Others – especially the 'ordinary people' who are the bearers of lay knowledge or everyday experience of how a service works – may be recruited and enrolled: but they may also become marginalised in the 'business of governance'.

Vignette: what do governors govern?

This vignette is drawn from research by Cowan, McDermont and Prendergrast on the governing bodies of Registered Social Landlords. These were formed to take over the ownership and management of formerly 'public' (local authority owned) housing stock following large scale voluntary stock transfers. RSLs are run by 'independent' governing bodies within the regulatory framework of the Housing Corporation (and its successors). As such they represent one example of the shift of control from democratically elected citizen representatives to governing bodies. Membership of these bodies is drawn from three constituencies: one third tenants, one third councillors, and one third 'independents'. Governance frameworks espouse a 'neutral allegiance' model which means that the decision-making capacity of members is strongly focused on the needs of the organisation, potentially subordinating other interests or perspectives.

Data from this study shows the importance of understanding the interplay of different forms of expertise within governing bodies. While tenants brought forms of expertise based on their experience and understanding, and councillors that of local communities, these operated alongside the professional expertise of lawyers, solicitors, accountants and surveyors – serving as 'independent' members of the Boards. These different forms of expertise were hierarchically ranked, with financial expertise dominant. This meant that

> [T]here appears to be little acknowledgement for a plurality of perspectives on what the RSL as a social landlord should be doing. The training programme, for example, was designed by the officers to impart the necessary skills and understandings to run a large business. On the RSL board, New Public Management values were reiterated time and again, from the regulator, the officers, the training, and even the tenant board member who had inspected other landlords and knew what the regulator wanted. Managerialised values had taken hold. The concept of the 'well managed organisation' is taken for granted (Clarke and Newman, 1997: 143) and political decisions become de-politicised in the skilled and expert board.
>
> So we have to ask the question, to what extent can the governors govern? The narrowing of vision imposed by neutral allegiance and expertise means that there is a danger that the board just becomes a reassurance that managers have made the right decisions. The possibility for challenge, alternative paradigms, and resistance to the direction proposed by managers is heavily circumscribed and, during the period of our fieldwork, remained latent (Cowan et al., forthcoming: MS p. 20, 21).

This returns us to the recomposition of power and authority. Such governing bodies, in our terms, might be considered as assemblages of different forms of expertise, different conceptions of representation and 'presence', and different technologies of decision-making. Thinking of them as assemblages constantly in the making as relationships and practices are negotiated creates the possibility that new voices may be heard, new logics of decision-making may emerge, and new actors may be 'empowered'. In the research on which this vignette is based, we can see different tenant members claiming distinctive kinds of expertise, and some element of contestation around the tension between local authority councillors' roles as 'neutral' board members and as democratically elected representatives of the wider community. Elsewhere we can see other forms of expertise-based power bringing governance failures to public attention. For example 'whistleblowers' in health services have frequently highlighted the strategies used by managers and clinicians to distort statistics on performance against government targets. And the resignation of over 100 lawyers from the UK Police Complaints Authority in February 2008 highlighted 'increased dismay and disillusionment ... at the consistently poor quality of decision-making at all levels of the IPCC' (*The Guardian*, 25 February 2008: 1).

We can also see the discursive power of managerialism operating within the governance institutions that supposedly privilege the notions of good governance described earlier. It would seem that the norms of accountability, participation and performance are shaped in ways that, at least in the RSL example, support the business agenda of the organisations concerned. This does not mean that governing bodies are ultimately reduced to performative and symbolic functions (c.f. Freeman and Peck, 2007a); nor that managers always succeed in dominating decision-making processes. Rather, we suggest, it means highlighting ways in which the constitution of governance actors is framed in ways that privilege managerial logics and forms of expertise.

Beyond the Managerial State?

In *The Managerial State* (1997) we argued that managerialism was becoming a dominant mode of power, coordinating a fragmented field of action as state power was dispersed across multiple actors and agents. But it is evident from previous sections of this chapter that governance comprises multiple and disparate forms of power that are uneasily aligned, producing tensions and dilemmas within – and between – organisations. What, then, of the power of managerialism? Is it being subordinated to the increasingly dominant norms of 'good governance', 'user empowerment' or 'partnership'?

Contemporary reassessments of the New Public Management offer at least two different narratives. The first suggests that NPM can be understood as periodised (see, for example, Hood and Peters, 2004 on its 'middle ageing', or Christensen and Laegreid, 2007, on 'post NPM' reform strategies); the second claims that we can now look 'beyond' NPM to network-based governance in which collaboration is valorised alongside competition (Klijn and Kopperjan, 2000; Rhodes, 1997). Both narratives imply the possibility of a reassertion of 'public' values. However both also suggest a linear conception of change, the first evolutionary, the second suggesting some form of paradigmatic change, in which one set of ideologies and practices is displaced by another. Neither, then, takes account of the continuities that underpin managerial action and authority. The focus on efficiency gains, the use of market logics, the valorisation of business-like techniques imported from the private sector, are continuing imperatives that condition and shape the ways in which 'partnership' and 'governance' are understood and enacted.

Our focus on the dispersal of power, and on managerialism as a calculative logic of decision-making, offers a different theoretical approach to the idea of NPM as a unified template of reform applied 'from above' that may now be receding. The conception of managerialism as a set of discourses, practices and technologies that can be assembled and re-assembled with other forms of power offers, we think, a better framework for understanding change as dynamic and contested (rather than as a template that can be adopted or adandoned). So we now turn to questions of *how* managerialism is being assembled with other forms of power. The vignette on the governance of housing above suggested that managerial forms of expertise were privileged where financial and legal considerations took precedence within a governing body. The following vignette offers an insight into the privileging of managerial discourse in other settings.

> **Vignette: the governance of partnerships**
>
> Skelcher, Mathur and Smith (2005) investigated the relationship between the design of partnership institutions – what they term 'collaborative spaces' – and democratic practice. Partnership bodies have weak ties to representative democratic institutions, enabling them to operate with greater degrees of flexibility, but opening up problems not only of accountability but of democratic engagement and legitimacy. Their empirical work analysed the underlying discourses structuring the governance institutions of a range of partnership bodies in two UK municipalities. The research traced the interaction between three significant discourses of partnership: managerial, consociational and participatory. Managerial discourse privileges managerial action and increased discretion for managers with respect to the political process. Here 'questions of public participation and accountability are constructed in terms of their potential to facilitate the implementation process . . . rather than as matters of citizenship rights or good public governance' (2005: 578–9). Consociational discourse 'provides for a coalition between the varieties of social groups in an elite decisionmaking structure' (Ibid: 579); while the participatory discourse 'is seen to provide policymaking authority to a wider community of actors' (Ibid: 579). The results of the research demonstrated the dominance of managerialist discourse and its associated practices,
>
> > with partnerships being subject to clear operational and corporate rules of central control, but also 'disarticulating' from notions of deeper democracy. This disarticulation presents a semblance of an open space in which new actors are able to deliberate rules for moving ahead with the governance of their communities, however the constraints played by powerful yet subtle control ensure a dominant governance trajectory (2005: 592).

Such examples suggest how the new architectures of governance often involve a double dynamic. On the one hand, governance arrangements seek to bring multiple interests into the business of governing public services. Often, representatives of the public/lay/user perspectives are central to these new architectures. But the valorisation of some forms of knowledge and expertise over others – the knowledges of 'how to manage' or 'how to be businesslike' – can be seen in the work of Ball ('can do' types of people) and Cowan, McDarmont and Prendergrast (what do you need to know?). The dispersed, complex – even baroque – architectures of public governance 'take account' of diverse constituencies and types of representation, but are driven towards a 'practical' conception of doing the business of the public. Indeed, managerial rationalities are not necessarily forced from above but may be sought from below as actors seek new alliances, sources of legitimacy and plausible recipes for survival and success.

We want to take this argument a little further. Managerialism, we suggest, is not only positioned as the dominant rationality in 'flex' organisations (because competitive success is the key determinant of survival and growth); but it also provides the knowledges, skills and technologies essential to the process of flexing itself. That is, managerialism provides a coordinating logic through which multiple forms of power and authority are combined and articulated, enabling business rationalities to be aligned with the alternative rationalities of state bureaucracies, 'third sector' organisations, social movements or community groups.

Governance regimes are, then, 'structured in dominance' through managerialism. It offers 'business-like' templates through which organisational power can be exercised. It infuses new rationalities of organisational leadership appropriate to coordinating complex partnership, network-based or 'hybrid' organisational forms. It is the basis for the knowledges and skills into which 'self-governing' actors have to be tutored. Community-based organisations have to acquire skills of financial management and 'good governance' in order to be eligible to bid for contracts. Service users may have to learn the language and logics of producers in order to engage effectively in 'co-production' activities. And, as the housing vignette suggested, 'lay' publics serving as participants or representatives in governing bodies not only have to learn new languages but have to translate their own perspectives and interests into them.

Managerialism – as an assemblage of practices, strategies, techniques and knowledges – is demonstrating its capacity to colonise other forms of power, reassembling alternative rationalities within its own logics. Governing at a distance, we suggest, is made possible by the growing power of managerialism. Yet we need to be careful to avoid any sense that this is somehow simply imposed from above. Indeed, managerial rationalities may be proliferating as actors undertake management education and leadership training programmes, network with other organisations, or seek out solutions from the growing cadres of management consultants (Sahlin-Andersson and Engwall, 2002; Pollitt, 2007). 'Governing at a distance' does not necessarily imply a spatial dispersal of power (though this is certainly evident, as we argued in Chapter 2); it is associated with the 'empowerment' of actors to make choices and to innovate. It also assumes that they will make the *right* choices (and systems of inspection and evaluation work to ensure this).

Such processes of empowerment may mean that managerialism can be adapted and shaped around a range of political, professional or social purposes. There is a strong body of work that argues that alternative rationalities associated with service user groups, social movement organisations, public service professionals and others 'working for the public' are likely to become incorporated into dominant managerial rationalities as they encounter managerial power (Glendinning et al., 2002; Newman, 2001, 2005e; M. Taylor, 2003). However, there is also evidence to suggest that organisations and services may be inflected with ideas and principles derived from social movements, community-based action or other 'alternative' spaces (Holland et al., 2007). At worst, these may be little more than marketing devices, or the opening up of a new entrepreneurial space. But such principles may also be a source of legitimacy as organisations 'flex' to different stakeholders, including states (as funder, auditor, or policy-maker). And they may be carried in the orientations and actions of those working for the public in different sites – whether as social entrepreneurs, frontline staff, volunteers, professionals, senior managers. In the next chapter we explore attempts to defend – and enlarge the scope of – such 'counter logics' in public services.

Conclusion: Managing publicness

Reviewing the arguments of this chapter we might wonder whether it is any longer sensible or possible to talk about *public* services. The proliferation of new forms of organisations and service configurations, the dominance of managerialism and the methods, sensibilities, tactics and values of entrepreneurship are now well entrenched in public service organisations, whether rooted in the public, private or not for profit sector, or – more likely – in some hybrid form. The blurring of the boundaries between public and private, between state professional and service user, between governance and management, produces multiple dynamics of organisational 'shape shifting' that make it difficult to discern what might mark the publicness of public services.

However, the transformations we have described here are also open to a more ambiguous reading. The complexity of organisational forms and combinations of public and private authority represents not simply the demise of the public but is also a condition of its proliferation. Forms of public finance, public authority and public governance have become key assets in many businesses. As such, the public is 'invited in' to the new assemblages of discourses, practices, skills, resources and reputational assets that are the key determinants both of good governance and commercial success. Publicness may be inscribed in new forms of organisation, new templates of governance, new regimes of partnership and participation, and may be a crucial element of organisational legitimacy. The public itself might be implicated in new forms of co-production in 'personalised' services integrated through digital and web-based technologies. However, the meanings and practices of publicness are limited by their association with – and subordination to – managerial forms of power.

This has crucial implications for our understanding of the politics of the public. We have seen how forms of state power are implicated in attempts to shape new practices of governance, reaching into the management of new organisational forms, developing technologies appropriate to governing at a distance, constituting actors as both the agents and subjects of governing, and summoning publics to voice. In each we can see governing logics and strategies as partly displacing or subordinating politics. However, we must also note the intractability of politics as claims about what is and is not a public issue, who can speak for and on behalf of publics, and what are legitimate forms of expression of public action. These continue to trouble new governing logics and rationalities.

6 | Valuing publics? The dilemmas of public work

In chapter 1 we highlighted the unsettling of sedimented formations of publicness in nation, state and the liberal public sphere. Here we focus on public services as mediating these processes of unsettling, but also of recomposition. Public services, as we noted in the Introduction, help constitute the changing 'sphere of publics'; but are also themselves being re-constituted within the political transformations of both nation and state. In returning to this theme at this point of the book we do not offer a story of the revival and resurgence of public norms and values after the supposed demise of the New Public Management; nor provide heroic tales of resistance as actors struggle against intractable forces. Rather, we try to unravel the multiple ways in which a politics of the public is being played out in specific sites. In doing so we engage with the possibilities they create for public values or an ethic of publicness. Despite the rise of managerialism and the privileging of business models for the delivery of public services, questions of value have repeatedly demanded attention. For example, the two quotations below articulate the idea of *public value* as a foundation for public service work. The first is from the work of the US scholar Mark Moore, the second from a more recent Work Foundation Report in the UK:

> We know the aim of managerial work in the private sector: to make money for the shareholders of the firm . . . In the public sector, the overall aim of managerial work seems less clear: what managers need to do to produce value far more ambiguous; and how to measure whether value has been created far more difficult. Yet, to develop a theory of how public managers should behave, one must resolve these basic issues. Without knowing the point of managerial work, we cannot determine whether any particular managerial action is good or bad. Public management is, after all, a normative as well as a technical enterprise. (Moore, 1995: 28).

> The challenge of how to marry the new culture of individualistic consumerism with the ethic of public services (necessarily more solidaristic and oriented around citizenship) besets all advanced economies. . . . The concept of public value . . . offers a resolution to what otherwise would seem to be two apparently irreconcilable cultures and belief systems. (Hutton, 2006: 10).

Next, an IPPR pamphlet titled *Public Services at the Crossroads* reflects the 'progressive agenda' for public services noted in the Introduction to this volume, and argues that, to promote social justice, public services should:

• support equal, effectively exercised rights of citizenship,
• help secure a decent social minimum, defined in respect of basic levels of education, health, housing and security,
• ensure equal opportunities to access services . . . and
• aim to achieve a fair distribution of outcomes, paying particular attention to the narrowing of unjust inequalities. . . .

(Brooks, 2007: 5)

Each of these interventions raises questions about the relationship between public services and a liberal public sphere, as in the third of the discursive chains set out in Chapter 1:

Public = legal and democratic values = Public Sphere

The 'liberal legal and democratic values' at the core of this discursive chain – such as openness, equality, impartiality, tolerance, and justice – were, in different combinations, inscribed in the bureaucratic norms and codes of the organisations that largely made up the public sector. Critiques of the debasement of the public sphere or the demise of the public sector often point to the loss of such values (e.g., Gamble, 2004). However there are considerable doubts about how far such values were ever realised in liberal democracies and welfare states. Cooper (2004), Brown (2006), Fraser (1997) and others have also challenged the values themselves, highlighting how norms of impartiality and shared interests 'have worked simultaneously to protect and obscure the interests of dominant social forces' (Cooper, 2004: 99). Feminism and other social movements brought into question the solidity of the boundary between public, private and personal, surfacing the gendered and heterosexist subtexts of the relationships between them (Warner, 2002). In particular western liberal values have signally failed to address contemporary questions of culture, faith and identity (Cooper, 2004; Hesse, 2001; Lewis, 2000b; Parekh, 2000a; Newman, 2007a). The discursive chain centred on liberal values, then, offers a relatively narrow politics of the public sphere – one that has trouble acknowledging new claims for voice and justice. It was also open to challenge from the failure of liberalism as a template for achieving equality and progress on the West's own terms. As Brown comments:

> Liberal universalist and progressive principles have been challenged by anti-assimilationist claims of many current formations of politicized 'differences', including those marked by ethnicity, sexuality, gender and race; by a political ethos promulgating agonistic social relations associated with

these cultural differences, as opposed to a model of pluralistic conflicting interests on the one hand, or of general social harmony on the other; and by the patently mythical nature of a progressive political worldview that presumes steady improvement in the general wealth, felicity, egalitarianism, and peacefulness of liberal societies. Undermined by historical as well as intellectual events in the late 20th century, the seamlessly egalitarian social whole constituting liberalism's vision of the future now appears problematic both theoretically and practically. (Brown, 2001: 20–21)

The limits of a discourse of equality tied to national citizenship and entitlements of a national welfare state are now well recognised (Fraser, 2005). Public service organisations were – and continue to be – key sites of struggle around the alignment of equality and difference. 'Equal opportunities', 'managing diversity', 'community empowerment', 'multi-cultural education' and other practices associated with contested compositions of the public emerged from, rather than being imposed on, public service practice. Public services also mediated changing norms and values, translating them into new discourses, decision-making templates, job descriptions, training manuals, complaints procedures, customer service units and other technologies. This did not happen without conflict, however. The following vignette suggests some of the strategies in play as a group of public service professionals in the mid-1970s in an English city confronted the limits of liberal norms of practice. The vignette focuses on public libraries. These are significant mediums of publicness in their own right, in that they serve as spaces of public communication and as transmitters of public culture. Public libraries were – in principle – open to all; were inscribed with bureaucratic norms of equality and fairness; and held themselves to be professional and neutral in their treatment of different interests in, for example, the selection of books and other materials. Their response to challenges to these values, and the practices in which they were inscribed, exemplify some of the discursive shifts that were involved in reassembling publics in the second half of the twentieth century.

Vignette: remapping the public: public libraries and the public sphere

A study of transformations in professional practice in one large municipal library service in the 1970s and 1980s traced how liberal discourses of equality, openness and neutrality were challenged. There was a realisation among some professionals that the doctrine of openness was insufficient given the failure of the library service to reach many population groups, and that a more proactive approach was required. Similarly the doctrine of neutrality meant that public libraries could not respond adequately to growing inequalities. At the same time equality itself was being challenged by a new awareness of social diversity in this increasingly multi-ethnic city.

These different challenges produced a reworking of the founding liberal values of public librarianship into an emerging discourse of 'community'. This formed a mobilising discourse for the transformation of public libraries in a number of ways. First, it signified an emerging professional logic as librarians began to reach out to 'new' publics beyond the library doors rather than to restrict the service to the existing public who came through them. . . . Community was used variously to denote outreach services; services to the 'disadvantaged'; and services that looked to the locality rather than to the centre. Second, community was defined as the antithesis of what was seen by some professionals as bureaucratic and inward-looking mainstream service. Respondents spoke of the personal impact on them of taking services out to the local Mosque, of reading stories to children on a glass-strewn playground in a run-down council estate, of giving talks about books to groups of teenage mothers in a Family Centre, of trying to develop a service to support community action groups and a local Immigration Advice centre . . . As librarians began to engage in such 'outreach' activities they inevitably came into contact with very different publics and attempted to carry their voices – highly mediated – back into the mainstream service. Third, community represented a new form of professional practice and group of professionals (community librarians); and new technologies (ways of organising books and information). A new community information service was designed to provide information on local services; to promote participation in local initiatives; and to support emerging networks of voluntary, self help and social movement groups. Finally – and perhaps most significantly – community formed a template for 'remapping the public' into a series of discrete groups with particular needs; including groups defined by a complex mix of race, faith and culture in the emerging discourse of multiculturalism (adapted from Newman, 2007b: 898–9).

The original article considers the fate of this 'turn to community' in public libraries in the face of Thatcherite and subsequently Blairite politics in Britain. But in the 1970s 'community' provided a way not only of 'respatialising' services to address population changes but also of engaging with emerging social movements making new representative claims. It offered more dynamic and contested conceptions of the public, and facilitated new forms of identification that challenged the bureaucratic and paternalistic power bases of a conservative profession.

This vignette points to processes of *translation* that were condensed in the remaking of professional practice. Notions of multi-culturalism and community did not necessarily supplant prior norms and values – such as equality, openness and tolerance – but transformed their meaning by more active association with notions of multiplicity and exclusion. Such ideas were translated into professional practice not through a 'top down' process of implementing new policy prescriptions through hierarchical methods of control. Rather they arrived through a set of practices that were invented, developed and refined in encounters between relatively low level staff; between staff in different local authorities; between different professionals; and between professionals and 'new' publics (groups and movements seeking both recognition and resources).

These processes highlight the importance of viewing translation as work. New discourses were, over time, translated into new administrative systems and professional technologies – the setting up of special collections and new classification processes, the invention of systems appropriate to 'community' libraries, the production of guides to 'multi-cultural' books for schools, and so on. It was through such work that difference was made 'manageable' by its incorporation into working styles and practices. The elision of 'difference' and 'community' enabled such approaches to become part of the mainstream, rather than marginal, work of librarianship (Black and Muddiman, 1997) – although this remained in tension with the idea of the public library as the bastion of a public culture defined in terms of a liberal, western aesthetic.

This vignette offers one small example of how multiculturalism was promoted by many public service professionals concerned to make services more 'relevant' to the diverse needs and experiences of different 'minority ethnic groups'. As we saw in Chapter 2, new translations are currently in play as multiculturalism is in turn being displaced by ideas of social cohesion. Tensions between the liberal value of equality, with its associations of fairness and neutrality, and the implications of social differences and divisions continue to pervade public policy and public services. For example, responses to social diversity in the allocation of public housing in England have led to concerns about unfair procedures and the production of new forms of inequality (Cantle, 2006; Dench et al., 2006; see also Milton and Phillips, 2008). Conflicts around the extent of local authority freedom to decide local priorities are also played out around competing definitions of equality and fairness: for example, should local authorities be able to determine responses to local needs and to develop services in line with local priorities, even if this produces national inequities (McKee and Cooper, 2007)?

Those working in public services often hope to contribute to social justice – 'making a difference' through ameliorating inequalities, targeting services to 'disadvantaged' groups or engaging with questions of social diversity. But modernising governments have avidly seized on arguments about the limitations of 'old fashioned' conceptions of equality in their attempts to legitimate programmes of reform (see Brodie, 2008). In the UK, public service reform deployed this imagery of modernity:

> Many of our public services were established in the years just after the Second World War. Victory had required strong centralised institutions, and not surprisingly it was through centralised state direction that the immediate post-war Government chose to win the peace. This developed a strong sense of the value of public services in building a fair and

prosperous society. The structures created in the 1940s may now require change, but the values of equity and opportunity for all will be sustained. The challenges and demands on today's public services are very different from those post-war years. The rationing culture which survived after the war, in treating everyone the same, often overlooked individuals' different needs and aspirations . . . Rising living standards, a more diverse society and a steadily stronger consumer culture have . . . brought expectations of greater choice, responsiveness, accessibility and flexibility. (Office of Public Services Reform, 2002: 8).

Here we can see the liberal idea of equality as access for all on an equal basis linked to 'centralised state direction' and a 'rationing culture', both now displaced by greater social diversity. Equality is subordinated to notions of choice, responsiveness, flexibility and accessibility. The rupture of this chain opens each of these concepts to the possibility of new inflections of meaning as they are juxtaposed with other ideas: in the quote above, for example, the positive coupling of equality and choice; or in Gordon Brown's notion of fairness as something to be earned: 'fairness not just for some but for all who earn it' (Brown, 2007).

Ideas of equality as a key element of citizenship have become more problematic as public services have been subjected to decentralising and marketising strategies, or targeted towards particular groups of customers. Inequalities between regions or localities, and between different categories of service user, have become more evident and opened up new sites of claim-making. Universalism has been undermined as a normative good as governments have set about modernising welfare states (e.g., New Labour's antagonism to services based on a 'one size fits all' philosophy). Openness has become more problematic as services in the new marketplace of public goods privilege notions of commercial confidentiality. Tolerance, too, has been recruited to imperial and integrationist usages through increasingly hegemonic discourses of (in)security and the fracture of the 'multi-cultural' settlement (W. Brown, 2006). The transformation of state bureaucracies into dispersed arrays of multiple service delivery organisations and economic enterprises weakens their role in sustaining social justice as they focus on their 'core busisiness'.

The reframings at stake here have been the focus of considerable professional anxiety, doubt and resistance, often played out in concerns about the sustainability of a public service ethos and/or the restatement of public service values. Given the fragmentations of the public sphere and the challenge to liberal values, how far can public services continue to be considered as a medium of publicness? How sustainable is their role in contributing to a socially just society? Or in promoting solidaristic forms of attachment? It is possible to trace a number of different responses, each of which deal explicitly with questions of value.

Remaking the professions

Whatever the inherent difficulties of the liberal values associated with the public sphere, they remain potent symbolic resources for those attempting to hold on to – or restate – the publicness of public services. However recent years have seen considerable debate about how far publicly oriented motivations can survive the transformations of the public sector (Le Grand, 2003; Lawton, 2005; Webb, 1999). The assault on state bureaucracy as wasteful and self-serving led to the spread of a 'dispersed managerial consciousness' that brought many public service professionals and workers into new regimes of power. Du Gay (2000) asks 'Is it really feasible to assume . . . that honesty and integrity in public management will take care of itself while the structures and practices that are generally believed to have helped constitute it – common patterns of recruitment, rules of procedure, permanence of tenure, restraints on the power of line management – have been reduced, diluted or removed?' (2000: 87).

Nevertheless the idea of the distinctiveness of public services remains a focal point both for public service workers and for the users of public services. Despite the decline in deference and the rise of mistrust, public service professionals continue to command a relatively high degree of public trust and confidence in surveys, especially by contrast with other occupations that sometimes claim the 'public interest' defence (politicians and journalists, for example; Clarke, 2005b). But such legitimacy now appears more fragile and more contextually contingent, rather than being available 'en bloc' to a public service organisation or occupation. As a result, the consent of those subjected to professional authority is more explicitly at issue in the encounters between the public and public services. In the process, 'negotiating' skills and strategies have come to the fore in both organisations and occupational formations.

The question of legitimacy is most obviously an issue for the relationships between public service occupations and the public, but it also has what we might call 'internal' aspects. These involve the plausibility and desirability of the stories that the occupation can tell to itself – and even how individuals can account for their own working lives to themselves and others (Cribb, forthcoming). There are some interesting examples from continental Europe of professionals and public managers attempting to reclaim – or remake – their legitimacy and authority. For example, Noordegraaf (2006) argues that, after widespread critiques of the NPM, a process of 're-professionalisation' is taking place among public managers, constructing more space and autonomy in which they can defend service ethics and demonstrate effectiveness beyond, as well as within, individual service encounters.

Re-professionalisation cannot be viewed simply in terms of the search for value-based alternatives to the NPM; it also reflects a search for a new legitimacy for those who work in public service following decades of assault on their credibility and status. But can professional practice be detached from old negative associations with paternalism and expert power and remade in the image of 'guarding publicness'? Professional power is often understood to be in tension with wider public values, weakening what Friedson views as the role of the professions as 'moral custodians', not only of the knowledge base of their disciplines but of 'transcendent values' associated with a sensibility of a wider public good (2001: 222). This rather idealised view of the professions is challenged by Duyvendak, Knijn and Kremer, who suggest that 'the very idea of a pure professional logic that can only be polluted by other logics is an overly theoretical, essentialist and pessimistic argument' (2006: 8). Furthermore 'professionals are not only passive objects of change; they themselves play a role in defining professionalism' (Ibid, p. 8). Professions in fields like social care and health have actively incorporated concepts such as public involvement, community participation, diversity, choice and service user empowerment, redefining professional boundaries and developing new skills (Clarke, 2006b; Newman and Vidler, 2006a, 2006b).

Such developments are sometimes self-consciously addressed towards the creation of more democratic relationships between public professionals/managers and the publics they serve. This requires the unravelling of the 'knowledge–power knot' of professional power (Clarke et al., 2007a). Moves in this direction have included attempts to create more 'knowledgeable' service users, to enhance 'voice' in the service relationship or to develop 'co-production' approaches. These have different implications, but they each set out to overcome some of the disparities of power and knowledge between professionals and publics, perhaps producing what Kremer and Tonkens (2006) term new logics of 'democratic professionalism' or 'civic professionalism'. These do not dissolve the boundaries between professional and client, but do give the service user more voice, and perhaps keep discussions and deliberations on the public good alive.

Emergent logics of professionalism point to the political ambiguities that are condensed in public service work. Old forms of professional authority have been challenged from a number of directions: managerialism, consumerism, user movements, participatory or co-production innovations. However, the recomposition of professional authority involves constructing relationships with different forms of power. Certainly, re-centring professionalism on relationships with people using public services is a critical dimension of this. Our own research showed people looking for relationships with public service that involved respect, fairness and forms of partnership, mutual deliberation and co-production (Clarke et al., 2007a; see also Needham, 2007). Such relationships might provide an alternative source of legitimacy and authority for professionals – but this still needs to be negotiated against older professional attachments to power over users, and against managerial and corporate powers that assert the overriding obligations of professionals to the employing organisation. In this condensed and contested context, there are risks that the weak power of a user-centred or civic focus may be overpowered.

Public service professions have ambiguous relationships with politics and power. At a minimum they are both public servants and governmental servants, working with and on publics. As such they are active in processes of classifying, constituting and managing publics. Some users, clients or communities are recognised as appropriate, worthy, desirable 'partners' in public service – invited to become expert patients, enabled to be independent, or allowed to have their needs recognised as legitimate. Others may need grooming – bringing under professional tutelage so that they might come to be partners, know their own condition or achieve the earned autonomy of being self-regulating. A further group may comprise the intractable, troublesome or anti-social. Ruppert (2006: 184-187) talks about the 'moral economy' of public planning in Toronto, where redevelopment aimed to solicit 'good' publics and exclude the less desirable. She argues that planning discourses articulated a distinction between public groups and non-public groups. Public groups included those who bring economic benefits: office workers, people with a higher disposable income, shoppers, entertainments seekers, high-end retailers, students, and tourists. Publics who were also solicited included social groups that were not likely to disrupt or threaten the social character of the economic regeneration project: residents of the area, the elderly, families and children. Non-public groups, in contrast, included categories such as teenagers, marginalised youth, vagrants, discount stores, drug dealers, loiterers, illegal vendors, gangs and 'interlopers'.

These are some of the 'practical categories' deployed in this particular field of professional discourse. Ruppert indicates how opposing discursive categories – citizens v denizens, students v teenagers, families v troublemakers – delineated a clear boundary between 'publics' and 'non-publics' within this public regeneration project, staffed by public professionals and reliant on public finance. As Ruppert notes, 'connections to race, class and ethnicity were never explicit; rather, they were implied in the discourse as something everyone knew' (2006: 185). Professional discourse and practices are bound up with 'governing the social' and this puts questions of social difference, inequalities and power at the centre – even if these are concealed by other vocabularies of public distinction (see also Burney, 2005 on anti-social behaviour and the imagery of anti-social people).

The discretionary spaces occupied by professionals may, then, have differential consequences for different publics. At the same time, however, the discretionary spaces that public service professionals have historically claimed (and sometimes infused with progressive or radical social orientations) has been increasingly constrained by other forces. We have discussed the increase in managerial power and its demands of corporate loyalty, but the reform of public services also brings other constraints, from the introduction of tighter eligibility criteria to intensified regimes of audit and inspection. Changing organisational forms subject professional discretion to new organisational and governance logics (see Garrett, 2008, on the 'modernisation' of social work practice). Professional discretion has been mediated not only through processes of democratisation and co-production, but also by the emphasis on consumerism and choice (see Chapters 4 and 8, and Needham, 2007). At the same time much professional work is being recast as 'behaviour change' policies become more significant (improving diet, work, parenting, curbing anti-social behaviour, promoting environmental sustainability and many more). Reconciling the idea of democratisation with the policy emphasis on authoritative interventions to change behaviour produces new kinds of dilemmas that cannot easily be resolved by recourse to professional ethics.

What kind of democracy is actually at stake in efforts to challenge traditional power relationships between public services and publics is the focus of the next chapter. Here we want to note how such processes of re-professionalisation (around a newly confident management cadre) and de-professionalisation (unravelling the 'knowledge-power knot' through processes of democratisation) assemble notions of 'public', 'management', 'profession' and 'politics' in new configurations. These open up multiple views not only about what 'working for the public' might mean in terms of ethical principles, but also about how public services can continue to act as mediums of publicness.

Remaking the public service ethos?

The previous two chapters have highlighted a number of challenges to the sustainability of a public service ethos: the organisational imperatives that result from the introduction of competition and choice; the more risky context of public service work; the new alignments of business and public rationalities in service delivery organisations; and the subordination of professional and bureaucratic forms of power to norms of 'good governance'. Nevertheless there have been a number of attempts to redefine a public service ethos for modern times (e.g., Aldridge and Stoker, 2003; Brereton and Temple, 1999; Pratchett and Wingfield, 1996), and some interesting attempts to set out new frameworks of public governance. Here we draw on the production of a new 'codex' in Denmark.

Vignette: the Danish Codex

2005 saw the publication of a code of practice for chief executives working in both central and local government in Denmark. The code was published under the title *Public Governance: Code for Chief Executive Excellence* (Forum for Top Executive Management, 2005: www. publicgovernance.dk). It was based on the work of a Top Executive Forum that, over two years, conducted surveys among chief executives, held workshops and seminars, organised a final conference and produced a glossy handbook. The forum's membership comprised chief executives from central and local government and academics from Denmark, the US and the Netherlands; it was supported by a secretariat from the Ministry of Finance and from the Danish Regions. Built into the report is a framework for translating such competencies into practice through self assessment against a checklist set out in the report; through 360 degree feedback mechanisms; through peer coaching by members of the Forum; and the use of professional coaches. In 2008 the forum was still active, concerned with dissemination and development activities.

We want to highlight several features of this initiative that recast the role of public management at senior levels. It establishes the concept of 'public governance' as a guiding principle of chief executive work. This distinguishes the role of senior public managers from that of senior managers in the private sector. The report states that:

> The public sector is characterised by some fundamental conditions which give rise to special ground rules for management, such as the public sector's democratic values, its many varied bottom lines, etc. Public Governance differs, in other words, from Corporate Governance in several respects, for which reason management perspectives, tools and inspiration drawn from the private sector cannot enjoy unlimited application to public sector management. The development of Public Governance in Denmark has been organised as a common management project for the entire community of public sector chief executives (Forum for Top Executive Management, 2005: 120).

It also acknowledges the existence of 'multiple competing management principles' rather than asserting a single management logic:

> The challenge for the public sector chief executive consists of mastering and being aware of the strengths and weaknesses, competing values and partially contradictory forms of logic that characterise the hierarchical, market based, profession based and network forms of management respectively . . . The interplay and combinations between these various forms of management can give rise to a number of independent challenges for chief executives. . . . The underlying legitimacy and value base for a given matter can be ambiguous . . . From the perspective of the chief executive, such a situation creates an 'ethical moment' in work and decision-making. These are situations in which laws and rules fail to provide clear answers and guidelines, and in which a public sector chief executive must take decisions which are based to a great extent upon the conscience, experience and current knowledge of the individual. . . . The question is how chief executives in their choice of management forms can combine, communicate and challenge the various competing and at times conflicting values that characterise the public sector organisation. How can the chief executive act as a bridge-builder between political decisions and values and professional values and implementation? (2005: 35).

This implies that public management is itself already an assemblage; no single logic (whether efficiency, performance or customer orientation) can suffice; and no single template of ethical principles can resolve the dilemmas of practice. Indeed it is the task of senior managers to assemble and reassemble competing managerial, professional and political logics to meet the wider requirements of public governance.

The Danish Codex addresses a series of 'new conditions and challenges' for chief executives and the politicians with whom they interact. These include changes in decision-making structures of the public sector, with the 'continued alternation between . . . decentralisation and centralisation'; the challenge of the 'expanded management universe', which includes internationalisation and public-private cooperation; and the challenge of the 'knowledge society' (2005: 23–4). These combine to produce the need for a new conception of public governance. Public Governance is inflected with a sense of the responsibility of chief executives to shape, as well as respond to, the context in which they work. That is, the work of top managers is not just that of managing organisations for high performance: the task is to ensure that 'the public sector organisation is on the one hand capable of handling the demands and expectations of the surrounding world, and on the other is itself in a position to shape developments' (ibid: 120). This proactive sense of engagement is a sign of a confident cadre of public managers seeking to delineate a clear role for themselves in the Danish public sphere; an event made possible, some have suggested, because of the sense that the NPM is no longer a single unassailable template of reform.

Dilemmatic spaces

An alternative to establishing a codified set of ethical principles that can be applied to different contexts and problems involves a more relational and negotiated conception of public service as ethical work. This offers a response to the difficulty of applying abstract criteria to the dynamic, contested and plural encounters that make up public service work in 'post-bureaucratic' organisations. Definitions of success in such contexts are ambiguous, boundaries are porous and the nature of the work itself is highly fluid. New problems and possibilities arise in heterogeneous encounters with clients, stakeholders, partners, inspectors, policy actors and with the wider public. Traditional authority relationships, whether in terms of manager/staff, professional/client or senior/junior ranks of the bureaucracy are weakened, intensifying both ambiguity and interdependence. Defining a public service ethos in this context focuses not on re-inscribing rules of conduct but on examining how ethical conduct is negotiated within diverse relationships across the plurality of sites and encounters in which public service work is conducted:

> Rather than an essential public service ethos, that can be enshrined in abstract principles, in practice public service workers constantly have to

negotiate the boundaries between such general principles, their own values and the particularist requirements of service users and different kinds of communities. Such tensions constitute the 'dilemmatic spaces' (Honig, 1996) of the street level bureaucrat (Lipsky, 1980; Hoggett, 2005). From the perspective of lived practice, what constitutes justice is therefore not abstract and immutable but has to be worked through, often case by case. (Hoggett et al., 2006b: 767)

Hoggett (2006) argues that public organisations – by virtue of their place in the public sphere – are the sites of continuous contestation of public purposes and value conflicts. The studies of Hoggett and colleagues focus on 'front line' workers but dilemmatic spaces, we suggest, permeate public work at all levels, including those occupying managerial or even newly empowered 'leadership' roles (Hoyle and Wallace, 2007; Wallace and Hoyle, 2007). Rather than the image of the neutral, objective public administrator, leadership is now imagined as more person-centred, bringing personal commitments and passions into the domain of work (O'Reilly et al., 2006). Strong values are viewed as an asset that transformational leaders deploy in fostering cultural change (Wallace, 2008). Rather than a separation between the person and the office, the person is integral to, and a key resource in, the office itself: he/she is its very material and spiritual embodiment (Newman, 2005d). As such they have space, it would seem, to shape the value base of organisations and to assert their wider public role.

Vignette: the ambiguities of public leadership

A small study of such leaders (Newman, 2005d) suggests some of the ways in which public service actors exercise agency in the context of dispersed and fragmented fields of governance. Responses from career entrants on MPA programmes suggested how actors were engaged in reworking traditional rationalities – based on the bureaucratic ethos of office – to deal with the dilemmas raised by the current contexts in which they were working. Their attempts to produce a statement of an ethos of office for public service leaders were full of inconsistencies, evident for example in the different concepts of accountability that they deployed. What stood out was the idea of wanting to 'make a difference' through their work.

Responses from practising senior managers suggested ways in which this idea of 'making a difference' was being enacted. They revealed different forms of cultural practice. Some deployed governmental discourse to strengthen managerial power; discourses of globalisation, consumerism and modernisation were frequently deployed to counter attitudes or practices associated with professional and bureaucratic power. But governmental discourses were also constantly being reworked and recombined. The discourses of social exclusion, public involvement, community capacity building, well being, restorative justice and so on formed potential points of such mobilisation, opening up new articulations between governmental discourse and professional aspiration.

These articulations brought 'local' goals into organisational missions or expanded the social or public dimensions of government policy. This cannot be viewed simply as forms of resistance or the exercise of discretion: the accounts suggest ways in which practitioners were constituted within, but also themselves deployed, government discourses, amplifying some strands and marginalising others.

Possibilities of innovation and translation emerged as established patterns of relationship and hierarchies of knowledge were being reconstructed, and new spaces and sites of action that could not be controlled from the centre opened up. Such spaces were formed out of a double process of change: the emphasis on delivering policy outcomes through networks, coupled with the new emphasis on 'transformative leadership' (Wallace, 2007). The latter meant that actors were discursively positioned as the agents as well as the objects of change.

Each of the examples discussed so far has an explicitly normative dimension and each suggests, albeit implicitly, that questions of ethos or value can be treated in isolation from a consideration of the changing conditions of public service work. While leaders may have enlarged discretionary space, they and those they manage are exposed to new forms of risk and insecurity. Ahmed and Broussine (2007) trace the increasing 'disempowerment' and loss of identity among mid-career managers in a study across six European countries: 'It seems that some European public service systems may be characterised by factors that create anxiety in managers' and workers' roles that in turn limits the potential for public servants to develop a full sense of personal agency' (2007: 6). These anxieties result from factors such as:

- internally driven performance management regimes that are driven by external targets;
- organisational change imperatives driven by a governmental ideology that 'change must happen';
- financial stringency and cuts;
- imperatives of partnership and intraprofessional working that produce a loss of professional and organisational identities;
- the privatisation of public service provision and associated questioning of the public service ethos;
- ambiguous and contradictory accounting structures.

(adapted from Ahmed and Broussine, 2007: 7).

In addition to such factors, we might point to ways in which the application of new technologies tends to delimit the discretionary spaces of professional and managerial work. And, as we have seen, the changing conditions of public work militate against forms of agency that might challenge managerial logics. Hebson, Grimshaw and Marchington's study of the impact of public private partnerships on the public sector ethos in local government and health in the UK, leads them to conclude:

> Our evidence suggests that workers have experienced a decline in working conditions and there has been some weakening of values associated with a public sector ethos. In particular, notions of loyalty have changed, with greater emphasis on loyalty to 'the service' and less to either the public sector as former employer (now as client) or to their new private sector employer. But workers' values of public interest and altruistic motivation seem relatively resilient. Emphasis on contractual performance targets often conflicts with workers' customary emphasis on working for the public interest. . . . Arguably, the full impact of a worsening of services provided under PPPs has been minimised because workers continue to meet the needs of patients and claimants in a way that involves working beyond what is required by the performance contract. However the material circumstances of limited resources and a performance based culture mean that they often cannot deliver what they want. (2003: 498).

The politics of publicness in public services, then, cannot be reduced to philosophical, moral or ethical considerations. Rather than exploring the sustainability of a public ethos as an ethical construct, attention has shifted in recent years to ways of securing public legitimacy by recourse to concepts of public value. This, as we will see, does not 'solve' the problem of the politics of the public but translates it (into a series of technologies) or displaces it (onto the public itself).

Public value and the politics of the public

Ideas of public value may offer new sources of legitimacy for public services in this complex arena. Public value is a concept that can be applied to any organisation, whether public, private or a hybrid form. Indeed its appeal is that it offers a means of reasserting the public role of organisations no longer securely positioned in a public sector. But, rather than resolving questions of value, this introduces yet another concept that is contested and a practice in which very different techniques, strategies and indeed values are condensed (Horner et al., 2006).

Public value creates the conditions for new forms of agency on the part of public managers, and the stakeholders and publics drawn into collaborative processes of definition and evaluation. But it may also be uneasily aligned with new governmental strategies. The approach in the UK, set out in a Cabinet Office paper (Kelly et al., 2002), owes much to NPM rationalities and techniques.

In contrast, the Work Foundation report cited earlier emphasises democratic legitimacy as the basis of public value:

> public value is what the public values, and it is the role of public managers to help determine through the democratic process of deliberation and public engagement what social outcomes are desirable. It is through such processes that public managers can help to articulate collective citizens' preferences and thereby redress the 'democratic deficit' between citizens (Hutton, in Horner, Lekhi and Blaug, 2006: 6).

This report proposes strong links between public legitimacy and deliberative democracy, in which questions of value and purpose are devolved to a plurality of sites and spaces – the governance bodies discussed in the previous chapter, local forums, service user forums and so on. We consider some of the issues that arise in these new encounters between governmental, organisational and 'public' powers in the next chapter. Here, however, we want to highlight ways in which specific forums – and the services that promote them - are situated in wider fields of power, circumscribed both by government policies and commercial considerations. This raises questions about how much can be achieved through managerial attempts to assess public value, and how far wider questions have to be addressed in order to create the conditions that might enable public elements to be inscribed in 'hybrid' service arrangements. Ota de Leonardis (2007) argues that these wider questions must include:

- how far welfare policies nurture democracy. For example, how far do policies, and their organisational enactment, work to produce individualised or 'collective' attachments and identifications? Such factors influence the power of the service recipient in their encounters with provider organisations;
- how the organisational forms through which welfare is delivered contribute to – or undermine – democratic values. For example, the transformations of 'civil society' organisations through contracts and through their reconstruction as businesslike service providers is diminishing their democratic functions. A crucial distinction, she argues, is between organisations based on 'management' and organisations based on 'membership';
- the character of organisational networks in the policy arena – how far these are grounded in aggregation or integration;
- how actors interpret, dispute, make compromises, and work to reframe the contexts in which they work; and what the effects of this might be on the organisation of democracy.

Such points underscore the importance of a wider politics of the public. That is, there are constraints on the ways in which public service workers can act in the 'dilemmatic spaces' highlighted in the previous section. This is perhaps closest to de Leonardis's final category (concerned with ways in which actors interpret their world); here there is a focus not just on how they resolve dilemmas, but how far they are able to 'reframe the contexts in which they work'. We can see such reframings taking place in examples such as the public library, the Danish Codex, the translations of leadership, and the remaking of professionalism explored earlier. But the material and discursive conditions – of public service finance, public service work and the inter-relationship with governmental power – shape the possibilities of such reframing. The space for 'transgressive' subject positions is limited by the determination of governments to deliver their reforms. A senior local government figure, interviewed by Newman, observed that, 'Finance and performance dominate. You have to make the budget work. You have to meet your government targets. Only then do you have the luxury of bringing any values to bear' (Executive Director Local Authority, London, March 2007).

However powerful new 'public' discursive formations such as public value might be, they are unlikely to be able to resolve such contradictions. This takes us back to the arguments in the previous chapter, where we suggested that different formations of power were assembled in specific sites, and may be structured in dominance. Any specific site in which workers negotiate tensions, forge partnerships, manage their performance and engage with the public – in all its complex forms – can be considered as a condensate in which different projects and forms of power coalesce. These produce 'governance paradoxes' – the dilemmas and tensions faced by organisations and those working for the public.

Governance paradoxes

We saw in the previous chapter how the dispersal of state power to newly 'autonomised' agents seeks to de-politicise the spaces in which professionals, managers and organisations make decisions. In the process, responsibility for managing tensions and dilemmas becomes devolved to individual agents. The dilemmatic spaces traced earlier tend to be experienced as personal, professional or ethical dilemmas. But they are rooted in wider tensions and contradictions, refracting the uneasy alignments between different regimes of governance. Different governance regimes are likely to co-exist in any specific site. Each regime is assembled from a range of specific technologies, discourses, practices, and 'empowered' actors. Each is also likely to privilege particular logics of decision-making and particular forms of practice. For example, a health service organisation may operate within multiple framings, shaped by:

- pressures towards efficiency and productivity (e.g., financial decision-making, competition and contracts: *managerial governance*);
- pressures towards enhancing cohesion and collaboration (e.g., team based decision-making, partnership working: *network governance*);

- pressures towards performance accountability (e.g., good governance, scrutiny, control: *hierarchical governance*);
- pressures towards 'co-production' with health service users (e.g., responsibility, capacity building, democratisation: *self-governance*).

We can see ways in which these different regimes of governance may coexist in some of the vignettes used in this and the previous chapter. For example, the Danish Codex recognises that senior managers will need to draw on different forms of governance that are appropriate to different kinds of problem, and that navigating between them is a key leadership attribute. The vignette on the governance of partnerships in Chapter 5 highlighted the interaction between managerial, consociational (network-based) and participatory (self-governance) discourses; while the vignette on social care included tensions between hierarchical governance (exercised through inspection and regulation bodies) and self-governance (represented in the move towards individual budgets and direct payments), alongside professional and managerial forms of power.

Figure 6.1. shows one way of mapping different regimes of governance and highlighting the tensions that emerge between them in specific sites:

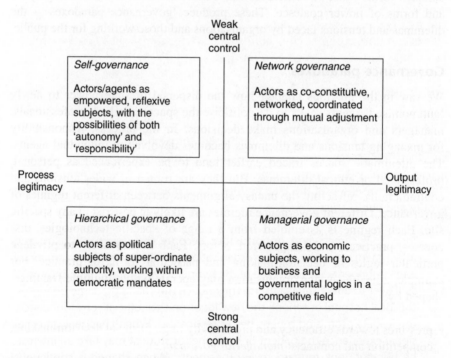

Figure 6.1. Regimes of governance. Adapted from Newman J., *Modernising Governance.* Sage, 2001.

Each regime mobilises and deploys different forms of power – or, more accurately, different combinations of forms of power. In each regime some forms of power organise and structure these combinations, so that in hierarchical governance political authority and bureaucratic power dominate the field of relationships, techniques, discourses and practices. In managerial governance, managerial power forms the organising or articulating principle; whereas self-governance relies on actors and agents being responsible and autonomous sites of authority. All of them, as the grid structure indicates, are regimes that are constituted by relationships of 'meta-governance' (more or less tight central direction, through different orientations to legitimacy). So, in any specific site, different regimes may combine and coalesce; and diverse forms of power will be mobilised, often in tense or uncomfortable relationships with others.

These regimes have positive and negative associations. *Hierarchical governance* is inscribed in the much-maligned bureaucracies of state, with all of the associations of inflexibility, proceduralism and slowness. It tends to be viewed as a constraint by those privileging managerial power or network governance: it gets in the way, gives rise to inflexible targets, imposes audit and inspection processes that produce high transaction costs, and so on. It is legitimised through representative democracy, which many have argued is unable to address the complex needs and interests of a diverse public. Its requirements for common standards (based on an image of a universal public with common entitlements and rights) squeezes the capacity for the devolution of authority and discretion. However it does ensure accountability, and privileges notions of public probity, procedural fairness and good governance.

We have already encountered many of the negative associations of *managerial governance*: it rests on an image of organisations as businesses and as actors as economic agents. The focus on competitive survival and success can mean that 'public' interests are marginalised: 'difficult' pupils excluded from schools, costs of 'expensive' patients or service users shunted onto other organisations, and short-term success privileged over longer-term sustainability. It also places a heavy emphasis on innovation and constant change. Pollitt, writing about 'hypermodernisation' in the UK, highlights the potential loss of organisational loyalty and public trust:

> Individual careers and opportunities become the dominant focus, and attachments to any particular organisation (or client group) are temporary and contingent. . . . The sense of the temporary-ness of everything can also spill over to affect service users. They notice the changing name boards on the local hospital or school; the new logos on their official correspondence, the leaflets promising a new, better service. . . . When change is an occasional experience the patient or pensioner or student may take an interest, be hopeful, look forward to improvements. When change is continuous it easily becomes a kind of irritating 'white noise', raising no particular

hopes or interest but generating an anxiety that the new could be a concealed cut, or at least may not be better, or may be hard to understand. (2007: 539).

However enthusiasts for managerial modes of governance insist that they 'deliver results': they have unlocked many of the paternalistic and patriarchal forms of power associated with welfare bureaucracies, opened up the possibilities of diversity of provision and user choice, and reduced the costs of public services, arguably augmenting the chances of their long-term survival in the context of global competition between nation-states.

Network governance has become the privileged mode in many analyses of the shifting regimes of power in recent decades, overcoming, it is supposed, the fragmenting effects of the NPM, and offering ways of drawing multiple stakeholders into the processes of delivering complex policy outcomes in a dispersed system. It has underpinned a series of policy initiatives directed to major social problems: urban regeneration, combating ill health, reducing child poverty, improving services to older people, and so on. And it gives rise to the popularity of 'partnership' in both governmental and professional discourse. Yet outcomes remain difficult to measure and attribute; the costs (especially in terms of time) are high; and accountability elusive. There are major lines of tension between network and hierarchical governance; and attempted resolutions tend to produce a proliferation of new strategies of governmental control (e.g., refinements to the ways in which targets are imposed or negotiated). Questions of accountability are particularly significant since networks are themselves the source of potential inequities – including inequities of access (who is included), voice (who gets heard) and legitimacy (what kinds of people and forms of expertise are valued).

The fourth regime – *self-governance* – is becoming increasingly prominent as a result of emerging frameworks for public service delivery. The self in self governance may be an individual, a collective (the self-governing community) or a corporate body (a self-governing trust). All these types of self are empowered and enabled to be self-governing in new arrangements: co-production, consumer choice, independent budgets, self-managing trusts or community-based services. This regime promises to deliver 'empowerment', freeing publics from the power of state bureaucracy and from professional paternalism. As we saw in the social care vignette in Chapter 5, this produces other lines of tension: with hierarchical regimes that require 'good governance'; with managerial regimes that attempt to incorporate them into new logics and rationalities; and with network regimes that privilege professional and stakeholder power. But there may be other difficulties. Self-governance is highly ambiguous: on the one hand, it promises 'empowerment' (for some), but on the other, it requires 'responsibility'– especially the shifting of responsibility of welfare services from the state to newly empowered, self-provisioning publics. We explore this further in Chapter 8.

The purpose of mapping these tensions is twofold. First, the matrix in Figure 6.1 highlights some of the structural tensions that give rise to the dilemmas experienced by those working for the public – dilemmas that tend to be experienced as individual and personal, but that derive from deeper contradictions. Second, it offers an analytical framework for understanding some of the problems or difficulties associated with 'reassembling the public'. For example, we might map some of the different inflections of 'public value' as shown in Figure 6.2.

This suggests that the different technologies or strategies for determining public value operate in a field of contestation; the concept itself is ambiguous, opening out different issues of politics (who decides) and power (what technologies are used to decide and measure value). Of course none of these 'ideal types' of governance exists in isolation from others – indeed our argument is that any specific site of practice is likely to be cross-cut by multiple and conflicting regimes of power and competing sources of legitimacy. As we saw in Chapter 5, actors are having to become increasingly skilled at facing in multiple directions, deploying different sources of legitimacy and perhaps playing one form of power off against others as they 'flex' organisational, governmental and public resources. But changing political and organisational contexts may shift the balance of forces, bringing a particular regime – or mix of regimes – into

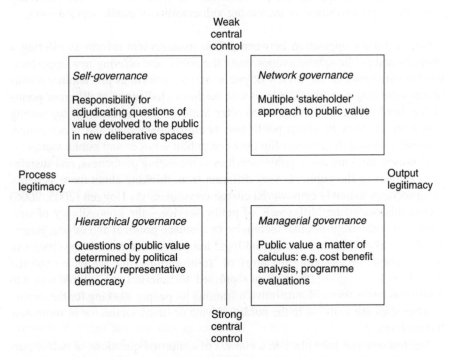

Figure 6.2. Governing public value? Adapted from Newman J., *Modernising Governance.* Sage, 2001.

pre-eminence. This not only changes the nature of the dilemmas but also the potential resources for dealing with them.

Conclusion: Mediating the public?

This chapter has explored how public services – and those who work in them – mediate values and principles of publicness. Ideas of the public sphere are important to understanding some of the reasons why many of the principles and values associated with a public service ethos, public purpose or public value are now deeply contested. But this does not mean that questions of value are no longer significant. In this chapter we have traced a proliferation of value-based concepts shaping public service work (public governance, co-production, the 'democratisation' of the professions, public value). Here we want to suggest two different perspectives on these developments:

- The new focus on ethics, democracy and the search for 'softer' or 'more democratic' forms of NPM restores questions of value and purpose and offers new roles for public leadership in delivering public value;
- This is merely rhetorical froth – a smokescreen that conceals and legitimates increasing marketisation and privatisation, the continued drive for efficiency and the impoverishment or increasing vulnerability of public service work.

Such a binary opposition between public management reform as offering a strengthened public sphere, empowering the public and offering new opportunities for participation, and a view of public service reform as just another means of strengthening neo-liberal rule, is one we have challenged at different points of this book. Here we have tried to offer a more nuanced reading, suggesting a number of ways in which publicness being disassembled and reassembled, especially around the relationship between public services and public values.

However, thinking about public services as mediating publicness, and sustaining a politics of the public, is very different from thinking about them as delivering services to newly empowered citizen-consumers. As Hoggett (2005, 2006) argues this marks the 'difference' of public service – the impossibility of subsuming it within regimes that technicise or displace political and ethical issues. Neither market value nor managerial logic has proved adequate to the challenge of publicness, necessitating the array of 're-inventions' that we have explored here. They testify to the tendency of repressed, technicised or displaced issues to return and be the focus of innovative reframing by people working for the public, whether they are working in the public, private or 'third sector', or in some new hybrid form.

But reinventions take place in a context of contested questions of public purpose and public value. Such questions pervade the unpredictable encounters between diverse and fragmented publics and diverse and fragmented arrays of public service providers. Their resolution is no easy matter given the changing pressures on public service, the unstable combinations of different governance regimes and the efforts to de-politicise, displace and technicise these questions of purpose and value. Our commitment has been to making these more visible and contestable, because such dilemmas cannot be reconciled on an individual basis in front-line – or managerial – work. They are political – part of a wider politics of the public.

7 Engaging publics: participation and power

The shifting character of publics takes on particular salience in relation to new processes of public participation. Most governments, it seems, are currently interested in enhancing public participation; and participation is central to the strategies of the EU, the World Bank and other institutions concerned with modernisation or development. There is no simple explanation of why public participation has become so significant in governmental discourse and practice. The dominant rationale focuses on the problems of sustaining governmental legitimacy in the face of an 'unengaged' public who are increasingly distanced from, and disenchanted with, formal political institutions and politicians (Stoker, 2006). But this intersects with a range of more radical projects of 'empowerment', especially of those viewed as disadvantaged, socially excluded or lacking voice. It also has links to with the turn towards consumerism in public services. This means that, like most of the other sites of proliferation and innovation we have considered in this book, participation is not a singular thing: not one process, practice, technology or institutional arrangement. Rather it is politically ambiguous, both in its conception and in its practices. To illustrate this, we begin with a vignette:

Vignette: varieties of e-democracy

Electronic forms of communication and participation have generated a considerable degree of excitement. Web-based technologies are viewed as both fostering public engagement, extending access to those who may be disillusioned by, or disenfranchised from, the political process, and disrupting traditional ideas of the public sphere (e.g., Leadbeater, 2008). They appear to be more open and inclusive – anyone with access to the web can participate, whether or not they have formal citizenship status. Their horizontal and connective qualities disrupt territorial boundaries, producing both transnational and community based encounters and mobilisations. They also disrupt the temporalities of public decision-making, offering an immediate exchange of ideas that may sit uncomfortably with the timelines of governmental procedures.

Such innovations suggest the possibility of overcoming democratic deficits, addressing the disaffection (especially of young people) from politics, and providing decision-makers with faster and more subtle feedback from diverse populations. New mediating organisations have proliferated; for example:

- *E-parliament* – a 'global forum in which democratic legislators [those elected to national parliaments] work together to exchange and implement good policy ideas' (*www.e-parl.net*, accessed 21-March-2008). This offers a 'virtual parliamentary process' comprising electronic polling, video-conferences, and international meetings of legislators.
- *Downing Street e-petitions* – through which publics can petition government through electronic polls. (*www.petitions.pm.gov.uk*).The polls are conducted by a charitable organisation – mySociety – that runs other political websites such as *HearFromYourMP.com* and *TheyWorkForYou.com*. Given a certain number of signatories relevant departments are required to write a response to each petition, justifying a policy or action or saying how the request will be responded to.
- *Scottish Parliament e-petitions (www.epetitions.scottish.parliament.uk)* – each e-Petition has its own discussion forum, where visitors and signatories can discuss the petition and surrounding issues online. In the Scottish Parliament e-petitions are governed by a Public Petitions Committee that adjudicates what petitions are admissible and what action should be taken, and that ensures results are communicated.
- *Centre of Excellence for Local E-democracy (www.icele.org*, accessed 21-March-2008) – launched by the UK government to encourage local authorities to use new technologies to interact with citizens.
- *YouGov plc* – a research and consulting organisation, pioneering the use of the Internet and information technology to collect data for market research, organisational research and stakeholder consultation; providing companies with 'a rounded view of their staff, customers, brands and investors as well as assessing opinion amongst the general public and the media'. (*www.yougov.com*)
- *E-democracy.org* – a US organisation (with UK links) that 'is a non profit, non partisan, volunteer based project whose aim is to expand participation and build stronger democracies and communities through the power of information and communication technologies and strategies' (*www.e-democracy.org*; accessed 21-March-2008).

The apparent similarities of technology in these initiatives mask a number of significant differences in the kinds of public sensibilities and political imaginaries that are invoked. Some mediating organisations are closely linked to existing representative institutions (electronic polls linked to Downing Street and the Scottish Parliament; ICELE) while others attempt to set up new ones (E-parliament). Many are government sponsored, while E-democracy.org prides itself on having a more 'grass roots' orientation. It promotes mobilisations around issue-based and local forums (leading, for example, to a campaign against the closure of post offices in Essex); supports groups in using new technologies to get information on local issues onto YouTube and other web-based platforms; and promotes both face to face and on-line discussions. YouGov and the electronic polls offered by parliaments have different origins, but both enable governments to refine their policies in the light of 'public opinion', and, in the case of government sponsored polls, to communicate directly with large numbers of voters and potential voters through a growing bank of email addresses. Some attempt to offer discussion and/or deliberation, and to introduce feedback mechanisms: but the dominance of e-petitions and other polling mechanisms suggests a more direct and populist form of participation.

There is no doubt that the internet offers new resources for engagement and mobilisation, potentially producing new forms of local and global activism and forming the basis for new counterpublics (e.g., Drache, 2008; Dryzek, 2006; Escobar, 1999). But the examples above suggest that the use of new technologies does not mean that publics can speak to governments in ways that are unmediated; nor does it get round the problem of negotiating different conceptions of democracy (direct, associative, deliberative, representative and so on). The diversity of initiatives, rather, highlights the continued significance of questions about who sets agendas, who claims to represent whom, and how different experiences, identities and interests can be given voice in the public domain.

This diversity of political imperatives is reflected in the range of literature that now seeks to explain, analyse or promote public participation. For some, it is viewed as capable of both deepening and enriching the thin institutions of formal democracy; for others, it is understood as a further extension of neo-liberalism, binding people into new regimes of power by making them willing accomplices of governmental projects; while yet others view public participation as a populist veneer concealing the deeper de-politicisation of contemporary societies. This points to the heterogeneous political projects that may be condensed in public participation initiatives. These, we argue, produce a series of tensions in the constitution and summoning of publics to the participation process: tensions between different conceptions of representation; between the valorisation of authenticity and expertise; between the recognition of publics and of counterpublics; and between cosmopolitan and parochial public imaginaries. The chapter begins by tracing the contours of these tensions, and the antagonisms they may produce. We then consider two key potential alignments: the first is with a populist politics, and the second with the managerial rationalities and modernising strategies highlighted in earlier chapters of this volume. Finally we consider ways in which public engagement necessarily refracts wider tensions in the polity. At various points we draw on the work of Nick Mahony, a doctoral student at the Open University at the time of writing this chapter.

The politics of participation

The rise of public participation initiatives is situated in concerns about the changing character of the public – apparently more differentiated, more individuated, more consumer-oriented and less trusting of politicians – and about the political process itself. It is also connected to the various displacement and dislocations of public institutions we have traced earlier and to the processes of depoliticisation accompanying them. Fung and Wright argue that:

> As the tasks of the state have become more complex and the size of politics larger and more heterogenous, the institutional forms of liberal democracy developed in the nineteenth century – representative democracy plus techno-bureaucratic administration – seem increasingly ill suited to the novel problems we face in the twenty-first century . . . Rather than seeking to deepen the democratic character of politics in response to these concerns, the thrust of much political energy in recent years has been to reduce the role of politics altogether. Deregulation, privatisation, reduction of social services and curtailment of state spending have been the watchwords, rather than participation, greater responsiveness, more creative and effective forms of democratic state intervention. As the slogan goes, 'the state is the problem, not the solution'.(Fung and Wright, 2003: 3–4).

This shifts attention beyond the usual focus on a disengaged public, highlighting wider processes of depoliticisation resulting from state projects of modernisation and reform. Fung and Wright are advocates of 'empowered participatory governance' which is based on three principles: a focus on practical, concrete concerns (especially the concerns of the most disadvantaged); the development of 'bottom up' participation (rather than control by technical experts); and deliberative solution generation. They explore a number of experiments – from Brazil, India and the USA – that demonstrate the possibilities and problems of empowered participatory governance. However there is a substantial body of empirical work that highlights the failure of participation to bring about the desired transformation of governance institutions or the revival of democratic engagement on the part of citizens (e.g., Barnes et al., 2007; Cornwall and Coehlo, 2007; Neveu, 2007b; Newman et al., 2004; Rowe and Shepherd, 2002). Such failures have led some to argue that public participation can easily coexist with neo-liberal rule; and indeed may be one manifestation of neo-liberal forms of governance. For example Abram (2007) speaks of 'participatory de-politicisation', suggesting that the explosion of public participation is only possible since the public sphere has itself become de-politicised, becoming little more than a 'weak counterweight' to the withdrawal of state services and the weakening of public accountability. She notes that participation has been closely associated with urban regeneration in the UK, which coincides with the shift of public investment from local authority control to various forms of public-private partnership with limited accountability and only tenuous commitment to community development. Abram argues that participation testifies to the hegemony of neoliberalism, serving as 'a sign that such neo-liberalism has truly taken hold' (Abram, 2007: 133).

This view of neo-liberal hegemony leaves unanswered the question about why it might favour participative techniques rather than mere marketisation or even coercive forms of rule. One possible response derives from the literature on governmentality. From a Foucauldian viewpoint public participation is understood within an array of strategies for 'governing the social'. Here the public is constituted as new kinds of governable subject:

> the currently popular discourses of 'participation', 'empowerment', and 'democratisation' . . . as strategies of governance rest on tutoring people to build their capacities and become self-dependent, responsible citizens who can take care of their own welfare and govern themselves. This provides yet another example of neo-liberal 'unloading' of public services onto empowered and 'responsibilised' selves and communities who. . . are thereby made complicit in the contemporary workings of power and governance. (Sharma and Gupta, 2006: 21).

Both of these arguments – that the expansion of public participation marks the success of neo-liberalism, and that it can be understood as a new set of governmental techniques directed towards governing the social – operate at a high level of abstraction, and raise some troubling problems. One lies in the question of evidence: how might it be demonstrated that new political projects have driven the expansion of public participation, rather than simply being a parallel development? Are those promoting new participative strategies simply the agents (or dupes) of neo-liberal rule, or might they have a range of different interests, identifications and political aspirations? Do participative spaces also constitute sites of contestation where new forms of political engagement become possible? A governmentality perspective may take too much for granted the capacity of strategies to constitute subjects, paying too little attention to the complexity of relationships and identifications that may be at stake in encounters between governments and publics (Chatterjee, 2004). While forms of inclusion and participation have the potential to bind citizens into governmental power, it is important to recognise that 'the active citizen may not act in the way envisaged by government' (Newman, 2005e: 134). This is not just a question of refusals or resistances, but of the multiple discourses that are implicated in the expansion of public participation. Public participation, then, should not just be dismissed as the 'smiling face' of neo-liberalism; it condenses a range of different possible projects, purposes and discourses, not all of which can be contained within a single, overarching governmental strategy or political project (Sharma, 2008).

Furthermore, governmentality perspectives often fail to engage with the geopolitical contexts in which public participation initiatives are framed. In contrast, Cornwall and Coelho (2007) stress the role of public participation in building democratic politics in Africa, India and Latin America – countries in which 'post-authoritarian regimes, fractured and chronically under-resourced state services and pervasive clientalism leave in their wake fractious and distrustful relationships between citizens and the state' (2007: 3). Like Fung and Wright, they describe the proliferation of 'new democratic arenas' at the interface between state and society, and argue that they 'are spaces of contestation as well as collaboration, into which heterogeneous participants bring diverse interpretations of participation and democracy and divergent agendas. As such, they are crucibles for a new politics of public policy' (Cornwall and Coelho, 2007: 2). At the same time, the participation agenda in the South emerges from what they term 'a confluence of developmental and democratisation agendas' in the discourses and policies of the World Bank, the United Nations and other transnational bodies.

This idea of a 'confluence' between different political projects is also addressed by Dagnino (2007) who describes the politics of participation in Brazil being shaped by a 'perverse confluence' between two different political projects. The first is the project of enlarging and deepening democracy produced as a result of the important role played by civil society actors and social movements in the struggle against military rule in the 1980s. In the 1990s, she argued, this success had produced a context in which the principle of participation became a distinguishing feature of a new settlement between civil society and the state, and marked the success of the political project oriented towards the creation of new public spaces, the extension of citizenship and the deepening of democracy. But since the 1990s, under neo-liberal strategies, the idea of a 'minimal state' has also taken hold: a state that is withdrawing from social responsibilities and transferring them to civil society. The last decade, then, has been 'marked by a perverse confluence between the participatory project and this neo-liberal conception. The perversity is located in the fact that, pointing in opposite and even antagonistic directions, both projects require an active, proactive civil society' (Dagnino, 2007: 335).

This idea of a 'perverse confluence' is compelling, illuminating the importance of understanding public participation as a condensate in which different political projects may be uneasily combined, thereby producing spaces that are ambiguous rather than being simply categorised on one site of a duality between the 'empowerment' and 'incorporation' of social actors. The transformative potential of public participation is conditioned and shaped through the interaction of different political orientations and practices in different contexts. Political orientations and origins are, in turn, mediated through the organisations, institutions and services engaged in promoting participation, and translated by the staff and publics who encounter each other in these new spaces. This brings us to the question of how such ambiguous spaces are occupied by citizens, officials, facilitators and others.

Inhabiting ambiguous spaces: tensions of participation

Much of the literature on public participation engages with Habermas's key work, *The Structural Transformation of the Public Sphere* (1989). His analysis has been widely critiqued, not least by feminists such as Fraser (1997) and Young (1990), who challenged a conception of rationality that marginalised affective, expressive and experience-based forms of discourse. Summarising these debates, Barnett concludes:

> The continuing salience of the public sphere concept depends on revising some cherished assumptions that often shape academic discourse about media and democracy. These include assumptions about what counts as rationality, acknowledging the diverse modes through which public issues can be problematised and addressed. It is also important to affirm the practical existence of counterpublics with different norms of access, conduct, participation and representation. These challenge a class- and gender-biased model of publicity that continues to underwrite ideals of undistorted communication, disembodied reason and universalistic ideal of undistorted communication as the singular form of public discourse. (Barnett, 2003: 79).

This points to a series of tensions in the politics of participation, beginning with contested views of *representation*. Participation initiatives range from those that involve a formal measure of social or demographic representation to those that select their members on a random basis (as in many citizen councils) or those that promote open access (as in most e-democracy projects). Across this spectrum, those organising initiatives tend to be deeply concerned about the representativeness of those that are selected in terms of specific sets of characteristics: age, gender, ethnicity, and/or membership of so-called 'excluded' or 'hard to reach' groups. Many different meanings of representation are condensed here: traditional forms of mandate; statistical representativeness against a general population norm; or a weighted sample designed with particular governance purposes in mind. Notions of representation and representativeness sideline what Young (1990) terms a 'politics of presence' – the significance of the bodily presence in decision-making forums of excluded or marginalised groups. The idea of representation also rests on an assumption that identity and interests are formed and fixed in the private sphere, and brought ready made in the public, rather than viewing communicative practices as a means through which identities are potentially formed or transformed. Deliberation, in the Habermasean ideal, has the capacity to transform interests and opinions: we would also argue that it is a process that shapes identifications – who people think they are.

> The concept of representation depends on a simple and static notion of identity: representation is sought on the basis of characteristics that are considered to define the individual and to enable a sufficiently broad range of participation. This fails to acknowledge either the differentiated nature of identity, or the significance of the processes of identity construction that

takes place across lines of difference through participation. . . . This is a process in which both citizens and officials are implicated. (Barnes et al., 2006: 205)

Representation, then, rests on a narrow view of politics and of identity. It essentialises identity itself, inviting people to 'stand for' specific categories: the young or old, black or white, male or female population, without taking any account of the dynamic relationships between the multiple dimensions of personhood. In the search for representatives, public officials engage in a process of categorising people into mutually exclusive groups: the 'usual suspects' versus 'hard to reach' groups; 'expert citizens' versus 'ordinary people'; 'community' versus 'business' stakeholders, and so on. This process of categorisation does not 'reflect' a pre-given public, but is constitutive of it: that is, both expert citizens and 'usual suspects' are made so through their contact with public bodies (Barnes et al., 2003). Marilyn Taylor's research on the role of voluntary and community sector participants in Neighbourhood Renewal programmes in the UK includes the following quotation from a respondent:

> Every time you keep hearing 'Oh we want the real people to be involved in this'. So we say 'OK, we'll help you get the real people'. They get the real people, they tell the real people you have to become organised . . . and they become a group and then they say 'Oh no, we don't want groups, we want real people'. (Taylor, 2007:18).

This focus on 'real people' echoes our argument in Chapter 3. Here it suggests publics engaged in participation initiatives may be asked to respond in terms of how they feel as an individual, abstracted from wider identities, allegiances and relationships, and from the forms of knowledge and expertise they carry.

This takes us to a second tension – between *authenticity and expertise*. Authenticity is a characteristic of lay participants: the ordinary people who are invited because they are not aligned with pre-existing interests or political positions. In health and social care discourses, one resolution is the view that people can be 'experts of their own condition'; that is, they bring an authenticity based on having lived with their long-term illness, their disability or their role as carer. Such expertise forms the basis of their participation in decisions about their own treatment or care and may even be solicited in service design processes. But these are always 'particular' sorts of knowledge, set in tension with more abstract or general types of expertise (managerial, business or professional: see Chapter 5).

Notions of expertise and authenticity may also be mobilised in deliberative forums in which citizens are invited to help make 'expert judgements'. This is a classic image of the deliberative process in which, it is assumed, prior assumptions or interests may be unravelled as a result of receiving new knowledge (perhaps through testimony from 'experts'), and by developing new understandings through communicative practice. Such assumptions are questioned in one important study by Davies et al. (2007).

Vignette: Assembling 'communities of practice'

Researchers at the Open University studied a Citizens' Council established to work with the National Institute of Clinical Excellence (NICE) in the UK. NICE is charged with making difficult decisions about what health treatments – including drugs – should be available within the NHS. From its inception it was much concerned to establish its legitimacy through engagement with a range of stakeholders and through a forum (the Citizens' Council) in which citizens were invited to deliberate on key decisions. Participants rarely spoke from a position of a pre-given or fixed set of interests. The emphasis in many – though not all – exchanges was one of collaboration rather than argument. This collaborative and exploratory style characterised exchanges both between Council members and expert witnesses, and among Council members themselves. The authors use the term 'community of practice' to describe this emerging process. For instance, citizens were invited to debate the proposals for the adoption of a new drug designed for treatment for pain in arthritis:

> Council members were emotionally and cognitively engaged; the discussion sessions facilitated the emergence of reasoning they could share, and the result echoed that of the appraisal committee itself. What are we to make of such a conclusion? Did this moment of practice serve to create an expertise space from which citizens could speak as citizens, or did it bring citizens as 'good pupils' into an appreciation of the expertise space of NICE itself, to produce an echo of the outcomes achieved there? (Davies et al., 2007: 206).

The construction of this 'community of practice' problematises distinctions between professionals and lay citizens, and between 'authenticity' and 'expertise'. The emphasis, in blurring these boundaries, was on achieving consensus. This masked deeper workings of power, in which lay members were positioned as 'good pupils' by the experts they encountered. However this did not foreclose the possibility of challenge: encounters between multiple forms of knowledge and different resources created ambiguous spaces.

Here we turn to the third tension – the antagonism between *publics and counterpublics*. Challenges to everyday, informal, taken for granted forms of power require alternative political repertoires, relationships and identifications. These emerge from what Nancy Fraser terms 'counterpublic' spaces in which everyday experience can be transformed into a shared political expertise (Fraser, 1989; see also Chapter 3). Service user and citizen controlled organisations, for example, tend to combine mutual aid, self-help and political action, and to have their own ways of working, strategies, and styles of decision-making. Such spaces, and those that inhabit them, are precisely those that officials tend to distrust most when they seek 'ordinary people' to speak to. As result, deliberative structures have tended to be set up separate from service user or citizen controlled organisations. But the evidence from the studies in Barnes et al. (2007) suggests that groups or movements who have deliberated in an autonomous public space are much more capable of contributing positively to the wider public sphere:

> It is notable that where groups with a prior existence (formed around community activism, social movement politics or in other alternative public spaces) were invited to participate. . . deliberation was more likely to produce challenges to the status quo and some element of transformation – if not in terms of quantifiable outcomes, then at least in terms of attitudes and orientations of public officials. . . . They also form sources of collective identity and oppositional politics that have the potential to reinvigorate and renew the public sphere (2007: 202).

The idea of counterpublics challenges the norms of representation discussed earlier. Instead, representation becomes a site of negotiation, involving confrontations between different sources of power and legitimacy. Such negotiations have become increasingly important as public bodies seek to enhance their legitimacy with particular publics. For example, police services in the UK, following charges of 'institutional racism' in the 1990s, set up extensive forms of engagement with black and ethnic minority 'communities', and some began to work with gay and lesbian networks in order to ensure more effective policing of hate crime. In each case counterpublics had to manage the tension between defending a space of oppositional politics, and being co-opted into partnership arrangements that enrolled them into formations of governmental power.

Co-option, however, suggests a singular purpose for governmental bodies. Our focus in the previous chapter on the complex negotiations over issues of public value and purpose suggests a rather different picture. Public participation initiatives create new kinds of dilemmatic space, producing discomfort for both facilitators and publics, as well as opening up tensions between them. For example, the NICE forum study, cited earlier, refers to a 'clapping incident' in which, when one member expressed a view that minority ethnic and disabled groups 'play the system' and that any 'special treatment' would be unfair, a number of other members of the Council applauded her stance. When the issue was addressed at a later meeting, with facilitators reiterating ground rules, several members objected to what they termed 'political correctness' and others clearly resented being 'told what to do or how to behave' (Davies et al., 2007: 144). The incident, the authors conclude, brought wider tensions of British public and political discourse into the deliberative spaces. Such spaces, then, cannot successfully be sealed off from the wider political culture; rather conflicts within that culture are likely to be refracted through them.

This takes us to a third tension – the antagonistic relationship between *cosmopolitian and parochial publics*. Ideas of citizen 'empowerment' through participation are often linked to spatial processes of decentralisation, providing one dimension of the processes of respatialisation discussed in Chapter 2 (see also Williams, 2004). Decentralisation is one of Fung and Wright's requirements for 'empowered participatory governance'; but they themselves highlight the difficulties of 'uncoordinated decentralisation' that isolates citizens into small units (2003: 22). The imperatives of decentralisation and of participation have been closely linked in the UK, producing a slippage between locality and community that may be detrimental to participation as a site of political agency. The focus on locality 'delimits the kinds of political identity that are given legitimacy in participative governance. The result may be a constrained, managed and consensus oriented political imaginary' (Newman, 2005e: 135; see also Neveu, 2007a). This makes it difficult for local participatory processes to make connections with wider transformations of the public domain. Taylor and Wilks-Heeg (2007), while advocates of greater locally based participation, note that:

> Alongside the introduction of new systems for local participation is the apparently contradictory drive for centralism and divestment of services to specialist agencies. Often carried out with the intention of achieving greater efficiency and cutting costs, many public services are being reorganised into larger geographical units and many have been put out to private tender. This is resulting in an increase in the remoteness of services and risks people feeling alienated and excluded from decision-making. (2007: 2).

We would take this argument further. The public that is constituted through local forums is one in which local identities are privileged, to the detriment of wider connections that individuals might bring to such settings: for example, those implicated in the politics of race, gender, sexuality, disability and more. While local forums may be of great value, the agendas seldom enable participants to make connections between local, city-wide, national and indeed global issues; for example, environmental issues and social justice concerns.

Vignette: challenging the limits of the local

This vignette draws on innovations in public participation in two London Boroughs. In Borough A, some power had been devolved to a series of local committees comprising elected councillors and representatives of a wide range of organisations. Nevertheless the decision-making process was deemed to be inefficient, hampering the Council as a whole in its capacity to meet central government targets. As a result the committees were abolished, to be replaced with a new local participative arrangement in which recomposed local committees could deliberate on decisions about the spending of devolved funds. At the same time, the membership of committees was changed: representatives were now sought from explicitly place-based groups (resident and tenants associations, and groups formed as 'friends' of local parks). The council then received numerous protests about the 'exclusion' of other kinds of representative who had served on previous committees: representatives of church-based organisations, women's groups, youth organisations and so on, each of which brought other possible identities and wider imaginaries to the deliberative process. This not only returns us to the contested nature of 'representation', it also suggests which categories of public tend to be privileged, and which viewed as less authentic, in local forums.

Borough B (one of Mahony's case study sites) decided to hold an 'Open Budget' exercise. This was a Borough wide event in which local residents were invited to deliberate on policy options that would inform future expenditure on a range of services. One such policy area was the future of waste management in the Borough. These deliberations were narrowly channelled. Participants were invited to select between two options: one focused on educating the public to recycle more of their waste, the second on incentives for new patterns of consumer behaviour (such as less frequent waste collections). However some participants responded by suggesting that a tax should instead be levied on companies responsible for the production and distribution of 'excessive' packaging materials. This was a challenge from the margins of a tightly managed event, in which the organisers retained the power to decide whether – or not – to respond to recommendations and challenges. We can see here the framing of what is – and is not – a public issue refracted through notions of locality.

Both examples demonstrate conflict around definitions of local participation. In the first, who is – and is not – to be considered a local public or (even more problematically) a 'local representative' can be seen as contested. In the second the focus of contestation was the framing of waste management as a 'local' issue, stripped of wider – even global – environmental concerns. The second also suggests a challenge around the definition of waste management as a matter of consumer behaviour rather than something situated in a wider field of public – and political – agency, including a potential challenge to corporate power.

The depoliticisation associated with local publics being invited to engage in deliberation on local issues is sharpest where participation is inflected through a communitarian politics. Community and locality are often conflated, posing questions about scale in the political imaginary (Neveu, 2007b; Newman, 2005e). The emphasis on the local tends to constitute the public into a series of particularised publics, narrowing the political imaginary and augmenting parochial, rather than cosmopolitan, allegiances. But the production of parochialism is not just a result of a politics of scale – it may also result from practices which produce an 'othering' of particular publics: minority ethnic groups, travellers, asylum seekers, mental health service users, and, increasingly, those who exhibit what is defined as 'anti-social' behaviour. Rather than such groups or individuals being accommodated in a larger imaginary of a liberal public realm, they may be positioned as 'outside' the particularities of the publics being summoned to voice in local participation initiatives – and indeed as the 'others' against whom populist forms of direct democracy are mobilised.

As we have shown, participation initiatives are cross-cut by a series of tensions and antagonisms that may be resolved in different ways or may even remain unresolved, producing a series of unstable encounters and unpredictable outcomes. Such tensions cannot be resolved by simply choosing the 'right' set of techniques for a particular purpose. They are essentially political, condensing the politics of social movements, service user or community activism alongside dominant political formations. We examine two of these – the politics of populism and the politics of managerialism – in the following sections.

Making governance popular

New forms of public participation are viewed as a means of engaging a public that is disenchanted with formal political styles and institutions. Ideas of 'dirty politics' and the perceived detachment of the 'political class' from everyday life play important roles in this disenchantment. There is a new emphasis on the informal and everyday, the use of new media and web-based technologies to reach out to the public, and the search for 'authentic' publics, untrammelled by the messy associations with a discredited political domain. This in turn invokes a 'politics of faith' rather than a 'politics of scepticism' (Oakeshott, 1996), or a politics of redemption rather than a politics of pragmatism (Canovan, 1999). Such politics are visible not only in the increasing use of public relations techniques (the satisfaction survey, the focus group, the marketing campaign) but also in new ways of addressing citizens though popular media and web technologies. For example Bang and Joergensen (2007) argue that

> we are witnessing the emergence of expert celebrity citizens . . . who depend for their success on the media endowing them with a certain degree of public visibility in their particular niches of expertise and power. . . . They also represent an explicit response to the political inadequacies of old collective forms of oppositional and legitimating participation in civil society (2007: 177).

Beyond the sphere of public policy, popular media have also sought to engage citizens through talk shows, opinion polls, feedback events and others (Coleman, 2003, 2005; Couldry, 2003; van Zoonen, 2005).

Vignette: Vote for Me

This was a reality TV programme studied as part of Mahony's research (Mahony, 2008). The programme, taking place, over five evenings in one week in January 2005, offered viewers in the UK the chance to select a prospective parliamentary candidate – 'a new kind of politician' drawn from the ranks of 'ordinary people'. The format echoed that of other reality TV talent shows, especially *Pop Idol*, with a series of daily programmes presenting candidates and their 'policies'. Viewers exercised their 'votes' by telephone, gradually eliminating candidates one by one, until the favoured candidate 'won' at the end of the week. TV producers permitted and encouraged a variety of modes of address, from right-wing ranting to left-wing posturing, from stripping to publicise the cause of brothel legalisation, to the airing of more traditional protest songs. Celebrity was fostered, and 'authenticity' valorised. The 'winner' was a right–wing candidate who had stood on a consistently anti-immigration platform, leading to difficulties for both presenter and judges. He subsequently stood for election in 2005 as a candidate for a party that he founded – the Get Britain Back Party – against the then leader of the Conservative party, losing heavily.

Political commentators and the Electoral Commission had greeted plans for this series with enthusiasm. On the front page of *The Observer* in January 2004 the paper's chief political correspondent announced the news that Peter Bazalgette, chairman of production company Endemol and creator of reality television show *Big Brother*, was in talks with broadcasters about a political version of the reality television show *Pop Idol*. 'Broadcasters have not yet had the chutzpah to commission a formatted popularity contest for politics, but we're now discussing it with them' (*The Observer*,4 January 2004, p.1). In a separate article in the same edition, Stephan Shakepeare, director of opinion research at YouGov, related the initiative to a wider set of contemporary developments including recent experiments with online deliberative polling, the UK Labour Party's 'Big Conversation' initiative and, the news of a poll that positioned Switzerland – 'which operates under direct democracy' – as 'the happiest country on Earth'. Forms of public participation such as these have the potential, Shakespeare claimed, to unleash 'consumer power' on the 'entrenched monopoly of the party political system'. 'Consumer power is the new revolutionary force . . . representative democracy, with its reliance on essentially tribal political parties, will soon face competition' (*The Observer*, 4 January 2004, p.28) Academic commentators such as van Zoonen (2005) and Coleman (2003, 2005) have also been optimistic about the potential of such techniques and formats to encourage individuals disenchanted with formal politics to participate in the political process.

As Mahony (2008) argues, distinctions between entertainment and politics appear to be collapsed here. Both have to address the problem of how to engage the attention of large numbers of people. The techniques used by programmes such as *Pop Idol* were viewed as having the capacity to repopularise the UK electoral system and empower those currently disenfranchised by the 'old' model of politics. But the elision between entertainment, politics and popular culture is not confined to events promulgated by the mass media. Mahony's research shows a range of populist strategies across widely differing cases of public participation (including *Vote for Me*, the *Open Budget* event referred to earlier, and a series of meetings linked to the European Social Forum). In each case, organisers, producers or facilitators constructed their appeal to potential participants by actively distancing themselves from 'official', formal, 'old-fashioned' modes of public governance and instead positioned themselves as facilitators or hosts, emphasising the informal, everyday, popular qualities of the events. 'Newness', 'informality' and 'authenticity' were key discourses, linked to a politics of affect, designed to invoke positive feelings, impressions and emotions. But each evoked a different meaning of the popular: the *Open Budget* in its appeal to everyday, informal and feeling-based repertoires of 'community'; *Vote for Me* in its use of a popular cultural genre; and the Social Forum in its strongly anti-establishment form of politics designed to outsmart their neo-liberal opponents by being as spontaneous, creative and unpredictable as possible in the siting and timing of their actions.

Each innovation thus challenged the Habermasean ideal of rational deliberation by appealing to a politics of authenticity: in the case of the European Social Forum, to an authentic politics, untainted by the institutions of government; in the *Open Budget* event, to the authenticity of people's experience of 'real life' in that borough; and in *Vote For Me* the authenticity of selfhood, i.e., the presentation of a 'true self' through reality TV. These appeals were not premised on any expectation that participants would necessarily be representing fully worked-through, considered or fixed positions. Rather they would be able to express their impressions and reactions: how they might be feeling about situations or topics as well as what they thought about them. There are notions here therefore of holding individuals and groups of participants accountable for performances of their own feelings – expressing their true, authentic selves – as well as for their more considered deliberations.

Each innovation also disrupted ideas of a unitary, spatially bounded public sphere based on liberal principles. Together they suggest an increasingly fractured and fragmented public sphere; fragmented not only in terms of interests and identities, but also in terms of the different media and technologies through which multiple publics are mobilised. The three cases carry different inflections of 'the popular' and cannot be collapsed into a general equivalence between public participation and populist politics. Nevertheless Canovan highlights some dangers associated with the 'redemptive' mode of democracy. One is the casting of 'ordinary people' against a privileged, cosmopolitan elite, thus allowing space in which 'illiberal' views to be surfaced and validated (as in the NICE forum cited earlier). Public participation may make space for the expression – and validation – of anti-elitist values, including those that challenge the presumed legitimacy of multi-culturalism, internationalism, feminism, and, more recently, environmentalism.

A second problem with the 'redemptive' style of politics is the valorisation of simplicity: 'Populists claim that all this complexity [compromises, negotiations, coalition building] is a self serving racket perpetuated by professional politicians, and that the solution to the problems ordinary people care about are essentially simple' (Canovan, 1999, 6). Politics, then, becomes a matter of simple choices – such as those presented to those attending the *Open Budget* event, watching *Vote for Me* or participating in various forms of e-democracy. We can see here clear links with politicians' attempts to develop new styles of direct engagement with citizens – webs, blogs, TV, phone-in programmes, chat shows, e-petitions – that bypass traditional democratic channels. We can also see the traces of a shift to a style of politics that may be both populist and consumerist. Taguieff points suggestively to how populist appeals promise to suspend temporality, effacing 'any distance between all desires and their realisation' (2007: 16, translation by JC).

Canovan does not dismiss what she terms 'redemptive politics': she argues that its aspirational qualities, its faith that the world can be made a better place, is essential to the survival and flourishing of democracy itself rather than its collapse into a series of pragmatic or instrumental practices. But here lies the danger: advocates of public participation frequently offer expressions of 'faith' in the capacity of participation to renew the public sphere, revive civil society and restore legitimacy to political institutions, without paying sufficient attention to ways in which public voices are mobilised and managed.

Managing participation

In Chapters 4 and 5 we highlighted the ways in which emergent forms of publicness – such as co-production, choice or participation – were potentially assembled with managerial power. This has several consequences. First, it produces a technical and procedural focus (in both the literature and in practice) rather than a political framing of participation. As the participatory imperative has gathered force it has produced a proliferation of mediating devices: models of best practice, handbooks, rhetorics, professional managerial routines, all promoted by a new corps of consultants, facilitators and market-makers. Second, participation may come to be framed by organisational rationalities, with citizens constituted through their relationship to a particular organisation – the hospital, the school, the police service, the municipality, the partnership board – rather than a wider sphere of publics. This means that participation may be particularised as well as localised: issues not the concern of the organisation are excluded or marginalised (Williams, 2004).

Third, participation may also come to be aligned with the expansion of consumerism in public services. This has been a key discourse driving through modernisation reforms, producing an expansion of consultative mechanisms on the part of service delivery organisations positioned in an increasingly competitive field, and indeed of governments seeking to enhance their legitimacy. The process of consultation here tends to become subject to managerial technologies of power: the survey, the market research exercise, the opinion poll and the focus group. It is certainly the case that forms of consultation – including e-petitions – can help shape agendas, keeping governments more closely attuned to 'popular' sentiments and service organisations responsive to the changing needs of their users. But publics are positioned as individual customers rather than political subjects. For example, the invitation to participate in electronic polls elicits – and aggregates – individual responses rather than enabling more active and deliberative forms of engagement (a problem partly addressed by parallel discussion forums). Citizens are positioned as little more than the customers of governments increasingly anxious to elicit feedback and to engage in direct forms of marketing that bypass an increasingly sceptical media (Needham, 2003). In the case of service-based forums, power is rarely shared: decision-making tends to remain firmly in managerial hands, and service users tend to be involved individually and fleetingly, despite some exceptions, and so have little opportunity to develop a collective voice (Harrison and Mort, 1998).

Fourth, the managerial logics discussed in Chapters 5 and 6 produce their own temporal imperatives. Consultation and participation events are routinised as episodes in political cycles of decision-making (the annual budget, the performance plan) or managerial templates of project management (in which consultation tends to be a single step in a linear temporal sequence). For example, Abram (2007) notes the difficulties in participative planning exercises created by the entry of new participants who had not been part of earlier participatory decision-making outcomes and who wanted to set new agendas. She also describes the difficulties of combining participatory planning with local government cycles of decision-making. There are clear links here to the process of 'projectisation' noted in Chapter 3: participation becomes a temporally bounded event rather than an ongoing process of engagement that might be linked to alternative modes of power.

Finally, managerial rationalities of efficiency, as we have seen, help drive the offloading or outsourcing of public services onto private or not-for-profit enterprises. Participation may continue; indeed may be enhanced. However its meaning may change for those involved. Writing about Brazil, Dagnino notes that the increasing reliance on civil society organisations as the providers of public services means that '[t]he crucial meaning of participation, conceived by the participatory project as an effective sharing of power between State and civil society through the exercise of deliberation in new public spaces, is radically redefined as and reduced to management (*gestão*)' (Dagnino, 2007: 361).

Conclusion: Participation and power

The pervasiveness of public participation in the remaking of public services nevertheless represents a new set of aspirations, including those of professionals and public managers seeking to transform service organisations in ways that offset some of the impoverishments of the new public management (Chapter 6). Although it may be most easily be assembled with consumerist or populist tendencies, it also offers alignments with more democratic movements, and can contribute to alternative framings of 'voice', 'co-production' or 'empowerment' that offer connections between publics rather than further processes of individuation. However it is deeply entangled with forms of managerial forms of governance that have the capacity to reduce, rather than enhance, the meanings and practices of citizenship.

Many of the arguments of this chapter suggest the potentially de-politicising consequences of public participation initiatives. Constituting the public for the purpose of participation may seek to make the public manageable within the bureaucratic and organisational contexts to which they are invited. The sites and technologies of participation – the citizens' forum, the neighbourhood council, the open budget exercise, the police liaison group, the electronic poll – seek to produce neutral, manageable spaces. Decisions about what issues may be opened up, and what technologies are to be deployed, are mostly made outside the participative process. This is not however a straightforward process of de-politicisation that can be attributed to neo-liberal forms of 'governing the social' (Chapter 1). The range of different political projects that are condensed in the expansion of public participation means that it forms an ambiguous assemblage. Different interpretations of public and private are played out in assumptions about the identities that people bring to the participative process. Publics are mobilised in different ways, bringing multiple experiences, identities and forms of agency to the participative process. Processes of mediation and translation challenge the boundary between 'officials' and 'lay' publics, potentially producing new 'communities of practice' that are not containable within organisational rationalities. Spaces of participation are opened up in ways that can enlarge – or constrain – the political imaginaries of those occupying them. And, as we have argued, identities are not brought ready made into the public domain but are shaped and negotiated in 'public' interactions. What might be the consequences of new encounters and interactions for the remaking of publics – as consumers, service users, communities and participants in partnerships and governing bodies? How is public participation reshaping the 'dilemmatic' spaces inhabited by those attempting to engage – and even 'empower' – publics? And what is happening as the boundary between 'official' and 'lay' identities and forms of expertise becomes more ambiguous and contested? Such questions are not easily answered – but they point to public participation as a site of unpredictable encounters and unstable reworkings of power.

Such questions raise challenges for both research and practice. For researchers, they highlight the significance of 'getting under the skin' of discourses and strategies to explore how meanings are negotiated within specific sites – and raise the challenge of how to generalise from such detailed work.

For those engaged in policy development or the translation of policies, it opens up a series of dilemmas or difficulties that will have to be negotiated. There is, in short, no single model of 'best practice' that can be transferred unproblematically from one location or policy domain to another. Rather, the transformative potential of public participation is conditioned by the way in which a series of political and policy tensions are negotiated. To tease out the dynamics of participation this chapter has explored some of these recurring dilemmas whose resolution may tilt participation towards different resolutions of political and managerial imperatives, or orient it towards the strengthening or loosening of established regimes of power. Such tensions, and the antagonisms they produce, may have to be negotiated within specific initiatives or sites; but they stem from deeper fault lines in the reconfigurations of publics, politics and power traced in this book. It is through these reworkings of power that spaces and sites are both opened up and – if they become too difficult – closed down.

The ambiguities we have highlighted leads us to take a position of being 'critical enthusiasts' for the emergent politics of public participation in many countries. We are enthusiasts because, in complex, diverse societies, it is no longer possible (if indeed it ever was) for different experiences and voices to be accommodated in formalised processes of representative democracy. We are also enthusiasts because many of the people – citizens and officials – we have met in the new sites and spaces of participation are themselves enthusiasts. They want to make a difference; are willing to spend their time and energies in helping to make a difference; and the difference that they want to make is usually one that will, they hope, be of benefit to others. That is, the act of participation – of being a particular kind of active citizen – can be regarded as a gift that many people bring to the public domain, however fraught the experience may be in practice.

But we are *critical* enthusiasts for several reasons. First, we are suspicious about the close association between the proliferation of new sites of participation and the policies and politics of some Western governments. We might consider public participation as an attempt to forge a new settlement that aligns, however uncomfortably, the heritage of the social movements that struggled for voice in the twentieth century with the newer rationalities of consumerism in the twenty-first: rationalities that tend to individualise difference and displace the more politicised imaginaries formed in the spaces of counterpublic mobilisations (Clarke et al., 2007a, see also Duggan, 2003). Second, we are sceptical about the transformative potential of new sites and technologies of civic engagement as they are de-politicised, technicised and managerialised. Third, as we have argued, public participation may produce a form of politics with an extremely narrowed political imaginary: one that is highly particular, highly localised, or framed in ways that offer an extremely thin form of engagement. Fourth, it may be that it is the public themselves who are the subject of transformation rather than the institutions that they confront – a theme we return to in the next chapter.

Perhaps we have ended up being rather more critical than enthusiastic in our assessment. This reflects a concern that public participation may end up widening the democratic deficit rather than overcoming it. Those invited to encounters with power in its many forms may go away disheartened – perhaps power did not listen, or listened but took no notice, or took notice but failed to tell citizens what they had done (or not) as a result. Or perhaps citizens misunderstood the nature and extent of the power being offered to them. But the very proliferation of new sites in which citizens encounter institutional and political power encourages possibilities that cannot be easily contained, controlled or managed. The result is unpredictable, open to new challenges and new definitions of what is – and is not – a matter for public interest and attention. But for the transformative possibilities of participation to be realised, three political alignments need to be disrupted: that of populism (in the search for 'authentic' people who politicians can communicate with directly); that of parochialism (that reduces the public sphere to a series of bounded localities and responsible citizens); and that of consumerism (in which public services and governments become predominantly concerned with feedback from individualised customers). Only then might it be possible to engage the public in ways that foster and renew the 'sphere of publics'.

8 Remaking citizens: transformation and activation

Many of the processes of remaking publicness work on, and through, citizenship, changing its character, conditions and consequences. Citizenship occupies a central place in these processes because it articulates formations of nation, state and the liberal public sphere; the three core elements of the discursive chains of publicness with whose unsettling we began. As national formations are disturbed, as the state is decentred as a site of publicness, and as the established orientations of a liberal public sphere become contested, we should not be surprised to see citizenship being revised and reworked into new configurations. Citizenship condenses a variety of political, governmental and cultural projects: those that seek to restore national identity and belonging as well as those that attempt to re-invent relationships between people and the state, not least in rewriting relationships between 'rights' and 'responsibilities'. Above all, the figure of the citizen embodies changing conceptions of the public.

For some, these changes form a story of decline and abandonment, in which what were once welfare states increasingly expose their citizens to the revived power of markets, leaving them to endure the violence and vicissitudes that markets create (Clarke, 2005d). This decline is manifest in the evacuation or diminution of citizenship: its shrinking political and social substance, and the greater conditionality of access to citizenship and of its provisions (Dwyer, 2000). The continuing challenges to the social basis of citizenship, with lines of connection and solidarity eroded by the twin processes of individuation and consumerism, attest to the weakening of a public domain of citizenship engagement and action. But this focus on the demise of citizenship does not tell the whole story. In contrast, some commentators focus on transnational expressions of citizenship that transcend the nation state – from ideas of a post-national citizenship grounded in a universalising regime of human rights (Soysal, 1994) to the possibilities of a transnational civil society and a 'deliberative global politics' (Dryzek, 2006) or global 'defiant publics' (Drache, 2008). Others focus on the potential of the market to offer a means of enacting citizenship through consumer, rather than political, power (Sassatelli, 2007).

At the same time, governments have been intensifying some types of interaction and engagement with citizens, seeking to make them 'active' in different ways. Citizenship has become a prime focus of strategies of modernisation and reform, with discourses of active citizenship, responsible citizenship, citizen-consumers citizen empowerment and participation, all crowding the policy landscape. In many places, citizenship has been addressed by policies concerned with the promotion of social cohesion and social inclusion, re-articulating ideas of belonging, identity and social solidarity. Its national character is currently being made more visible through the introduction of citizenship education, citizenship ceremonies and the specification of the duties of 'responsible' citizens. Alongside narratives of decline, then, proliferation is also a critical dynamic as states come to demand more of their citizens – and more people demand to become citizens. This proliferation of citizenship discourse reflects an unstable terrain of new citizenship claims (for recognition, resources and rights) as well as new governmental strategies associated with modernisation and development. Citizenship is, then, a prism through which our focus on the twin processes of public decline and proliferation can be made visible. This means that we see citizenship not as a static and solid entity, based on a clearly defined set of civil, political and social rights, but as a figure that is traversed – pulled in different directions, and into different shapes – by multiple political projects that aim to make it mean something new.

Contesting citizenship

Citizenship has always been a focus of political struggles. Despite the critiques of the limited character of bourgeois citizenship as a universal model, the idea(l) of citizenship has been mobilised by different projects seeking to reconstruct social and political relationships – some transforming the substance of citizenship in the process. Ever since 'first wave' Western feminism demanded the 'rights of man'; since the property-less proletariat insisted that equality extended rights beyond the possession of those with property; since slave rebellions insisted on humanity as a common condition that underpinned equality, citizenship has been one of the most salient and most contested images in the political lexicon. Recent struggles have seen groups demanding citizenship rights in relation to other dimensions and dynamics of exclusion: continuing 'gender troubles'; forms of sexuality; the distinction between able-bodied and disabled people; age discriminations; cultural citizenship; genetic citizenship and so on (see Lister, 2007).

Such developments highlight the ways in which citizenship remains both politically desirable and politically problematic. It always involves more than just a recurring dynamic of inclusion/exclusion. Dominant political projects often try to recoup citizenship struggles to a containable model of individual rights, and to accommodate them within a normative universalism (Duggan, 2003). This normative image centres on the self-possessed, self-directing self of liberal personhood, however much this is expanded to include those who were not previously recognised as 'fitting' this image. Yet many of these struggles threaten to remake the norm – changing the public realm, rather than merely demanding admittance to its current form.

We want to distinguish two ways in which citizenship is contested: the first is expansive, focusing on questions of access and inclusion; the second is transformative, challenging the legitimacy of the social and political arrangements of the social body itself. In the first, citizenship is contested by multiple political projects demanding access to the public realm. This has sometimes resulted in legislative attempts to inscribe formal equality – for women, for black and ethnic minorities, for disabled people, for gay and lesbians and others. Such legislation has required public bodies to adjust their own practices to enable access by previously marginalised groups to public services and public service employment, producing a proliferation of equal opportunity policies and guidelines. The formalisation of new claims in legislation and in bureaucratic rules has, however, not necessarily resolved the demands for recognition and justice. Mainstream cultures and institutional practices have often remained relatively resistant or unchanged (Breitenbach et al., 2002; Itzin and Newman, 1995). Equal opportunity legislation, guidelines and procedures have primarily addressed issues of access by excluded groups to the liberal public domain of citizenship (Clarke, 2004c). As such, they fail to problematise the values of the public domain itself, and leave unchallenged the way in which the boundaries between the public domain and the 'private' realm of personal and domestic life are drawn.

Feminist politics and scholarship in particular has challenged the separation of a public world of citizenship and justice from the private world of relationships and care, noting how such a separation has bracketed care and other contributions to social well-being from wider public recognition (Lister, 2003; MacKinnon, 1989; Uberoi, 2003). One result has been the attempt to expand a 'feminist ethic of care' from the private to the public domain (Tronto, 1993; Sevenhuijsen, 1998). The attempt to make care a public issue has had limited success; despite decades of public care services, their funding has remained precarious and social care is currently the site of attempts to 're-privatise' care to personal and familial domains. Care services, however, have also been the focus of claims by particular groups – disabled people, people with learning difficulties – for recognition as citizens rather than 'dependents'. Struggles around care are one vital location of the conflict between expansionist and transformative citizenship claims.

While many struggles have been about expanding access to citizenship, they have often blurred into struggles that contest the larger social architectures of power, inequality, and structured forms of domination and subordination. Citizenship has considerable potency as a mobilising term for challenging particular social architectures of inequality, subordination and exclusion. It offers a powerful discursive device through which the legitimacy and sustainability of specific social arrangements can be called into question. For example, while early feminist struggles centred on political franchise and legal status, second wave feminism offered a transformative, rather than merely expansive, conception of citizenship. Citizenship and gender were reworked through the insistence that the 'personal is political' – a device that radically re-invented distinctions between public and private realms (e.g., Lister, 2003; Williams, 2000). Feminism thus expanded the terrain on which equality claims could be made, shifting the focus from equal legal and political status to address inequalities within the domestic sphere and to raise questions about the social organization of care work, reproduction and sexuality, bringing debates about body rights into the public domain. As with subsequent struggles around sexual citizenship, the focus shifted to social and cultural transformation. Such claims for citizenship are not merely demands for access to the juridical status of citizen (legal person-hood) but imply reforming the social body itself. They seek to transform both who is/can be a member of the society and what relations between members must exist to form the 'good society'. To illustrate this, we turn once again to the work of Evelina Dagnino:

Vignette: citizenship and social relations in Brazil

Writing about citizenship struggles in Brazil, Dagnino argues that the end of the military dictatorship was both driven by, and made possible, a politics of citizenship that was both expansive (including more people as citizens) and transformative (contesting the social, political and cultural orders of Brazil):

> the recognition of the cultural dimension of politics led to a broadening of the scope of citizenship beyond incorporation into the political system in the restricted sense of the formal/legal acquisition of rights. The struggle for citizenship was presented as a project for a new sociability: a more egalitarian framework for social relations at all levels; new rules for living together in society and for the negotiation of conflict; a new sense of public order and public responsibility; a new social contract. A more egalitarian framework for social relations at all levels implies the recognition of the 'other' as a subject-bearer of valid interests and legitimate rights. It also implies the constitution of a public dimension of society, where rights can be consolidated as public parameters for interlocution, for debate on and negotiation of conflicts, making possible the reconfiguration of the ethical dimension of social life. Such a project unsettles not only social authoritarianism as the basic mode of social ordering in Brazilian society, but also more recent neoliberal discourses, which erect private interest as the measure for everything, obstructing the possibilities for an ethical dimension of social life . . . (Dagnino, 2006: 154).

It is important to underline how social and political movements like those in Brazil worked through – and expanded – the discursive repertoire of citizenship to construct alternative social and political imaginaries: conceptions of how society might be re-ordered in the face of existing systemic oppression, inequality and subordination. Citizenship provided a discursive resource for imagining how social relationships might be ordered in ways that are inclusive, egalitarian and participatory. So concepts of equality, rights, justice and participation in economic, social and political life have a powerful political-cultural resonance. Dagnino goes on to argue that the neo-liberal forces have been obliged to engage with – and transform again – the idea of citizenship precisely because of its 'symbolical power' and 'mobilising capacity' (2006: 156).

Neo-liberalism's project is not merely a matter of 'rolling back' the previous expansive enlargement of citizenship. Rather it has also been engaged in a 'transformative' politics of its own, seeking to remake as well as retrench citizenship. Public services occupy a significant place within these multiple, overlapping and contradictory conceptions of citizens and citizenship. The expansion of claims for recognition unsettled public service conceptions of 'their' publics, producing a proliferation of tailored services designed to reach particular groups (as in the public library vignette in Chapter 6). For example, education services responded to the needs of migrant children, traveller children, children with 'special needs' and other groups. Police services attempted to respond to women's concerns about rape and domestic violence, and to gay and lesbian concerns about 'hate crime'. Social services redesigned their provision around the claims for recognition of mental health service users, people with learning disabilities and others struggling for recognition as citizens rather than dependents. Each expansionary claim has possible transformative implications – not just about who can access services, but concerning the basic cultures and practices of public service organisations. Public services, then, have had to negotiate these expansive and transformative claims, while encountering the pressures to manage with less resources, offer better value for money, become partners, and act competitively in a tightening fiscal climate, as we saw in the vignette on social care in Chapter 5. One way of reconciling expansive and transformative citizenship demands with the market-centred reform of public services has been through re-inventing the citizen as a consumer of public services (Clarke et al., 2007a).

Consuming citizens

Just as expansive/inclusive contestations of citizenship have their parallels in politics of retrenchment that seek to shrink and constrain citizenship, or make its scope and substance more conditional, so the transformative politics of citizenship has its parallels, notably in what Dagnino refers to as the 'neo-liberal project'. In this we can see the attempt to transform the discursive repertoire of citizenship towards a very different social imaginary – a society of individuals who are treated, and understand themselves, as private rather than public figures, who owe 'responsibilities' to the economy, the state and the nation, who have a limited array of 'freedoms' that can be exercised in market or market-like institutions, and whose core rights are 'spending one's own money' and being 'hard-working'.

In chapter 4 we examined Bobbitt's (2003) concept of the 'market state' and its corollary: market citizenship. The idea of the market state carries both descriptive and normative claims. Like many equivalents, it claims to describe the dominance of markets and market relationships and it celebrates their superiority over 'old-fashioned' models of public provision (with their statist, monopolistic, and fordist tendencies). Such normative narratives translate very easily into policy discourse. In the UK, New Labour located the mission of reform in just such an account of social change:

> Thirty years ago the one size fits all approach of the 1940s was still in the ascendant. Public services were monolithic. The public were supposed to be truly grateful for what they were about to receive. People had little say and precious little choice. Today we live in a quite different world. We live in a consumer age. People demand services tailor made to their individual needs. Ours is the informed and inquiring society. People expect choice and demand quality (Alan Milburn, then Secretary of State for Health, 2002).

Here, 'a consumer age' becomes the term through which struggles around citizenship, difference and inequality are translated and enrolled into a discourse of 'individuals' different needs and aspirations' that attaches such individuals to the preferred mode of individualism. 'Choice' then emerges as the means through which these benefits are to be realised (Le Grand, 2007). Root (2007) neatly summarises the argument:

> Choice is identified in market citizenship as the key mechanisms by which markets can function efficiently. It is also seen as the means by which citizens can exercise power and control over important aspects of their lives, and, also, more controversially, the tool by which greater equality and social justice can be achieved in the wider society. It is argued that choice, leading to personalised public services, increases equity and social justice more than other allocative mechanisms. ... Following from this, market citizenship involves treating the citizen as a consumer or customer. The market, not the state, is seen as the key institution to provide more choice and improve public services. The market is said to be preferable to the state because it breaks up monopolies, and provides the means by which low-quality services or incompetent providers can be identified, and gives an opportunity for intervention and the closure of inferior suppliers (Root, 2007: 57).

Such ideas can readily be traced in UK political speeches and documents of the late twentieth and early twenty-first centuries. One critical part of New Labour's inheritance from the period of Thatcherite conservatism was this populist view of 'the people versus the state', with the people needing rescue from an over-bearing, intrusive and dominating public power (Hall, 1989). Government took up the role of 'People's Champion' against the state with its intractable bureaucracy, its excessive interference, and its domination by 'producer interests' rather than those of 'consumers' (Clarke and Newman, 1997). The view of citizens as consumers of public services was a consistent and expanding focus, based on the claim that social changes towards a 'consumer culture' had created both experiences and expectations of individualised choice among the population. Against these standards, public services were judged backward, inadequate and dominated by producer paternalism. Choice was translated as a desirable condition in its own right, as a means of responding to difference, and as a means of empowering citizens – especially those who had been relatively disadvantaged in 'producer-driven' services:

> In reality, I believe people do want choice, in public services as in other services. But anyway, choice isn't an end in itself. It is one important mechanism to ensure that citizens can indeed secure good schools and health services in their communities. Choice puts the levers in the hands of parents and patients so that they as citizens and consumers can be a driving force for improvement in their public services. We are proposing to put an entirely different dynamic in place to drive our public services; one where the service will be driven not by the government or by the manager but by the user – the patient, the parent, the pupil and the law-abiding citizen.
> (Tony Blair, quoted in *The Guardian*, 24 June 2004:1)

Of course choice had long been inscribed in 'pillarised' welfare provision in some continental European states. However the current reworking of the choice making citizen in the UK – and beyond – has been challenged for the ways in which it seeks to de-collectivise the public and its relationship to public services, preferring to treat citizens as individuated agents pursuing selfish interests (Needham, 2003). Root summarises such conceptions as 'thin' citizenship that privileges rights over responsibilities, is passive rather than active, promotes dependence rather than interdependence, is legal rather than moral, and that offers freedom through choice rather than through the exercise of civic virtue. It also views the state as a 'necessary evil' rather than promoting a view of a political community (not necessarily the state) as the foundation of the good life. However, Root suggests, market citizenship weakens some rights (civil liberties, rights to asylum) while strengthening others (consumer rights, rights to information, and rights to express cultural differences and identities).

Market-based citizenship implies a different kind of public sphere, one in which choices and preferences are expressed through the marketplace rather than through the electoral process and public deliberation. For example, Hajer (1997, 1999) considers claims that the public, by exercising choices that move in the direction of a better environmental quality of life, produce new environmentally oriented policy discourses and give manufacturers an incentive to improve technologies that protect the environment. Sassattelli argues that consuming itself can be politicised: 'Just as it becomes clear that there is nowhere else to go outside of the market, the market itself appears, on the one hand, less natural and neutral; and, on the other, a site of politics to which consumers may actively contribute using their purchasing power' (2007: 186). She traces both the ways in which traditional consumerist organisations and other social actors – environmental groups, Fair Trade organisations, organisations concerned with ethical finance, organic food and many others – are framing consumer action in more political terms:

> It is not easy to draw an inclusive map of the issues contained within the boundaries of critical and alternative consumption. However, the starting point of these initiatives is that consumer choice is *not universally good* and it certainly is *not a private issue* . . . rather, it is framed as a consequential and momentous practice, capable of expressing consumer sovereignty only if consumers take full responsibility for the environmental, social and political effects of their choices (Sassatelli, 2007: 186–7; emphasis in original).

Consuming may also offer new ways of expressing solidarities, and exercising political power, both within and beyond the polities of individual nation-states. Rather than dismissing the introduction of market mechanisms and choice into public services as just another example of the growing hegemony of neoliberal rule, we can see that it both draws on and translates some of the citizenship claims traced in the previous section.

Vignette: assembling the citizen-consumer

In *Creating Citizen-Consumers* (Clarke et al., 2007a) we considered the hyphenated citizen-consumer as an assemblage that brought together multiple identifications and the social relations these implied. We noted that the figure of the consumer (as user of public services) did not represent the wholesale dismantling of more collective terms: UK discourse on the reform of public services continued to speak of the public, of communities, service users, passengers, patients, parents alongside – and intimately interwoven with – the consumer. Indeed 'it was this interlocking net of themes and identities that enabled the consumer to play such a central and organising role in New Labour discourse of public service reform' (2007a: 45). We examined the citizen-consumer as a hybrid form in which these different identities and social relationships were condensed, asking 'but what are we to make of such hybrids? How does hybridisation work in political and governmental projects? Do the elements – whether neo-liberalism or communitarianism – retain their essential character, or are they transformed in the encounter with other discourses and positions?' (2007a: 45). In response, we drew attention to the ways in which political projects are forged in the face of paradoxes, tensions, incompatibilities and contradictions, rather than being coherent implementations of a coherent discourse or plan. This pointed to two important features of the hyphenated citizen-consumer. 'The first is that the hyphen denotes the focus of political work: the effort to give the 'citizen' new meanings through its articulation with the consumer. The second feature of this hyphenated articulation is that neo-liberalism comes to take on a particular local/national character precisely through its necessary encounters with other political discourses, oppositions and projects' (2007a: 45–6).

The citizen-consumer, then, did not represent an abandonment of citizenship, but its reworking, changing its meaning to make it more compatible with the wider political project of New Labour governments in the UK. It did so by drawing on, and giving voice to, older conceptions of citizenship (expressed through notions of equality, entitlement and access to public services) while transforming them through their articulation with the image of the consumer. 'The consumer appeared as the dominant identity by being able to represent all these other positions. . . . As a result, the citizen-consumer named new forms of relationship between producers and publics, between government and services providers, between those commissioning services and those making choices in a marketised field of services. In its attempts to reconcile conflicting forces through a discourse centred on the citizen-consumer, New Labour can be viewed as attempting to articulate a national interest, purpose and sense of direction that 'took account of' other positions and projects. . . . But it did so while articulating them as subordinate and supporting voices – tying them to the 'mission' and attempting to dissolve their differences (and thus their status as alternatives) in the process' (2007a:46).

The citizen-consumer is, then, a distinctive assemblage, enrolling divergent political and cultural resources while claiming to offer a coherent (and progressive) strategy for public service reform that uses choice as a device for shifting forms of power and authority (as we saw in Chapter 4). This strategy aims to engage public services and their users in new forms of relationships and identifications – though the evidence of its success is mixed (Clarke et al., 2007a; Needham, 2007). But it forms only one strategy in a larger field of governmental re-inventions of the citizen.

New model citizens

Ideas of the market-state and citizen-consumers suggest a reduced role for nation-states in relation to their citizens. But at the same time, states have been busy in reconstructing citizenship – and activating citizens. Several images of the ideal citizen swirl around contemporary policy discourses. These include:

The empowered citizen

This figure takes several different forms. In Northern 'post-welfarist' states, empowerment tends to mean freeing individuals from the dead hand of bureaucratic administration and professional paternalism, enabling them to define their own needs and engage in decisions about their own care and welfare. Thus, 'choice' becomes a means of empowering individuals in their encounters with public services, while participation/consultation becomes a means of empowering individuals, communities and stakeholders in political and policy settings (as we saw in the previous chapter). In countries of the South, strategies of empowerment are associated with development logics, in which people are to be released from cycles of poverty, or perhaps from the tyrannical constraints of oppressive governmental regimes, and enabled to deploy their new power both for individual benefit and for the wider process of development. The two versions overlap in the rise of models of 'participatory planning' for local development projects (see, *inter alia*, Li, 2007b; Hickey and Mohan, 2005; Sharma, 2008).

The worker-citizen

Here unemployed people are targeted for governmental attention, and supported in their entry, or re-entry, to the labour market. Welfare dependence is thus reduced as citizens become more economically self-sufficient and become more self-reliant in other areas of their life. Labour market activation is also viewed as a means of overcoming social exclusion – that is, marginal groups of citizens are both reconnected to the wider economy and polity, and given access to opportunities that, it is hoped, help address cycles of poverty and exclusion (Lister, 2002; Rosanvallon, 2000). Rather than a primary emphasis on social protection, the policy focus shifts to one of investment in skills and capacities. Such investment promises to enable citizens to contribute to economic growth and to overcome patterns of marginalisation that both produce welfare dependence and that challenge the idea of a socially cohesive society. In the process, the new images of citizenship involve a shift from rights and entitlements towards responsibility, productivity and performance. The idea of the worker-citizen has, in the process, been extended beyond the conventional male worker who formed the core Fordist labour force. Although much activation policy began with the young unemployed (e.g., New Labour's New Deal for Young People), activation now seeks to include 'diverse' subjects into waged work: lone mothers, disabled people, people receiving incapacity benefits and older people. The worker-citizen is an equal opportunity figure.

The contracted citizen

The idea of a new contractual relationship between citizen and state extends across a range of policy areas. Rose has argued that 'the politics of the contract' is central to welfare reform (1999: 165; see also Monteleone, 2007). Andersen (2004), writing about the Danish experience, highlights the introduction of contracts around parental control of children as well as in labour market activation policies. He draws direct analogies between market-based contracts and what he terms 'social' contracts, but goes on to describe the particular characteristics of the latter:

> [T]he social contract is about mutual empowerment. Only through the making of the citizen into a negotiating partner is it possible for the administration to access the self relation of the citizen and negotiate his or her sexuality, self integration, motherhood, personal development, self responsibility etc. ... Through its communicative demarcation of obligations it presupposes that the participants are free to commit themselves and free to translate obligation into commitment (Andersen, 2004: 284).

The 'social' contract, then, invokes new forms of governmentality that are based on the inculcation of new forms of governable subject, in which the person – his or her 'inner will' – becomes a resource enabling the transformation of welfare states. However, homologies between economic contracts between organisations and social contracts may be flawed. Newman (2007c) argues for the importance of distinguishing between the extension of purchaser–provider contracts and agency–citizen contracts, and points to the problems of conflating strategies of institutional and personal governance. As we noted in Chapter 4, these 'social' contracts are not between equal partners and involve a degree of compulsion, using state power to enforce acceptance and compliance.

The responsible citizen

Citizens are encouraged to let go of expectations that the state will provide and protect them in the ways that welfare states promised. Instead, citizens will take greater degrees of responsibility for their own care and welfare, and for that of their family. This carries a double agenda. Eating more healthily, stopping smoking, being good parents, saving rather than spending, investing for one's old age, all bring individual benefits. But it also brings benefits to the state, reducing costs on health systems, pension funds, social care and child protection services and so on. However, the responsible citizen is not only charged with individual responsibility for their own – and their family's – well-being; they are also impli- cated in other strategies for 'governing the social'. Citizens who are both active and responsible look after the well-being of communities, participate in civic decision-making, engage in voluntary service activity, and work in partnership with public service agencies to co-produce social services, ensure the security of neighbourhoods and renew their social fabric.

The conditional citizen

The benefits of citizenship, especially social or welfare entitlements, have become subject to increasing conditionality (Dwyer, 2000; Gould, 2005). A vari- ety of tests has been deployed by states anxious to make citizens responsible for themselves and to manage the costs of public spending. These include toughened eligibility criteria for benefits or services (e.g., examinations of need and vulner- ability for domiciliary and residential care for elderly); an enlarged scope for means-testing; a greater use of tax systems (for credits or benefits directed to the 'working poor'); and devices that allow the 'targeting' of benefits or services on those in 'genuine need'. Forms of 'contract' between services and service users also make citizenship benefits conditional on 'performance'. Such things as job search, morality tests, drug use, attending work or parenting classes and many other performance criteria become thresholds for access to the substantive benefits of citizenship. Citizenship is thus made both more conditional and more contin- gent. It requires more of the citizen and implies the construction of a governmen- tal capacity to sift the worthy, deserving and productive from the rest. Such political projects and governmental practices involve the work of identifying and constructing new 'subjects of value' (Goode and Maskovsky, 2001; Smith, 1997).

The active citizen

Most governments have developed an enthusiasm for active citizens. Studies of activation have focused on labour market policies that aim to produce 'job seek- ers' and we discuss some aspects of activation in the following section. However, active citizenly behaviours are solicited in many other forms. New governance arrangements linked to activation, empowerment, consumerism and choice high- light the need for services to be de-standardised and differentiated, adapted to individual circumstances (individualisation or personalisation), or be co-pro- duced in a partnership between users and service providers. Service users are viewed as individual customers in a quasi-market of competing service providers; but also as reflexive, competent citizens elaborating their individual life projects. In the UK, New Labour liked to see its citizens being busy. Active citizens were viewed as a means of reducing cost and activity pressures on the National Health Service: becoming 'expert patients', taking on managing their own lifestyles and well-being, and requiring less direct attention from hospitals and general practitioners. Active citizens 'volunteer' and create mutual self-help were viewed as the basis for community activation and regeneration. They embrace the spirit of 'Do-It-Yourself': staying active in old age or taking over some of the work of assessment or service coordination in 'co-production' arrangements (Klein and Millar, 1995; Needham, 2007).

However, it would be wrong to treat the active citizen as though this figure was the product of a single and coherent governmental strategy. Such a singular view does not do justice to the ways in which divergent political projects are condensed in the commitment to produce active citizens. Hvinden and Johansson (2005) point to liberal, republican and communitarian formations of active citizenship. For example, a republican reading of active citizenship would emphasise democratic participation and civil society activism; a liberal model of active citizenship privileges the individual worker citizen and citizen-consumer; and a communitarian model centres on an image of the responsible citizen acting to sustain the moral fabric of community and to foster the bonds of civil society (see also Hvinden and Johansen, 2007; Lewis and Surrender, 2004; Van Berkel and Valkenburg 2007). Such different conceptions of the relationships between states, societies and citizens are condensed in different strategies of creating active citizens.

We do not think this list exhausts the range of re-inventions of citizenship but it points to something of the diversity of sites, forms and techniques that are in play. These are sometimes separate and even contradictory tendencies, but they may also be bundled together in particular strategies. For example, as we argue below, activation policy may combine conditionality, contracting, empowerment and responsibilisation.

Activating citizens

The concept of active citizenship condenses many different political and cultural inflections. But each opens the citizen to rationalities and forms of power that attempt to shift the meaning of citizenship from a status carrying rights and entitlements towards individualised notions of responsibility and self-sufficiency. Citizenship thus becomes individuated – and typically combines two models of the individual. On the one hand, the individual is conceived of as the object of therapeutic interventions, as described by Rose (1999) and Schram (2000). On the other, the individualised citizen is seen as an autonomous decision-making and calculating figure, whose performance as a citizen may be evaluated and judged, as Valkenburg (2007) indicates:

> Citizenship is no longer described primarily in social terms, referring to protection against the risks of general (economic) developments. It is described in individual terms, referring to the risks the unemployed individual creates for themselves in their relation to the labour market and to

activation policies. The right to protection is determined by the behaviour, choices, attitudes and motivations of the individual. The emphasis shifts from the collective responsibility of the welfare state to the individual responsibility of the individual citizen. (2007: 30)

Although this individualisation of citizenship is a widespread tendency, we think it remains important to distingish the different conceptions, projects and strategies that come together in this movement. Activation condenses very divergent models of citizenship and has been enacted through differing governance regimes and practices. Even where they share conceptions of citizenship and the mechanisms of activation, different national or regional strategies differ in their social contexts. To activate a citizen in Norway, with a high wage, high taxation, high public expenditure economy still shaped by political and ethical principles about low income differentials, is different from activation in more neo-liberal contexts, characterised by low-waged and contingent work, low personal and corporate taxation, reduced labour market regulation and widening income and wealth differentials. Although there is no simple mapping of different strategies in different states, in the process of assembly different models are combined, producing distinctive formations each with their characteristic sets of tensions and ambiguities. While models of activation share things in common, we doubt that they can be reduced to a common tendency.

Treating activation as a singular governmental strategy also risks over-stating the coherence or integration of strategies, policies and practices. As we argued in Chapter 3, we think it is important to explore the processes of translation and mediation that shape policy and practice.

Vignette: Translating activation

Van Berkel and Valkenburg highlight possible tensions produced by the intersection of two different discourses of activation: the 'active welfare state' discourse and the 'new governance' discourse. These do not necessarily share the same conception of the citizen and their relationship to the state. In the active welfare state discourse, the focus is on individual responsibility for preventing unemployment and achieving self-sufficiency through labour market participation. This is to be achieved through the individual action plan, with monitoring taking place and sanctions possibly applied in cases of non-compliance or under-performance. In the new governance discourse that underpins public service reform, individual responsibility is inflected with notions of choice, participation and user involvement. As a result, 'the process of individualising the provision of services may take place against the background of two rather different and potentially contradictory discourses: one focusing on enforcement and discipline, the other of a more empowering and enabling nature' (2007: 13).

This assemblage of different discourses produces strains and antagonisms. The process of condensing different political and governmental projects into a single strategy makes them ungainly, and tends to push the resolution of such tensions into the service delivery process (which is itself the focus of reform). Van Berkel and Valkenburg argue that the analysis of activation needs to address both policy developments and new governance arrangements and how they coincide – more or less comfortably – in practice:

> These new forms of governance are often legitimated, although not necessarily motivated . . ., by pointing to the need to improve the accessibility, responsiveness and quality of social services on the one hand, and to reconsider the role of citizens-as-service-users and their position vis-à-vis service providers on the other. The introduction of new modes of governance leaves its own marks on the individualisation of service provision, at least at a rhetorical level. Thus, the development of individualised social services in general, and of activation services in particular, takes place at the intersection of social policy and governance reforms and transformations (2007: 5).

One effect of these new governance arrangments is that activation policies involve high levels of discretion on the part of service organisations – and their staff (Hvinden and Johansson, 2007; Wright, 2002, 2006). Van Berkel and Valkenburg argue that

> Social workers working at the front line.. are the lynchpins in putting the transformation process . . . into actual practice: without transforming the work of managers and frontline workers, no welfare state or governance transformation is feasible. This raises questions concerning the conditions under which social workers do their work; the caseloads they have to deal with, the targets they have to meet, the availability of social services, the characteristics of the target groups in terms of the nature of problems of exclusion and unemployment, their professional identities and so on. It also raises questions about the coping strategies that the people working in the service providing organisations develop (2007: 15).

The focus on governance, as well as policy content, draws attention to processes of mediation and translation at the interface between staff and citizens. Halvorsen et al. (2007: 86) note how in Norwegian and Swedish models there has been a lack of central regulation of the content, process and structuring of the interaction between front line staff and unemployed citizens. They point to the ways in which claimants responded to the new constraints and to the new subject positions they were offered:

> Open as well as hidden strategies of negotiations, adjustments and resistance on the part of claimants in their interactions with the staff meant that these claimants were de facto co producers of the activation measures and their results. . . . Moreover, claimants did not remain passive in the face of constraints or about the ways in which front line staff perceived, categorised and treated them. Instead claimants actively sought to define the situation in a way that was consistent with their self image, preferences and priorities. (2007: 92).

Here we can see how activation policies condense some of the strains, tensions and antagonisms at stake in remaking the public. Public services are charged with projects that are intended to change the public, producing new subjects through behaviour change strategies, the discipline of social contracts, and the monitoring and sanctioning of citizens. But at the same time public services are themselves in the process of transformation as a result of governance reforms that emphasise personalisation, flexibility and choice. And it is through public services that the tensions between different meanings of active citizenship have to be resolved, some of which constitute 'empowered' citizens as the co-producers of services, while others seek to induce compliance to new norms of responsibility and self-reliance; some of which privilege economic activity and others moral responsibility. The tensions between these different political formations of citizenship create areas of ambiguity – spaces which can be occupied by citizens enacting their parts in ways not envisaged by governments. The remaking of citizenship is not only a concern of states: struggles for access to, and transformations of, citizenship have produced change 'from below'. Such tensions create dilemmas for public services, and open up 'spaces of translation' in which policies are interpreted (by staff) and negotiated (between managers, staff and citizens).

New politics and policies around citizenship are thus implicated in changing the public, changing public services and redrawing the distinctions between public and private (as more issues become private responsibilities). As we argued at the start of the chapter, the citizen is a public figure – embodying particular configurations of publicness. The condensed and complex entanglement of citizenship in these processes of decline and proliferation is, then, not surprising. But so far, our examination of citizenship has remained within the confines of national publics, nation states and their governmental strategies. As we argued in Chapter 2, however, these national conditions are themselves unsettled. Given citizenship's strong connections with questions of nationality, how is citizenship being remade in the re-assembling of the national?

Re-nationalising citizenship

Earlier we explored ways in which the national framing of publicness had become unsettled by a variety of economic, cultural and spatial dynamics that disturbed the taken-for-granted stability of the national space. In the last decade, though, the national character of citizenship has been reasserted by governments across the north, particularly in relation to perceived 'threats' to national identity, security and solidarity. As we saw earlier, migration, mobility and terrorism have troubled the 'nation' and have been used to pose the problem of 'defending it' from these multiple threats (which are combined in the image of the radical islamist/fundamentalist). The rise of the category 'Muslim' to a central status in European and US political discourse after 2001 reflects the intensity of this combination (Mamdani, 2004). It works through a series of elisions:

- Muslim = migrant (i.e., non-national);
- Muslim = traditional (i.e., non-modern, non-cosmopolitan);
- Muslim = fundamentalist (i.e., non-rational; non-secular);
- Muslim = other loyalties (attached to other nations, religious communities or political groups, i.e., non-national).

This Muslimisation of the 'threat to the nation' is overlaid on previous (and persistent) racialised and ethnicised conceptions of nationhood. The dynamics of globalisation are producing both new movements of people and increased competition and vulnerability for those who are not mobile, particularly where public resources and public services have diminished (e.g., in the provision of public or social housing). For example, Kalb argues that the forms of openness and flexibility being demanded in national adaptations to the economic and political dynamics of globalisation have provoked oscillations between openness and closure, including an 'upsurge of counter-narratives of nationalism, localism, religion and tradition … often of a male-chauvinist and paternalist persuasion' (2005: 187). In the process:

> Places and popular identities were becoming hamstrung between an intensifying dialectic of infinite openness and reactive and fearful closure. Instead of helping to create a cosmopolitan public sphere, neo-liberal globalization tended to generate 'culture talk' …, insider/outsider fights, populist paranoia, and intense struggles for 'place making' in general … The dynamics of cultural closure embedded in the contradictions of neo-liberal globalization got an extra push from increasing competition for scarce resources in land, labor, housing, education and sometimes marriage markets. (Kalb, 2005: 187).

As a result, a series of ugly dynamics became interwoven. The acceleration of social and economic inequalities has combined in unpredictable ways with governmental concerns to accommodate 'diversity' and promote 'social cohesion'. At the same time, nationality has been the focus for new racialising projects, including the (re)discovery of 'white working class' as an ethnicised and exoticised group (Skeggs, 2004). This 'whiteness' has been typically constructed in opposition to migrant populations (see, for example, Dench et al., 2006 and the discussion in Clarke, 2009). The rhetorical opposition of 'indigenous/white' and 'migrant/other' has provided a durable foundation for cycles of popular and political discourses around the 'problem of migration', visible across much of Europe and the USA. Such discourses are intimately linked with 'securitisation' – the intensified management of borders, boundaries and the populations that traverse them (Huysmans, 2006). Borders thus take on a new governmental significance:

> Within a more assertively geo-political frame, globalisation and related developments such as transnationalism and immigration are increasingly perceived as dangerous streams that risk flooding the protective and protected lands of domestic sovereignty. In this context, the desire to control and reclaim space has found new political adherents and partisans. Reflecting the latter, the dikes of control and containment have rather been re-strengthened and re-built over the past years . . . (van Houten et al., 2005: 2).

However, they go on to argue that this is not just a matter of restoring old borders and their stronger management. Rather, border work is a focus of invention and innovation, with new agents and agencies, new practices, new technologies and new locations (see also Kramsch, 2002; Ramajar and Grundy-Warr, 2007). The border management of problematic populations increasingly takes place at sites far from the geographical borders – requiring countries of origin and countries of transit to do the work of containment and people processing for the EU and countries within it. As Balibar (2004) argues, borders have been simultaneously externalised and internalised within Europe as 'problem populations' – notably migrants from former colonies – are subject to forms of surveillance, regulation and intervention that treat them as illegal/temporary/out of place.

Such identification and management of migrant populations is accompanied by a reassertion of citizenship-as-national, in which the cultural and political articulation of 'difference' is increasingly challenged by demands for integration. As we argued in Chapter 2, integration is a demand placed on 'others' that requires them to 'join in', acquire and demonstrate cultural competences, indicate that they are self-sufficient and productive subjects, and can perform appropriate shows of national attachment and loyalty. 'Earning' and 'performing' citizenship has been enacted through a variety of protocols, tests and demonstrations administered by anxious governments: from language tests to 2007 French proposals for DNA testing to 'prove' the genetic basis for family reunion; from oaths of loyalty to citizenship ceremonies; from proving that one is not 'a burden on public resources' to tests of national history and culture. Such willingness to 'integrate' has become one of the signifiers of the limits of 'acceptable' or 'tolerable' diversity (see, *inter alia*, Brown, 2006; and Hyland, 2006, on the verb to integrate).

But the problem of defending national conceptions of citizenship in a globalising world produces complex challenges of responding to the claims – and needs – of 'hidden' populations (illegals or *sans papiers*). How far, for example, should health or education services attempt to meet the needs of those with no formal citizenship status, or with conditional citizenship rights (Clarke and Fink, 2008; Morris, 2002; Morrisens and Sainsbury, 2005)? Public services have a role in policing and managing hidden populations; and are also implicated in constituting the boundary between legality and illegality in the course of their everyday decisions about who gets access to what services; who is sought out for special treatment; who is passed on to other agencies; and who is to be abandoned.

Through such changes, citizenship is being re-nationalised. The citizen is being revived as a figure of nation-building/nation-securing programmes. S/he is being invested with a history, values, and a culture that must be 'shared'. Citizenship is being increasingly viewed as a process of recruitment that is calculative, cultural, and disciplinary. These processes of nationalising and governmentalising citizenship are, of course, differentially applied. They bear most forcefully on those who would become citizens – migrants, refugees and asylum seekers. But the enforcement of citizenship's obligations and the performance of its duties are also unevenly distributed – as failing citizens, under-performing citizens, uncivil citizens and the like require interventions to discipline, improve or contain them.

Conclusion: Instabilities of citizenship

Across the different processes we have considered in this chapter we can see some ways in which the remaking of citizenship is 'structured in dominance': the reassertion of 'legitimate membership' of the national community and the greater 'policing' of citizenship rights; the emphasis of being active and responsible as elements of conditionality; and the dominance of 'work' (or labour market readiness) in the construction of new 'subjects of value'. Public services are shaped by these tendencies both in terms of objectives (the outcomes sought) and in terms of organisational/governance processes: engaging the public as citizens, workers, consumers and as active participants in the business of public services. However. we want to note three other issues that citizenship raises for our arguments here. First, despite the structuring in dominance of contemporary forms of citizenship, it remains an identity and status that has been, and is being, traversed and contested by very different political and cultural projects, including ones that construct international and transnational solidarities against the processes of re-nationalisation. Citizenship is desired by many agents and many projects attempt to enrol it and remake it.

Second, we need to be attentive to the limits of governmental and political projects in practice. Put simply, plans and strategies do not always produce their intended results. This may be the result of a variety of factors: they were not very good plans, or not very well implemented. Perhaps they were put to work in the same space as other plans with contradictory objectives or implications: for example, the happy assumption that women's labour is infinitely expandable and flexible underpins a range of policies that anticipate their greater involvement in waged labour; their improved performance as expert parents/mothers; their greater substitution for the declining state provision of care services; and their greater role in volunteering, community-building and so on (Newman, 2005c). But it is also the case that projects find it hard to produce the subjects they desire, because subjects embody different forms of recalcitrance (Clarke, 2004a; Clarke et al., 2007b). Subjects may perform the identities on offer enthusiastically and willingly, becoming self-sufficient and self-directing new model citizens. They may do so in a condition of calculating compliance, feeling that 'there is no alternative'. They may perform in grudging and foot-dragging ways, believing they are entitled to something better. Or they may dissent – in either passive or active ways – because they do not recognise themselves, understand themselves and their world in different ways, or are engaged by other commitments, imaginaries and possibilities.

Third, we want to raise the question about what happens if such individualising, empowering and autonomising citizenship projects are 'successful'. The political, social and even psychic consequences may not be an orderly realm of enterprising selves. The competitive production of winners and losers (and the increasingly unequal division of rewards and resources) produces social and personal strains – as does the process of making individuals 'responsible' for their successes or failures. The antagonisms arising from such changes are usually thought of as political and social matters. But Engin Isin (2004) has speculated about what might be called the psycho-social dynamics of producing the neo-liberal citizen. He argues that the corollary of the enterprising and self-directing citizen is the 'neurotic citizen' – the product of phantasies (in the Freudian sense) that bundle desires, powers and promises in unstable and unrealisable ways. Isin points to some of the unstable outcomes of this combination, suggesting that the neurotic citizen is a locus of anxiety, anger and projected hostility (directed at those who seem to block or thwart its desires and expectations):

> Thus the neurotic citizen is thrown into chronic discontent. The neurotic citizen is an uncertain citizen because it is confused about rights. The neurotic citizen has been promised so much and developed such an unrealistic sense of its rights that it becomes confused about its actual and actualisable rights. The formation of neurotic claims reproduces illusions of the neurotic citizen and enables it to shift responsibility to objects outside itself with hostility. (Isin, 2004: 233)

This is a speculative argument but it points to some of the psychic, social and political instabilities that the neo-liberal remaking of citizenship puts in play. The unstable mixture of promises, desires and responsibilisation might well produce frustration, anxiety and a sense of entitlements denied (for example, in the annual panic that surrounds secondary school choice in England as parental choices fail to materialise). It might also be at stake in the populist or demotic discourses in which conceptions of the social oscillate between individual/familial responsibility and freedom, and the demand that 'the government should do something'. If this view is even partly correct, it points to the reform of citizenship, not as installing a new order, but as producing a set of dynamic disorders in which relations between citizens and states, and among citizens, become increasingly dangerous. The renationalisation of citizenship looks, in part, like a response to a mixture of both governmental and popular fantasies about control, ownership, entitlement and security.

9 Conclusion: a politics of the public?

We began this book with the paradox of decline and proliferation as a way of addressing the dismantling of previous institutionalised formations of publicness and the remarkable flowering of new sites, policies and practices. We see this paradox as a genuinely important analytic and political puzzle: how can we account for the contemporary enthusiasm for new forms of publicness and what is their political value or significance? By this point, it should be clear that we approach views that can only see decline with considerable scepticism. They are, at least, empirically incorrect and seem wedded to an essentialised view of publicness that can recognize it only in the 'golden age' institutional formations of European welfare-nation-states. While we understand the sense of loss associated with the dismantling of such formations, we cannot share the sense of nostalgia or melancholy that infuses these stories of decline. Our own personal and political developments were shaped in opposition to those formations, so being asked to view them as the high-water mark of publicness is troubling.

What, though, are we to make of the new and emergent formations? How is publicness being imagined, invented and institutionalised in new assemblages? What forms of power and politics are at stake in them? We know that there are some simple and compelling responses. Perhaps they are the expressions of a 'progressive politics of the public' – restoring publicness to centre-stage after the battering of privatisation, individualisation and marketisation. Recent initiatives here include *Politics for A New Generation: the Progressive Moment* (Pearce and Margo, 2007); *Public Matters: the Renewal of the Public Realm* (Diamond, 2007); *New Publics with/out Democracy* (Bang and Esmark, 2007); the Compass programme of renewal, and many other publications from think tanks and centre-left governments. On the other hand, they might be the products of neo-liberalisation, masking the recomposition of power and assuring the conditions of capital accumulation (see chapter 1). In contrast, our exploration of new assemblages of publicness has revealed multiple sources and resources, dragged into complex, uncomfortable and contradictory alignments that produce unstable formations and may have unpredictable consequences.

For us, the three A's – ambiguity, articulation and assemblage – offer a means of examining the alignments of power and politics in these new formations of publicness. They expose the political work that goes into dismantling and reconstructing: creating alignments, enrolling political-cultural ideas and images, identifying problems and failures, producing new solutions, and, above all, articulating social and political alliances that make new assemblages imaginable, plausible and even popular. In the first part of this concluding chapter, we want to look back over the different dynamics that we have identified as central to the remaking of publicness:

• Re-assembling the nation;
• Displacing the public;
• Making up markets;
• Boundary blurring;
• Valuing publics;
• Engaging publics;
• Remaking citizens.

Each of these chapter titles intentionally uses the gerund form of verbs to foreground processes and dynamics of change. For the most part, these are continuing, rather than completed, processes. Nations are still in (contentious) process of being re-assembled; publics are still being displaced from their identification with nation-states; and citizens are still subject to diverse projects of remaking. Each phrase implies the effects of unsettling and dismantling processes that undermined the apparent solidity of earlier formations of publicness in their national, state-centred and liberal realm assemblages. Here we consider their individual and combined implications for publics and publicness (what we described earlier as the combinations of things, ideas, issues, people, practices, relationships and sites that are understood as public, p. 2).

We began with questions of the national formation of publicness, in part because these are often concealed behind the attention given to the state/market distinction (and its assumed equivalence to public/private). These national formations have proved unstable along two axes: the assumed social/cultural unity of the people as a national public; and the assumed territorial coherence of the national level as the scale at which publics are formed, act and are governed. The re-assembling of nations involves efforts to find new sorts of coherence, including the recentering of nationalism in assimilationist, integrationist and revanchist forms, as a precondition for managing diversity and mobility. But it also involves new scalar formations as localities, cities, and regions become 'empowered' through processes of rescaling that seek to secure the nation's economic and social development. Such processes of re-assembling are, however, partial, uneven and unfinished: scalar politics of devolution, decentralisation and subsidiarity regularly encounter centralising political and governmental tendencies (especially, but not only, in the UK). Such governmentalised scales are themselves cross cut by internationalising, globalising and transnationalising dynamics: regions, cities and localities are spatially related to other sites beyond the nation. New scalar and political-cultural assemblages try to manage and

contain contradictions and antagonisms – for example around migration, difference and inequality – but do not always succeed. They also bring into play new
antagonisms and instabilities that become the focus of contention and conflict.

For us, processes of assembling are concerned with the search for solutions:
how to overcome existing and anticipated disruptions, blockages, failures and
conflicts that get in the way of an improved order of things. Governmental and
political projects may try to reform problematic sites of publicness (making
states 'leaner and meaner' or creating 'leadership' for failing organisations) or,
as we argued in Chapter 3, they may displace problems and desires to new sites
viewed as better able to 'deliver'. Enrolling community, civil society and voluntary organisations into the creation of economic and social development, social
cohesion and public well-being is not just a matter of finding functional substi-
tutes for the provision of public services. Rather, popular resourcefulness is
regarded as a source of non-state, non-political and spontaneous (if carefully
tutored) value creation – from neighbourliness to civility, from cohesion to
development. The double movement of displacing and de-politicising aspires to
avoid conflict (or at least localise it and contain it in non-political locations) and
to construct self-governing and self-provisioning agents (individuals,
families/households, communities). As we saw, enrolling such sites – all with turbulent and contested characters – is by no means simple, and nor are the desired
results guaranteed. On the contrary, civil society, community, and voluntary
actors may well 'behave badly' – taking their empowerment too literally, too
seriously or too much to heart. As all those working with psychoanalytic
perspectives know, objects of desire always prove problematic in practice.

These attempts to mobilise popular resourcefulness (especially in formations
around social capital or economic value) marks points of elision between displacement from the state and the rise of markets as a dominant discursive and
institutional form. We have tried to emphasise the multiple ways in which markets feature in the re-invention of publicness, rather than assuming that change
has been organised around a simple state/market binary. In particular, it is important to insist that sending things to market (privatising public resources) is not
the same as introducing internal markets which is not the same as the spread of
economic discourse and imagery, even though they are related and the spread of
thinking like a market certainly enables the other two processes. These
different elements have certainly changed the place, role and significance of
markets globally, and within different national reform projects. Nevertheless,
writing this conclusion in April 2008, we are struck by three rather different
observations. First, some of the gloss has been removed from markets by the
crises emanating from the US financial services sector, not least because of
the resulting demands from banks and others for government assistance, subsidy
and rescue. At the same time, the commitment to cheap commodity consumerism has increasingly visible effects – most evidently in environmental
terms, but also in other ways: corrupted food chains; new globalised patterns of

labour exploitation; and an upsurge in product recall measures for safety/quality reasons. Second, despite the dominance of market discourse (or Frank's 'market populism') in political and policy terrains, its hold on popular understandings of publicness and public services seem less than wholly hegemonic. Two recent British studies of popular attitudes to public services reveal a refusal of consumerism and marketisation on the grounds that using public services is 'not like shopping' (Clarke et al., 2007a) and that, even where people were dissatisfied with public services, their dissatisfaction 'did not lead participants to want them to be more like private services, but rather more like what they felt public services should be . . . fair, consistent and needs- rather than profit-based' (Needham, 2007a: 193).

The third point emerges at the intersection of Chapters 4 and 5: 'markets' are themselves enrolled in new 'hybrid' formations, in which competition and contracting co-exist (not always easily) with forms of partnership, collaboration and cooperation in pursuing the business of the public. No doubt, some of these formations are dominated by processes of privatisation, outsourcing and models of private finance. And, as Janine Wedel has argued, the creation of 'flex organisations' that work across public-private boundaries produces the conditions for troubling forms of corruption and collusion as the search for power and profit eludes both public and private forms of scrutiny and accountability (2001; see also the UK Office of Fair Trading's revelations about 'bid rigging' by over 100 construction companies bidding for public tenders: OFT, 2008). But emergent assemblages of publicness involve more heterodox principles and commitments than markets can provide. Anxieties about diversity, social cohesion and security (of many kinds) promote new combinations of innovative organisational forms, including the re-solidification and extension of forms of state power.

We might note two features of these new assemblages. First, they are heterogeneous (in their sources, resources, organisational forms, social/spatial locations and the types of agent they recruit or enable). Second, they are structured in dominance in the ways these heterogeneous elements are combined. The articulatory principles tend towards some common features and organising assumptions;

- that markets are superior to states;
- that economic interests are the strongest motivating forces and that they are legitimate motivations for an increasingly wide range of activities;
- that being businesslike is a desirable quality;
- that publics have become more diverse, individualised and consumerist;
- that people are naturally resourceful, energetic and entrepreneurial (or at least hard working);
- that there are experts whose 'knowhow' makes organisations successful, effective or efficient;
- and that the 'bottom line' is that 'what counts is what works' (the distinctive epigram of dogmatic pragmatism).

But if these are the articulatory principles that tend to dominate, they have to find ways of co-existing or cohabiting with others:

- that people believe they have rights, as well as responsibilities;
- that ideas of equality, social justice or fairness continue to circulate around publicness;
- that scepticism and cynicism haunt popular attitudes to both politics and corporate enterprise;
- that people expect governments to be responsible and states to 'do something' about a whole array of problems, crises and anxieties;
- that people have expectations of being involved and having their (multiple) voices heard about things that matter to them;
- and that people are more than ready to exploit new technologies for public mobilisation and political action.

These are more than residual elements of publicness, even if they are fragmentary and contradictory. Across Chapters 6, 7 and 8 we have examined a range of different strategies for remaking publics and publicness. These involve governmentalised organisations in practices of mediating, engaging and activating publics in different sites and through different technologies. Such strategies, and the organisational practices through which they are enacted, construct problematic, incoherent and unstable sets of relations to publics. They oscillate – not predictably – between being enabling/empowering and being constraining/controlling (in which they are often backed by expanded disciplinary powers). They engage in complicated public business, sifting populations into subjects of value, potential subjects of value and subjects of no value. As we have seen subjects of value come in different forms: as workers, parents, as active citizens and communities, as leaders and representatives, as stakeholders and lay voices. Value is not only to be found in economic forms: social, organisational and governmental forms of value are also desired and discovered.

But this explosion of new sites and practices of producing and managing publics are themselves unstable formations. There are translation problems: between strategic thinking and policy-making; between policies and the organisations chosen to implement them; and between organisational imperatives and the orientations of managers and staff. In particular, the encounters between staff and their publics (individually and collectively) are settings in which outcomes are negotiated, not always amicably. Policy is co-produced by many actors, not necessarily in line with strategic thinking. Nevertheless, even this view of translation leaves 'strategic thinking' as if it is a singular and coherent point of origin. We have tried to indicate ways in which political projects and their governing strategies are less than pure. They are also assembled, condensing multiple political desires, diverse discourses and repertoires of governmental devices.

This is why we have found assemblage such a valuable concept: it points precisely to the work of enrolling ideas, images, agents, organisations, devices and technologies into something that is presented as coherent, integrated and logical. Assemblages produce something more like what Althusser once memorably called a 'teeth gritting harmony' – a forced coherence that is only more or less plausible and more or less sustainable. In short, assemblage reminds us that strategies for remaking the public in governable form have no singular force or logic, nor any guaranteed results. The heterogeneity of assemblages also points to one of the preconditions for their unsettling or dismantling: the reassertion of the differences between their elements. There are two other preconditions: the production of new antagonisms, disaffections, contradictions on which people may act; and the effects of empowerment, such that people take their new freedoms (too) seriously and act as if they have power.

Towards a politics of the public

So, how might a politics of the public take shape? Clearly, the proliferation we have described indicates that there are already many politics of the public: projects seeking to remake, expand or re-invent publicness. Many of these lay claim to being 'progressive' – from libertarian anti-statism through progressive community/civil society oriented conservatives to centre-left attempts to reclaim democratic citizenship. So how might we want to turn our analysis here into a more assertive view about a politics of the public? We want to begin by clearing a path through other attempted ways of formulating such a politics. We want, for example, to avoid a *politics of nostalgia*. We see no reason to revive earlier formations of public in the nation (and the ways in which they suppressed difference), nor the public in the state (with its associated problems of inclusion, exclusion, coercion, bureaucratisation and professional power). Nor do we want to restate the public in the liberal public sphere, whose values and principles have been challenged as particular rather than universal, and which have proved unable to sustain encounters across difference, inequality and power (that point to a sphere of publics rather than a public sphere; Calhoun, 1997). The nation, the state and liberalism provide the histories/traditions to which very different political projects lay claim. This is not to say that we can make the questions of nation, state and liberalism go away, but nor do we think that they can be restored – as if untarnished by their real histories – as the jewels in the crown of publicness.

But nor can we begin from a *politics of purity* that would search for formations or elements of publicness that are untainted by neo-liberalism or other dominant strategies. The list of social, political and economic phenomena to which the adjective 'neo-liberal' has been added is enormous (Clarke, 2008). Developments as diverse as Human Rights legislation, community, audit, good governance, nongovernmental organisations have been dismissed as the tools, sites or practices of neo-liberalism: as smokescreen, as programme or as govern-mentality. We have used the concept of assemblage to escape this political labelling: different ideas, practices and sites have heterogeneous histories, rather than an essential political character. Their enrolment in neo-liberal political and governmental strategies certainly tries to fix and naturalise a particular meaning – but critical scholarship should not allow, or reproduce, such attempted naturali-sations and essentialisations. In that sense, a counterpolitics of publicness needs to recover the alternative meanings, affinities and potential alliances of sites, ideas and practices (rather than denouncing them). Such a politics would itself be about assemblage – trying to imagine alternative assemblages that enrolled, recruited and connected ideas, ideals and publics.

While neo-liberalism is at issue, we should add that we do not find totalising critiques of neo-liberalism a helpful foundation for thinking politically. Analyses that project an omnipresent and omnipotent neoliberal project are immobilising. As we have argued elsewhere, accounts of the successful installation of neo-liberalism as a global hegemony leave little room for politics, and tend to add 'resistance' on as an afterthought or rhetorical closing paragraph (Clarke, 2004a: 158). Instead, we want to underline three rather different points. First, neo-liberalism is one political project among many – and has to find ways of coming to terms, or co-habiting with, others (in alliances, or through incorporation or subordination). Second, political projects are, in part, attempts to overcome previous problems (contradictions, resist-ances, refusals, disjunctures). Resistance shouldn't just be viewed as the effect of power plays (always after the event): it is one of the preconditions for the emer-gence of political projects and governmental strategies. Third, as we have kept insisting, political projects are not always and not necessarily successful. They suffer implementation gaps, translation problems and encounter more or less com-pliant subjects, producing a fractured, uneven and potentially unruly social field – a field in which, of course, the elements of alternative imaginings of the social and its better ordering might be found.

Just as we do not think there can be a politics of purity, so we are also anx-ious about the view that there might be a *politics of authenticity*, involving a search for real publics, untainted by engagements with power. This is a politi-cised version of the de-politicising enrolment of 'ordinary people' that we dis-cussed in Chapters 3 and 7. At different times and in different places, the real working class, true ethnic subjects, natural communities or indigenous people have provided the touchstones for a politics of authenticity. Embodied virtue is a difficult basis for politics, and it often fails to appear in the desired form or at the right time. Authenticity is itself a political device, refusing political engage-ment by claiming a pre-existing state of virtue that is pre-emptive. As such, authenticity is the focus of both claims and attributions – contested processes of representation and mediation (see, for example, Li, 2007c). Instead we might see authenticity as one element in a field of political and popular discourses in which publics are imagined and summoned, and claims to resources and power are negotiated (see Chapter 7). As a result, paying political attention to the vernaculars in which people construct, refuse and contest collective identities might be important.

The question about collective identities also points to some problems of a politics of publicness that is bounded by institutions. While institutions – public services, media, cultural spaces and so on – are sites of mediating practices, they also tend to settle previously constructed conceptions of publicness. They are where the marks of earlier struggles and projects can be found, but usually stripped of their history and politics (the bureaucratisation and individualisation of equal opportunities, for example). Bifulco addresses this difficulty by adopting what she terms a process-based perspective: 'The uncertainty as to what is public in fact hints towards shifting our attention from given realities – the public understood as characteristics of actors and organisations – to the processes through which arenas, actors and issues could become public' (Bifulco, 2006: 4). This points to a politics of the public that engages the conditions and dynamics of becoming – what makes it possible for people to think of themselves as publics or counterpublics? Alongside the usual suspects of interests, identities and institutional rationalities, we might also consider affective dimensions, such as the anxieties and desires that connect and mobilise people.

Finally, this view 'beyond the institutions' needs also to avoid a static politics that assumes publics are already existing sociological entities, waiting to be spoken to or spoken for. This assumes a singular and reflective voice – rather than a heteroglossic, and potentially conflicted, view of potential or emergent publics. Ideas of 'summoning' or 'convening' publics (Barnett, 2007a; Warner, 2002) point to the political work of imaging potential 'we's' and finding ways of inviting or recruiting them into collective, public, action. Once imagined and summoned, we should not be surprised if they don't turn up (or don't return), if they think they are someone else, or if they find another 'we' that enthuses, enthralls or engages them more. Assemblage is, as we keep saying, a contingent process, involving attempts to construct apparently coherent and effective unities out of diverse, if not heterogeneous, resources. Even successful assemblages are still contingent, vulnerable to the risk of coming apart under internal strain or the force exercised by alternative attractions. Why would the work of politics be any different?

Imagining publics?

Throughout this book we have highlighted a range of difficulties of engaging with a politics of the public. Yet publicness – and the struggles around it – still matters to us does because it marks a domain in which critical issues about the organisation of social life are condensed and contested. Jacques Rancière (2006) has suggested that the politics of publicness condenses two types of struggle. The first set of struggles seek to *enlarge* the public sphere by constructing issues, people, relationships and conflicts as public rather than private matters. Here the effort to contain things and subordinate them to private authority (within the contract, within the organization, within the family or within the master/slave relation) conflicts with the search to make them public and contestable. The second set takes place *within* the public sphere – between democratic politics and the logic of efficient government. At stake here is the conflict between the desire to make things political and the desire to de-politicise them (make them technical).

As a result, the sphere of publics itself is not and, indeed, cannot be stable – it is always assailed by two contradictory tendencies. On the one hand, we see the efforts to de-politicise and de-publicise. On the other, there is the constant emergence of counterpublics and new publics that both demand entry and change the rules of engagement (not unlike the expansive and transformative contestations of citizenship discussed in Chapter 8). Such dynamics produce temporary settlements that (sometimes) become sedimented or institutionalised in authoritative apparatuses, discourses and practices. In public authorities, public inquiries, and public services we encounter the sedimented forms produced by struggles to create publicness that are now forgotten, repressed, rendered dull and habitual. To borrow from Joe Painter (2006), the 'prosaics' of publicness – in their heterogeneous and sedimented forms – are the traces of earlier attempts to make things public, to enlarge the public sphere and to constitute publics.

We have talked about the political work that is involved in summoning or soliciting publics, but what sorts of principles might be at stake in trying to re-invent publicness, not least for shaping the continuing struggles over public services? Let us begin from a rather modest observation. Publicness needs to be oriented around concerns for fairness, equality and social justice. These seem to us to be the banal stuff of popular engagements with public issues, policies and services. Almost every political project and policy initiative pays at least lip service to such values, even when they are in fact proposing something unfair, unequal or unjust. In one sense, then, this implies a political discursive struggle to contest and define the meanings of such terms. In current UK politics, that might mean detaching 'fairness' from being enmeshed in conditionality ('fairness for those who earn it', Gordon Brown, 2007); insisting that the equity of due process is not the same as equality (of opportunity, much less outcome); or arguing that popular sensibilities about fairness, justice and equality cannot only be mobilised against migrants, but might be reconnected with their historical origins and addressed to ruling concentrations of wealth and power. In doing so, fairness might be restored as a potent connective and mobilising theme.

Of course, such concerns with fairness and social justice lead to political difficulties, controversies and conflicts, not least in terms of arguments about what sorts of inequalities can be combated, and to whom justice is owed. Questions of who 'we' are, and how we can find ways of living together – locally, nationally and globally – run into such questions quickly. Many inequalities have been legitimised, justified and naturalised, not least, the deepening of global and national inequalities in the last three decades. But this, too, involves political discursive work. It requires public strategies for de-naturalising and de-legitimising the forms of difference and inequality that currently command the social field.

One axis of the discursive possibilities of fairness and social justice is the challenge of building on, and deepening, current transnational and intergenerational sensibilities. These have emerged in part from the unpredictable conjunctions of cultural cosmopolitanism, diasporic networks and environmental globalism. They refigure the formations of both space and time in which public concerns, identities and orientations are formed – not consistently, not without antagonisms and not hegemonically. But they certainly identify the lineaments of imagined solidarities that stretch beyond the local or national and have a demonstrable (if uneven) capacity to engage or enroll new publics: both things and people, objects and subjects.

All of this implies the political work of making things public. This is the delicate and elusive intersection between what is political and what is public. We have argued throughout for an understanding of politics in its largest sense – that 'everything is political' – and there are contestations that consistently seek to depoliticise things, people, policies and practices, rendering them technical, private or natural. Any project of re-politicisation must have, therefore, a double character: one aspect is the political struggle to make things and people public; the other is installing a recognition that – at every point – the issues that are at stake in making things public involve conflicts of politics and power. This means making contestation, conflict, and contradiction visible and debatable, both about the large issues and about the practices of publicness. Our discussion of 'dilemmatic spaces' in chapter 6 points to the significance of this latter point: sites and spaces of public action are intrinsically dilemmatic. What matters is to make the 'dilemmas' visible and available for being acted upon, rather than compressing and displacing them into the difficult choices of individual actors (whether workers or users of public services).

This points us back to public services and their conditions and consequences for an expansive and political sense of publicness. Public services have had a critical role in producing publics and mediating publicness. Their reform has certainly undermined some of its established and institutionalised versions. But public services remain a focus of collective aspirations and desires – perhaps all the more so in times of growing inequality, division, anxiety and uncertainty. So can they be reconstructed or re-assembled again in ways that both reflect and summon emergent publics? Of course, we believe they can – and that they are worth struggling over for both their material and symbolic effects. Public services are worth struggling for because they hold the possibility of de-commodifying goods, services and, above all, relationships. In some contexts they can enact principles of open access, fairness and equitable treatment. More importantly, they also carry the possibility of remedying or challenging economic, social and political inequalities through transfers, services and goods produced and distributed on equalising principles.

Finally, public services have the potential to make people feel like 'members of the public' – offering a sense of belonging, connection and entitlement. This means, minimally, the importance of equitable treatment. More expansively, it points to questions of how members of the public experience their encounters and relationships with public services. In our study of citizen-consumers, issues of being treated as a person, with respect, and as a partner in the business of trying to solve the problem were recurrent themes. Such words – like fairness – sound banal, and they have been enrolled into political projects and strategies that diminish their value. But they nevertheless speak to the mundane qualities of publicness that people value and desire.

We do not think such aspirations for an expansive and egalitarian publicness are readily achievable. But we do think that they are imaginable – and not just in the abstract process of writing academic books. Rather we think that these imaginary relationships, commitments and forms of solidarity are themselves rooted in popular sensibilities. They are, as Gramsci might have said, the 'good sense of common sense' (1971: 324-5). They do not have to be invented or imposed from the outside; rather they need to be nurtured, sustained and voiced in ways that enlarge their reach and appeal. Recognising popular doubts and desires, aspirations and anxieties and making them public is a crucial part of the politics of publicness. Such an approach directs us to the problems of intervening in everyday popular and political discourses, rather than standing outside them.

Many terms – equality, bureaucracy, welfare, and, not least, public – have been the focus of sustained critique from multiple points of the political spectrum. But if we reject them out of hand, rather than thinking about them as continued sites of contestation and potential re-mobilisation, we lose some of our capacity to speak. This does not mean, however, that their use is unproblematic – rather that they have to be the focus of re-articulation in order to recast their meaning. We might point to two examples. The first is work by Davina Cooper on the politics of diversity. As we have seen at various points of this book, diversity – a term that represented the success of collective struggles on the part of marginalised groups – is readily depoliticised in its inflections towards individualisation, personalisation and choice. It is also a term that lends itself to a relativist conception of difference in which all claims must be considered to be of equal value. Cooper highlights three issues that disrupt this apparent equivalence: first, how difference is linked to the 'social production of unequal positions'; second, how the structuring principles of inequality are linked to 'modes of power and institutions'; and third, how inequalities are reproduced through 'particular social dynamics' (2004: 60). In this way, she restores the relationship between difference and inequality to the heart of debates about diversity. This reasserts the repressed social and political underpinnings of diversity as a concept and makes it more resistant to its articulations with neo-liberal, individualising forms of rule.

Our second example comes from Wendy Brown in her sustained and powerful critique of the concept of tolerance. She argues that the contemporary deployment of tolerance tends to suppress the articulation of 'inequality, abjection, subordination and colonial and post-colonial violence' (Brown, 2006: 205). However, she refuses demands to abandon the term, arguing instead for an engagement which demands a 'political intelligence' that

> does not entail rejecting tolerance outright, declaring it a necessarily insidious value, or replacing tolerance with some other term or practice. Rather becoming perspicacious about the contemporary operations and circuits of tolerance suggests a positive political strategy of nourishing counterdiscourses that would feature power and justice where antipolitical tolerance talk has displaced them . . . In short, without foolishly positioning ourselves 'against tolerance' or advocating 'intolerance,' we can contest the depoliticising, regulatory, and imperial aims of contemporary deployments of tolerance with alternative political speech and practices. (Brown, 2006: 205)

We find this a compelling statement that might just as readily be addressed to the problematic politics of publicness. The commitment to nourishing counterdiscourses, refusing de-publicising and displacing strategies, and contesting de-politicising, regulatory and imperial deployments capture many of our concerns. So, too, does the way in which a project of resisting de-politicising deployments is combined with a commitment to reconfiguring issues and conflicts through 'grammars of power' (2006: 205). These are the preconditions for articulating expansive and egalitarian assemblages of publicness. As Brown herself notes (2006: 205), such work 'constitutes a modest contribution' to the great political challenges of our time – but in these times we need such modest contributions to the re-articulation of publics, politics and power as a matter of urgency.

Postscript (October 2008)

By the time we were dealing with the final proofs of this book, the troubles of the financial services sector we noted in April 2008 (p. 177) had turned into a global crisis, threatening systemic failure of the world economy. As we suggested above, the effect was to undermine the myth of the market and to elevate states into new roles – as the rescuers of failed financial institutions and panicked markets, institutions, investors and savers. This sudden reinvention of public interests and institutions as the potential saviours of global capitalism has been marked by many of the paradoxical dynamics of assemblage that we have traced in this book. Emerging realignments of states and markets are overshadowed by unresolved questions about how governance, regulation and calculating logics can be reshaped as ways of out of the crisis. Is the public interest merely the restoration of 'business as usual' or has the 'business model' become untenable?

We do not know how these contradictory tendencies might play out – though we would be surprised if they were settled in any simple or singular form. But we do know that their impact on forms of publicness is likely to be immense. The growth of public borrowing (in order to bail out private debt) will impact heavily on the funding for public services (however they are provided). While the current public interest is being assembled around restoring 'financial security' to institutions, shareholders and savers, what might the effects be on those whose lives were already (or may become) insecure in other ways, or who do not have a 'foothold' on property ladder or financial system? At a time when unemployment, indebtedness and vulnerability are likely to increase dramatically, the retrenchment of all sorts of public services can both worsen individual circumstances and fuel a renewed growth of inequalities. There remains much at stake in reassembling publicness.

Bibliography

Abram, S. (2007) 'Participatory depoliticisation: the bleeding heart of neo-liberalism', in C. Neveu (ed.), *Cultures et Pratiques Participatives: Perspectives Comparatives.* Paris: L'Harmattan, pp. 113–34.

Agyeman, J. and Neal, S. (eds) (2006) *The New Countryside? Ethnicity, Nation and Exclusion in Contemporary Rural Britain.* Bristol: Policy Press.

Ahmed, Y. and Broussine, M. (2007) 'Leadership and anxiety in public services: implications for management education', Paper to the *European Group of Public Administration Conference*, Madrid, 19–22nd September.

Aldred, R. (2007) *Governing 'local health economies': The case of NHS Local Improvement Finance Trust (LIFT).* PhD thesis, Goldsmiths College, University of London.

Aldridge, R. and Stoker, G. (2003) *Advancing a New Public Sector Ethos.* London: New Local Government Network.

Alesina, A. and Glaeser, E. (2004) *Fighting Poverty in the US and Europe: A World of Difference.* Oxford: Oxford University Press.

Alexander, C. (2007) 'Cohesive identities: the distance between meaning and understanding', in M. Wetherell, M. Lafleche and R. Berkeley (eds), *Identity, Ethnic Diversity and Community Cohesion.* London: Sage.

Allen, J. (2003) *Lost Geographies of Power.* Oxford: Blackwell.

Allen, J. and Cochrane, A. (2007) 'Beyond the territorial fix: regional assemblages, politics and power', *Regional Studies*, 41(9): 1161–75.

Allen, J., Massey, D. and Cochrane A. (with J. Charlesworth, G. Court, N. Henry and P. Sarre) (1998) *Rethinking the Region.* London: Routledge.

Alvarez, S., Dagnino, E. and Escobar, A. (1998) *Cultures of Politics/Politics of Culture: Revisioning Latin American Social Movements.* Boulder, CO: Westview Press.

Andersen, N. A. (2004) 'The contractualisation of the citizen – the transformation of obligations into freedom', *Zeitschrift für Soziologische Theorie*, 10 (2): 273–91.

Andersen, N. A. (2008) *Partnerships: Machines of Possibility.* Bristol: Policy Press.

Andrews, G. (2006) *Not a Normal Country: Italy after Berlusconi.* London: Pluto Press.

Appadurai, A. (2001) *Globalization.* Durham, NC: Duke University Press.

Arditi, B. (2004) 'Populism as a spectre of democracy: a response to Canovan', *Political Studies*, 52: 135–43.

Bache, I. and Flinders, M. (eds) (2004) *Multi-level Governance.* Oxford: Oxford University Press.

Baldock, J. and Ungerson, C. (1996) 'Becoming a consumer of care: developing a sociological account of the New Community Care', in S. Edgell, K. Hetherington and A. Warde (eds.), *Consumption Matters.* Oxford: Blackwell/Sociological Review.

Baldwin, R. and Cave, M. (1999) *Understanding Regulation. Theory, Strategy and Practice*. Oxford: Oxford University Press.

Balibar, E. (2004) *We, The People of Europe? Reflections of Transnational Citizenship*. New Jersey: Princeton University Press.

Ball, S. (2005) *Education Policy and Social Class*. London: Routledge Falmer.

Ball, S. (2007) *Education Plc: Understanding Private Sector Participation in Public Education*. London: Routledge.

Balloch, S. and Taylor, M. (eds) (2001) *Partnership Working: Policy and Practice*. Bristol: Policy Press.

Bang, H. and Joergensen, S. (2007) 'Expert citizens in celebrity publics', in H. Bang and A. Esmark (eds), *New Publics with/out Democracy*. Frederiksberg, Denmark: Samfundslitteatur Press.

Banks, S. (2004) *Ethics, Accountability and the Social Professions*. Basingstoke: Macmillan.

Banting, K.G. (2005) 'The multicultural welfare state: international experience and North American narratives', *Social Policy and Administration*, 39 (2): 98–115.

Barnes, M. (2008) 'Is the personal no longer political?' *Soundings*, 39: 152–159.

Barnes, M., Newman, J. and Sullivan, H. (2006) 'Discursive arenas: deliberation and the constitution of identity in public participation at local level', *Social Movement Studies*, 5 (3): 193–207.

Barnes, M., Newman, J. and Sullivan, H. (2007) *Power, Participation and Political Renewal: Case Studies in Public Participation*. Bristol: Policy Press.

Barnes, M., Newman, J., Sullivan, H. and Knops, A. (2003) 'Constituting 'the public' in public participation', *Public Administration*, 81 (2): 379–99.

Barnett, C. (2003) *Culture and Democracy: Media, Space and Representation*. Edinburgh: Edinburgh University Press.

Barnett, C. (2005) 'The consolations of "neo-liberalism" ', *Geoforum*, 36: 7–12.

Barnett, C. (2007a) 'Publics and markets: what's wrong with neo-liberalism?', in S. Smith, S. Marston, R. Pain and J. P. Jones 111 (eds), *The Handbook of Social Geography*. London: Sage.

Barnett, C. (2007b) 'Convening publics: the parasitical spaces of public action', in K. Cox, M. Law and J. Robinson (eds), *The Handbook of Political Geography*. London: Sage.

Bauman, Z. (1998) *Work, Consumerism and the New Poor*. Buckingham: Open University Press.

Beckett, F. (2007) *The Great City Academy Fraud*. London: Continuum.

Benhabib, S. (1996) *Democracy and Difference: Contesting the Boundaries of the Political*. Princeton, NJ: Princeton University Press.

Benn, S. I. and Gaus, G. F. (1983) *Public and Private in Social Life*. London: Croom Helm.

Bennett, D. (ed.) (1998) *Multi-cultural States*. London: Routledge.

Beresford, P. (2008) 'Individual budgets could weaken the NHS', *The Guardian: Society Guardian*, April 16: 4.

Bifulco, L. (2006) 'Governance, the 'public' and public administration: notes from social policies', paper to the *22ⁿᵈ EGOS colloquium*, Bergen, July.

Bifulco, L. and de Leonardis, O. (2005) 'Sulla trace dell'aione pubblica', in L. Bifulco (ed.), *Le Politiche Sociali: Temi e Prospettive Emergenti*. Rome: Carocci, pp. 193–222.

Billig, M. (1995) *Banal Nationalism*. London: Sage.

Black, A. and Muddiman, D. (1997) *Understanding Community Librarianship: The Public Library in Post-Modern Britain*. Aldershot: Avebury.

Blair, T. (2003) 'Progress and Justice in the 21st century', *The Inaugural Fabian Society Annual Lecture*, London, 17 June.

Blomgren, M. and Sahlin, K. (2007) 'Quest for transparency: signs of a new institutional era in the health care field', in T. Christensen and P. Laegrid (eds), *Transcending New Public Management: The Transformation of Public Sector Reform*. Aldershot: Ashgate.

Blunkett, D. (2005) 'A new England: an English identity within Britain', *Speech to the Institute for Public Policy Research*, www.ippr.org.uk, accessed 16 February 2007.

Bobbitt, P. (2003) *The Shield of Achilles: War, Peace and the Course of History*. London: Penguin Books.

Bodi, L. and Laurie, N. (2005) 'Introduction to the working spaces of neoliberalism: activism, professionalism and incorporation', *Antipode*, 37 (3): 394–401.

Bourdieu, P. (1986) *Distinction: A Social Critique of the Judgement of Taste*. (Translated by R. Nice) London: Routledge.

Bovens, M. (1998) *The Quest for Responsibility: Accountability and Citizenship in Complex Organisations*. Cambridge: Cambridge University Press.

Bovens, M. (2004) 'Public accountability', in E. Ferlie, L. Lynne and C. Pollitt (eds), *The Oxford Handbook of Public Management*. Oxford: Oxford University Press.

Bovens, M. (2007) 'Analysing and assessing accountability: a conceptual framework', *European Law Journal*, 13 (4): 447–68.

Bovens, M., t'Hart, P. and Peters, G. (2004) *Success and Failure in Public Governance: A Comparative Analysis*. Cheltenham: Edward Elgar.

Brah, A. (1996) *Cartographies of Diaspora: Contesting Identities*. London: Routledge.

Bredgaard, T. and Larsen, F. (2007) 'Implementing public employment policy: what happens when non-public agencies take over?', *International Journal of Sociology and Social Policy*, 27 (7/8): 287–300.

Breitenbach, E., Brown, A., Mackay, F. and Webb, J. (2002) *The Changing Politics of Gender Equality in Britain*. Basingstoke: Macmillan.

Brenner, N. (2004) *New State Spaces: Urban Governance and the Rescaling of Statehood*. Oxford: Oxford University Press.

Brenner, N., Jessop, B., Jones, M. and MacLeod, G. (eds) (2003) *State/Space*. Oxford: Blackwell Publishing.

Brereton, M. and Temple, M. (1999) 'The new public service ethos: an ethical environment for governance', *Public Administration*, 77 (3): 455–74.

Brooks, R. (ed.) (2007) *Public Services at the Crossroads*. London: IPPR.

Brodie, J. (2008) 'We are all equal now: contemporary gender politics in Canada', *Feminist Theory*, 9 (2): 145–64.

Brown, G. (2000) Speech by the Chancellor of the Exchequer at the *National Council of Voluntary Organizations (NCVO) Conference*. Accessed at http://www.hm-Treasury.gov.uk./newsroom_and_speeches/speeches/chancellorexchequer/sppech-chex-902000.cfm (accessed on 19 June 2006).

Brown, G. (2007) 'Together to win', *Progress Online*, 02.06.2007: http://www.progressonline.org.uk/magazine/article.asp?a=1815 (accessed 18.04.2008).

Brown, M. P. (1997) *Replacing Citizenship: AIDS Activism and Radical Democracy*. New York: Guilford.

Brown, W. (1995) *States of Injury: Power and Freedom in Late Modernity*. Princeton, NJ: Princeton University Press.

Brown, W. (2001) *Politics out of History*. Princeton, NJ: Princeton University Press.

Brown, W. (2005) *Edgework: Critical Essays on Knowledge and Politics*. Princeton, NJ: Princeton University Press.

Brown, W. (2006) *Regulating Aversion: Tolerance in the Age of Identity*. Princeton, NJ: Princeton University Press.

Bullivant, B. (1981) *Race, Ethnicity and Curriculum*. Melbourne: Macmillan.

Burney, E. (2005) *Making People Behave: Anti-social Behaviour, Politics and Policy*. Cullompton, Devon: Willan Publishing.

Buss, D. and Herman, D. (2003) *Globalizing Family Values: The Christian Right in International Politics*. Minneapolis, MA: University of Minnesota Press.

Calhoun, C. (ed.) (1992) *Habermas and the Public Domain*. Cambridge, MA: MIT Press.

Calhoun, C. (1997) 'Nationalism and the public sphere', in J. A. Weintraub and K. Kumar (eds), *Public and Private in Thought and Practice*. Chicago: University of Chicago Press, pp. 75–102.

Campbell, D. and Vincent-Jones, P. (eds) (1996) *Contract and Economic Organisation: Socio-Legal Initiatives*. Aldershot: Dartmouth Publishing Company.

Canovan, M. (1999) 'Trust the people! Populism and the two faces of democracy', *Political Studies*, XLVII: 2–16.

Cantle, T. (2006) *Community Cohesion: Report of the Independent Review Team*. London: The Home Office.

Castells, M. and Himenan, P. (2002) *The Information Society and the Welfare State: The Finnish Model*. Oxford: Oxford University Press.

Castles, F. (2004) *The Future of the Welfare State: Crisis Myths and Crisis Realities*. Oxford: Oxford University Press.

Castles, S. and Davidson, A. (2000) *Citizenship and Migration: Globalization and the Politics of Belonging*. Basingstoke: Palgrave Macmillan.

Cerny, P. (1997) 'Paradoxes of the Competition State: the dynamics of political globalization', *Government and Opposition*, 32 (2): 251–74.

Charity Commissioners for England and Wales (2004) *The Hallmarks of an Effective Charity*. London: Charity Commission.

Charlesworth, J., Clarke, J. and Cochrane, A. (1996) 'Managing mixed economies of care', *Environment and Planning 'A'*, 74 (1): 67–88.

Chatterjee, P. (1993) 'The nation and its fragments: colonial and postcolonial histories', in A. Sharma and A. Gupta (eds), *The Anthropology of the State*. Oxford: Blackwell, pp. 211–42.

Chatterjee, P. (2004) *The Politics of the Governed*. New York: Columbia University Press.

Christensen, T. and Laegreid, P. (eds) (2002) *New Public Management: the transformation of ideas and practices*. Aldershot: Aldgate.

Christensen, T. and Laegreid, P. (eds) (2007) *Transcending New Public Management: The Transformation of Public Sector Reforms*. Aldershot: Ashgate.

Clarke, J. (1997) 'Capturing the customer: consumerism and social welfare', *Self, Agency and Society*, 1(1): 55–73.

Clarke, J. (2003) 'Turning inside out? Globalization, neo-liberalism and welfare states', *Anthropologica*, 45: 201–14.

Clarke, J. (2004a) *Changing Welfare, Changing States: New Directions in Social Policy*. London: Sage.

Clarke, J. (2004b) 'Dissolving the public realm? The logics and limits of neo-liberalism', *Journal of Social Policy*, 33 (1), 27–48.

Clarke, J. (2004c) 'Access for all? The promise and problems of universalism', *Social Work and Society*, 2 (2): 216–24.

Clarke, J. (2005a) 'Governance and the constitution of a European social', in J. Newman (ed.), *Remaking Governance: Peoples, Politics and the Public Sphere*. Bristol: Policy Press, pp. 39-58.

Clarke, J. (2005b) 'Performing for the public: doubt, desire and the evaluation of public services', in P. Du Gay (ed.), *The Values of Bureaucracy*. Oxford: Oxford University Press.

Clarke, J. (2005c) 'Producing transparency? Evaluation and the governance of public services', in G. Drewry, C. Greve and T. Tanquerel (eds), *Contracts, Performance Measurement and Accountability in the Public Sector*. Amsterdam: IOS Press.

Clarke, J. (2005d) 'New labour's citizens: activated, empowered, responsibilised, abandoned?', *Critical Social Policy*, 25 (4): 447–63.

Clarke, J. (2006a) 'Disorganizzare il publicco?', *La Rivista delle Politiche Sociali*, No. 2 (April–June): 107–26.

Clarke, J (2006b) 'Consumers, clients or citizens? Politics, policy and practice in the reform of social care', *European Societies*, 8 (3): 423–42.

Clarke, J. (2007a) 'Introduction: governing the social', *Cultural Studies*, 21 (6): 837–47.

Clarke, J. (2007b) 'It's not like shopping: relational reasoning and public services', in M. Bevir and F. Trentman (eds), *Governance, Citizens and Consumers: Agency and Resistance in Contemporary Politics*. Basingstoke: Palgrave Macmillan.

Clarke, J. (2007c) 'Diversity versus solidarity? Social divisions and post-welfarist societies', Paper presented at the TISSA conference on *Migration, Minorities and Refugees; Social Work under conditions of Diversity*, Messina, Sicily, August 28–31, 2007.

Clarke, J. (2007d) 'Subordinating the social? Problems of post-welfarist capitalism', *Cultural Studies*, 21 (6): 974–87.

Clarke, J. (2008) 'Living with/in and without neo-liberalism.' *Focaal: European Journal of Anthropology*, 51: 135–47.

Clarke, J. (2009) 'People and places: the search for community', in G. Mooney and S. Neal (eds), *Community: Welfare, Crime and Society*. Buckingham: Open University Press.

Clarke, J. and Fink, J. (2008) 'People, places and policies: identity, citizenship and welfare', in W. van Oorschot, B. Pfau-Effinger and M. Opielka (eds), *Culture and Welfare State: Values of Social Policy from a Comparative Perspective*. Brighton: Edward Elgar.

Clarke, J., Gewirtz, S., Hughes, G. and Humphrey, J. (2000) 'Guarding the public interest? Auditing public services', in J. Clarke, S. Gewirtz and E. McLaughlin (eds), *New Managerialism, New Welfare?*. London: Sage/The Open University.

Clarke, J. and Newman, J. (1997) *The Managerial State: Power, Politics and Ideology in the Remaking of Social Welfare*. London: Sage.

Clarke, J. and Newman, J. (2004) 'Governing in the modern world?', in D. L. Steinberg and R. Johnson (eds), *Blairism and the War of Persuasion: Labour's Passive Revolution*. London: Lawrence and Wishart, pp. 53-65.

Clarke, J. and Newman, J. (2006) 'The people's choice? Citizens, consumers and public services', Paper Presented to conference on *Citizenship and Consumption: Agency, Norms, Mediation and Spaces;* Cambridge, March.

Clarke, J. and Newman, J. (2007) 'Reluctant subjects: citizens, consumers and the reform of public services', in H. K. Hansen and D. Salskov-Iversen (eds), *Critical Perspectives on Private Authority in Global Politics.* Basingstoke: Palgrave Macmillan, pp. 110–27.

Clarke, J., Newman, J., Smith, N., Vidler, E. and Westmarland, L. (2007a) *Creating Citizen-Consumers: Changing Publics and Changing Public Services.* London: Sage.

Clarke, J., Newman, J. and Westmarland, L. (2007b) 'The antagonisms of choice: New Labour and the reform of public services', *Social Policy and Society*, 7 (2): 245–53.

Clarke, J., Newman, J. and Westmarland, L. (2007c) 'Creating citizen-consumers? Public service reform and (un)willing selves', in S. Maasen and B. Sutter (eds), *On Willing Selves. Neoliberal Politics vis-á-vis the Neuroscientific Knowledge.* Basingstoke: Palgrave Macmillan.

Clarke, J., Smith, N. and Vidler, E. (2005) 'Consumerism and the reform of public services: inequalities and instabilities', in M. Powell, K. Clarke and L. Bauld (eds), *Social Policy Review 17.* Bristol: The Policy Press.

Clarke, J., Smith, N. and Vidler, E. (2006) 'The indeterminacy of choice: political, policy and organisational dilemmas', *Social Policy and Society*, 5 (3): 1–10.

Cochrane, A. (2006) *Understanding Urban Policy.* Oxford: Blackwell.

Cochrane, A. and Etherington, D. (2007) 'Managing local labour markets and making up new spaces of welfare', *Environment and Planning A*, 39: 2958–74.

Cochrane, A. and Newman, J. (2009) 'Community in policymaking', in G.Mooney and S. Neal (eds), *Community.* Maidenhead: Open University Press/The Open University.

Cochrane, A. and Talbot, D. (eds) (2009) *Security.* Maidenhead: Open University Press/The Open University.

Coleman, S. (2003) *A Tale of Two Houses: The House of Commons, the Big Brother House and the People at Home.* London: Hansard.

Coleman, S. (2005) 'New mediation and direct representation: reconceptualising representation in the digital age', *New Media and Society*, 17 (2): 177–98.

Commission on Integration and Cohesion (2007) *Our Shared Future.* Wetherby: Commission on Intergration and Cohesion.

Cooper, D. (1998) *Governing out of Order: Space, Law and the Politics of Belonging.* London: Rivers Oram Press.

Cooper, D. (2004) *Challenging Diversity: Rethinking Equality and the Value of Difference.* Cambridge: Cambridge University Press.

Cornwall, A. and Coelho, V. S. (2007) 'Spaces for change? The politics of participation in new democratic arenas', in A. Cornwall and V. S. Coelho (eds), *Spaces for Change? The Politics of Participation in New Democratic Arenas.* London: Zed Books, pp. 1-29.

Couldry, N. (2003) *Media Rituals: A Critical Approach.* London: Routledge.

Coulson, A. (ed.) (1998) *Trust and Contracts.* Bristol: The Policy Press.

Coutin, S. B. (2006) 'Cultural logics of belonging and movement: transnationalism, naturalisation and US immigration politics', in A. Sharma and A. Gupta (eds), *The Anthropology of the State.* Oxford: Blackwell: 310–36.

Cowan, D., McDermont, M. and Prendergrast, J. (forthcoming) 'Structuring governance: a case study of the new organisational provision of public service delivery', *Critical Social Policy.*

Cowan, D. and McDermont, M. (2006) *Regulating Social Housing: Governing Decline.* London: The Glasshouse Press.

Craig, G. (2007) 'Community capacity building: something old, something new?', *Critical Social Policy,* 27 (3): 335–51.

Craig, G. and Mayo, M. (eds) (1995) *Community Empowerment: A Reader in Participation in Development.* London: Zed Books.

Craig, G. and Taylor, M. (2002) 'Dangerous liaisons: local government and the voluntary and community sectors', in C. Glendinning, M. Powell and K. Rummery (eds), *Partnerships, New Labour and the Governance of Welfare.* Bristol: The Policy Press.

Crawford, A. (2006) 'Networked governance and the post-regulatory state? Steering, rowing and anchoring the provision of policing and security', *Theoretical Criminology,* 10 (4): 449–79.

Creed, G. (2006) 'Reconsidering community', in G. Creed (ed.), *The Seductions of Community: Emancipations, Oppressions, Quandaries.* Santa Fe: School of American Research Press and Oxford: James Currey, pp. 3–23.

Cribb, A. (forthcoming) 'Professional ethics: whose responsibility?', in S. Gewirtz, P. Mahony, I. Hextall and A. Cribb (eds) *Changing Teacher Professionalism: International trends, challenges and ways forward.* London: Routledge.

Cruikshank, B. (1999) *The Will to Empower.* Ithaca, NY: Cornell University Press.

Cutler, T. and Waine, B. (1997) *Managing the Welfare State.* Oxford: Berg.

Cutler, T., Waine, B. and Brehony, K. (2007) 'A new epoch of individualization? Problems with the 'personalization' of public sector services', *Public Administration* 85 (3): 847–55.

Czarniawska, B. and Sevón, G. (eds) (1996) *Translating Organisational Change.* Berlin: de Gruyter.

Czarniawska, B. and Sevón, G. (2005a) 'Translation as a vehicle, imitation its motor, and fashion at the wheel', in B. Czarniawska and G. Sevón (eds), *Global Ideas: how ideas, objects and practices travel in the global economy.* Copenhagen: Liber and Copenhagen Business School Press.

Czarniawska, B. and Sevón, G. (eds) (2005b) *Global Ideas: How Ideas, Objects and Practices Travel in the Global Economy.* Copenhagen: Liber and Copenhagen Business School Press.

Dagnino, E. (2006) '"We all have rights but…" contesting concepts of citizenship in Brazil', in N. Kabeer (ed.), *Inclusive Citizenship: Meanings and Expressions.* London: Zed Books.

Dagnino, E. (2007) 'Participation, citizenship and democracy: perverse confluence and displacement of meanings', in C. Neveu (ed.), *Cultures et Pratiques Participatives: Perspectives Comparatives.* Paris: L'Harmattan; pp. 353–70.

Daly, M. (2002) 'Governance and social policy', *Journal of Social Policy,* 32 (1): 113–28.

Danish Globalization Council (2006) *Progress, Innovation and Cohesion: Strategy for Denmark in the Global Economy.* Copenhagen: Danish Ministry of Finance (see www.globalisation.dk – accessed 11/03/08).

Davies, C., Wetherell, M. and Barnett, E. (2007) *Citizens at the Centre: Deliberative Participation in Health Care Decisions.* Bristol: Policy Press.

Davies, H., Nutley, S. and Smith, P. (eds) (2000) *What Works? Evidence-based Policy and Practice in Public Services.* Bristol: The Policy Press.

Davies, N. (2008) 'Crisis at police watchdog as lawyers resign', *The Guardian*, February 25: p. 1.

Deacon, B. (2007) *Global Social Policy: International Organizations and the Future of Welfare.* London: Sage.

Deakin, N. (2000) *In Search of Civil Society.* Basingstoke: Palgrave.

Dean, H. (2004) 'The implications of Third way social policy for inequality, social cohesion and citizenship', in J. Lewis and R. Surrender (eds), *Welfare State Change: towards a Third Way?* Oxford: Oxford University Press, pp. 182–206.

Dean, M. (1999) *Governmentality: Power and Rule in Modern Society.* London: Sage.

Dean. M. (2007) *Governing Societies.* Maidenhead: Open University Press.

Defourny. J. (2001) 'Introduction: from third sector to social enterprise', in C. Borzaga and J. Defourny (eds), *The Emergence of Social Enterprise.* London: Routledge.

De Leonardis, O. (2007) 'Organisational variables affecting civicness and democracy in the governance and production of welfare services', Paper Presented at the seminar *Between State and Citizens – The Role of Civil Elements in the Governance and Production of Social Services,* Berlin, 30–31 March.

Dench, G., Gavron, K. and Young, M. (2006) *The New East End – Kinship, Race and Conflict.* London: Profile Books.

Dent, M., van Gestel, N. and Teelken, C. (2007) 'Symposium on changing modes of governance in public sector organizations: action and rhetoric', *Public Administration*, 85 (1): 1–8.

Department of Health (2007) *Social Enterprise: What are the Advantages of Social Enterprise?* http://www.dh.gov.uk/en/Managingyourorganisation/Commissioning/Socialenterprise/DH_4139126 (accessed 15.04.2008).

Department of Health (2008) *An Introduction to Personalisation.* http://www.dh.gov.uk/en/SocialCare/Socialcarereform/Personalisation/DH_080573 (accessed 16.04.2008).

Diamond, P. with Public Service Reform Group (ed.) (2007) *Public Matters: The Renewal of the Public Realm.* London: Methuen.

Dinham, A. (2008) 'Faiths, citizenships and publics: do we know who we are talking about?', Paper to ESRC seminar on *Faith and the Good Citizen: Key Debates and Perspectives,* Milton Keynes, 6–7 March, 2008.

Djelic, M-L. and Sahlin-Andersson, K. (eds) (2006) *Transnational Governance: Institutional Dynamics of Regulation.* Cambridge: Cambridge University Press.

Donald, J. and Rattansi, A. (1992) 'Introduction', in J. Donald and A. Rattansi (eds), *'Race', Culture and Difference.* London: Sage, pp. 1–10.

Downe, J. and Martin, S. (2005a) *Inspecting for Improvement? Emerging Patterns of Public Service Regulation in the UK.* Cardiff: Centre for Local and Regional Government Research, Cardiff Business School.

Downe, J. and Martin, S. (2005b) *Inspecting the Inspectors: An Analysis of the External Inspection of Local Public Services.* Cardiff: Centre for Local and Regional Government Research, Cardiff Business School.

Drache, D. (2008) *Defiant Publics: the unprecedented reach of the global citizen.* Cambridge: Polity.

Driver, S. and Martell, L. (1998) *New Labour: Politics after Thatcherism*. Cambridge: Polity.

Driver, S. and Martell, L. (2002) *Blair's Britain*. Cambridge: Polity.

Dryzek, J. (2000) *Deliberative Democracy and Beyond: Liberals, Critics, Contestations*. Oxford: Oxford University Press.

Dryzek, J. (2006) *Deliberative Global Politics: Discourse and Democracy in a Divided World*. Cambridge: Polity.

Du Gay, P. (1996) *Consumption and Identity at Work*. London: Sage.

Du Gay, P. (ed.)(2000) *In Praise of Bureaucracy*. London: Sage.

Du Gay, P. (2004) 'Afterword: the tyranny of the ephocal and work identity', in T. A. Jensen and A. Westenholz (eds), *Identity in the Age of the New Economy: Life in Temporary and Scattered Work Practices*. Cheltenham: Edward Elgar.

Du Gay, P. (2005a) 'The values of bureaucracy: an introduction', in P. du Gay (ed.), *The Values of Bureaucracy*. Oxford: Oxford University Press.

Du Gay, P. (2005b) 'Bureaucracy and liberty; state, authority and freedom', in P. du Gay (ed.), *The Values of Bureaucracy*. Oxford: Oxford University Press, pp. 41–62.

Duggan, L. (2003) *The Twilight of Equality: Neoliberalism, Cultural Politics and the Attack on Democracy*. Boston, MA: Beacon Press.

Dunleavy, P. (1991) *Democracy, Bureaucracy and Public Choice: Economic Explanations in Political Science*. London: Longman.

Dunleavy, P., Margetts, H., Bastow, S. and Tinkler, J. (2006) *Digital Era Governance*. Oxford: Oxford University Press.

Duyvendak, J. W. and Uitermark, J. (2006) 'When ideologies bounce back: the problematic translation of post-multicultural ideologies and policies into professional practice', in J. W. Duyvendak, T. Knijn and M. Kremer (eds), *People, Policy and the New Professionals*. Amsterdam: Amsterdam Universit Press.

Duyvendak, J. W., Knijn, T. and Kremer, M. (2006) 'Policy, people and the new professional: an introduction', in J. W. Duyvendak, T. Knijn and M. Kremer (eds), *Policy, People and the New Professionals*. Amsterdam: Amsterdam University Press, pp. 7–18.

Dwyer, P. (2000) *Welfare Rights and Responsibilities: Contesting Social Citizenship*. Bristol: The Policy Press.

Eikenberry, A. and Kluver, J. (2004) 'The marketization of the nonprofit sector: civil society at risk?', *Public Administration Review*, 64 (2): 132–40.

Elliot, A. and Lemert, C. (2005) *The New Individualism: The Emotional Costs of Globalization*. London: Routledge.

Ellison, N. (2006) *The Transformation of Welfare States?* London: Routledge.

Ely, G. (1992) 'Nations, publics and political cultures: placing Habermas in the 19th century', in C. Calhoun (ed.), *Habermas and the Public Sphere*. Cambridge, MA: MIT Press.

Elyachar, J. (2002) 'Empowerment money: the World Bank, non-governmental organizations, and the value of culture in Egypt', *Public Culture*, 14 (3): 493–513.

Elyachar, J. (2005) *Markets of Dispossession: NGOs, Economic Development, and the State in Cairo*. Durham, NC: Duke University Press.

Escobar, A. (1999) 'Gender, place and networks: a political ecology of cyberculture', in W. Harcourt (ed.), *Women@Internet: Creating New Cultures in Cyberspace*. London: Zed Books, pp. 31–55.

Esping-Andersen, G. (1990) *The Three Worlds of Welfare Capitalism*. Cambridge: Cambridge University Press.

Esping-Andersen, G. (2003) 'Against social inheritance', in M. Browne, P. Thompson and F. Sainsbury (eds), *Progressive Futures: New Ideas for the Centre-Left*. London: Policy Network.

Etzioni, A. (1995) *The Spirit of Community*. London: Fontana.

Etzioni, A. (1998) *The New Golden Rule: Community and Morality in a Democratic Society*. New York: Basic Books.

Everingham, C. (2003) *Social Justice and the Politics of Community*. Aldershot: Ashgate.

Farnsworth, K. (2004) *Corporate Power and Social Responsibility in a Global Economy: British Welfare under the Influence*. Bristol: Policy Press.

Farnsworth, K. (2007) 'Business, power, policy and politics', in S. Hodgson and Z. Irving (eds), *Policy Reconsidered: Meanings, Politics and Practices*. Bristol: The Policy Press.

Faulkner, D. (2006) 'Reflections on the Fabian New Year Conference: who do we want to be? The future of Britishness', *Runnymede's Quarterly Bulletin*, 346 (March): 6.

Ferguson, J. (1994) *The Anti-Politics Machine: 'Development', Depoliticization, and Bureaucratic Power in Lesotho*. Minnesota: University of Minnesota Press.

Ferguson, J. and Gupta, A. (2002) 'Spatializing states: towards an ethnography of neo-liberal governmentality', *American Ethnologist*, 29 (4): 981–1002.

Fergusson, K. (1984) *The Feminist Case Against Bureaucracy*. Philadelphia, PA: Temple University Press.

Fernandez, J-L., Kendall, J., Davey, V. and Knapp, M. (2007) 'Direct payments in England: factors linked to variations in local provision', *Journal of Social Policy*, 36 (1): 97–122.

Finalyson, A. (2003) 'Public choice theory: enemy of democracy', *Soundings*, 24: 25–40.

Flanagan, R. (2008) *The Final Report of the Independent Review of Policing, conducted by Sir Ronnie Flanagan*. London: Home Office.

Forum for Top Executive Management (2005) *Public Governance: Code for Chief Executive Excellence*. Copenhagen: Mkom Danmark Aps.

Fountain, A. (2003) 'Is the BBC fit for the 21st Century?', *Soundings*, 25: 21-40.

Frank, T. (2001) *One Market Under God: Extreme Capitalism, Market Populism and the End of Economic Democracy*. New York: Anchor Books.

Fraser, N. and Honneth, A. (2003) *Redistribution or Recognition? A Political-Philosophical Exchange*. London: Verso.

Fraser, N. (1997) 'Rethinking the public sphere', in *Justice Interruptus: Critical Reflections on the Post-Socialist Condition*. London: Routledge, pp. 69–98.

Fraser, N. (2005) 'Reframing justice in a globalising world', *New Left Review*, 36: 69–88.

Freeman, T. and Peck, E. (2007a) 'Evaluating partnerships: a case study of integrated specialist mental health services', *Health and Social Care in the Community*, 14 (5): 408–17.

Freeman, T. and Peck, E. (2007b) 'Performing governance: a partnership board dramaturgy', *Public Administration*, 85 (4): 907–29.

Freud, D. (2007) *Reducing Dependency, Increasing Opportunity: Options for the Future of Welfare to Work. An Independent Report to the Department of Work and Pensions*. Leeds: Corporate Document Services.

Friedman, T. (2005) *The World is Flat: A Brief History of the Globalized World in the Twenty-First Century*. London: Allen Lane.

Friedson, E. (2001) *Professionalism: The Third Logic*. Cambridge: Polity.

Fung, A. and Wright, E. O. (2003) 'Thinking about empowered participatory governance', in A. Fung and E. O. Wright (eds), *Deepening Democracy: Institutional Innovations in Empowered Participatory Governance*. London: Verso, pp. 3–43.

Fyfe, N. (2005) 'Making space for "neo-communitarianism"? The third sector, state and civil society in the UK', *Antipode*, 37 (3): 536–57.

Fyfe, N. and Milligan, C. (2003) 'Out of the shadows: exploring contemporary geographies of voluntarism', *Progress in Human Geography*, 27 (4): 397–413.

Gamble, A. (2004) 'Public intellectuals and the public domain', *New Formations*, 53 (summer): 41–53.

Garland, D. (2001) *The Culture of Control: Crime and Social Order in Contemporary Society*. Chicago: University of Chicago Press.

Garrett, P. (2008) 'How to be modern: New Labour's neoliberal modernity and the *Change for Children* programme', *British Journal of Social Work*, 38: 270–89.

Gewirtz, S. (2001) *The Managerial School: Post-welfarism and Social Justice in Education*. London: Routledge.

Gewirtz, S., Ball, S. and Bowe, R. (1995) *Markets, Choice and Equity in Education*. Buckingham: Open University Press.

Ghorashi, H., Salemink, O. and Spierenburg, M. (2006) 'The transnational construction of local conflicts and protests' (introduction to a themed section), *Focaal*, 47: 1–3.

Gibson-Graham, J. K. (1996) *The End of Capitalism (as we knew it)*. Malden, MA and Oxford: Basil Blackwell Publishers.

Gibson-Graham, J. K. (2006) *A Postcapitalist Politics*. Minneapolis, MA: University of Minnesota Press.

Gilroy. P. (2005) *Postcolonial Melancholia*. New York: Columbia University Press.

Gilling, D. and Hughes, G. (2002) 'The community safety "profession": towards a new expertise in the governance of crime, disorder and safety in the UK?', *Community Safety Journal*, 1 (1): 4–12.

Gingrich, A. and Banks, M. (eds) (2006) *Neo-Nationalism in Europe and Beyond: Perspectives from Social Anthropology*. New York, Oxford: Berghahn Books.

Gledhill, J. (2000) *Power and its Disguises: Anthropological Perspectives on Politics*. London: Pluto Press.

Glendinning, C., Powell, M. and Rummery, K. (eds) (2002) *Partnerships, New Labour and the Governance of Welfare*. Bristol: The Policy Press.

Goode, J. and Maskovsky, J. (eds) (2001) *The New Poverty Studies: The Ethnography of Power, Politics and Impoverished People in the United States*. New York: New York University Press.

Goodhart, D. (2004) 'Is Britain too diverse?', *Prospect*, 95 (February). http://www.prospect-magazine.co.uk/article_details.php?id=5835 (accessed 30.04.2008).

Gould, J. (ed.) (2005) *The New Conditionality: The Politics of Poverty Reduction Strategies*. London: Zed Books.

Gramsci, A. (1971) *Selections from the Prison Notebooks*. London: Lawrence and Wishart.

Gregory, D. (2005) *The Colonial Present*. Oxford: Blackwell.

Gupta, A. (1998) *Postcolonial Developments*. Durham, NC: Duke University Press.

Gupta, A. (2006) 'Blurred boundaries: the discourse of corruption, the culture of politics and the imagined state', in A. Sharma and A. Gupta (eds), *The Anthropology of the State*. Oxford: Blackwell, pp. 211–42.

Gupta, A. and Ferguson, J. (1992) 'Beyond "culture": space, identity and the politics of difference', *Cultural Anthropology*, 7 (1): 6–23.

Habermas, J. (1989) *The Structural Transformation of the Public Sphere*. Cambridge, MA: MIT Press.

Hackett, R. (2001) 'News media and civic equality: watch dogs, mad dogs, or lap dogs?', in E. Broadbent (ed.), *Democratic Equality: What Went Wrong?* Toronto: University of Toronto Press.

Hage, G. (2003) *Against Paranoid Nationalism: Searching for hope in a shrinking society* London: The Merlin Press.

Hajer, M. (1997) *The Politics of Environmental Discourse: Ecologic Modernisation and the Policy Process*. Oxford: Oxford University Press.

Hajer, M. (1999) 'Ecological modernisation as cultural politics', in M. J. Smith (ed.), *Thinking through the Environment: A Reader*. London: Routledge, pp. 364–72.

Hall, C. (2002) *Civilising Subjects: Metropole and colony in the English Imagination 1830–1867*. Chicago: University of Chicago Press.

Hall, S. (1989) *The Hard Road to Renewal*. London: Verso.

Hall, S. (2003) 'New Labour's double shuffle', *Soundings*, 24: 10–24.

Halvorsen, R., Nervik, J. A., Salonen, T., Thorén, T. and Ulmestig, R. (2007) 'The challenge of decentralised delivery of services: the scope for active citizenship in Swedish and Norwegian activation policies', in B. Hvinden and H. Johannson (eds), *Citizenship in the Nordic Welfare States: Dynamics of Choice, Duties and Participation in a Changing Europe*. London: Routledge, pp. 80–94.

Hancher, L. and Moran, M. (1989) 'Organising regulatory space', in L. Hancher and M. Moran (eds), *Capitalism, Culture and Economic Regulation*. Oxford: Clarendon Press.

Hansen, H. K. and Salskov-Iversen, D. (2005) 'Globalizing webs: translation of public sector e-Modernization', in B. Czarniawska and G. Sevón (eds), *Global Ideas: How Ideas, Objects and Practices Travel in the Global Economy*. Copenhagen: Liber and Copenhagen Business School Press.

Hansen, H. K. and Salskov-Iversen, D. (2007) 'Conclusions: the making of authority in global politics – towards the engagement of practice and micropolitics', in H. K. Hansen and D. Salskov-Iversen, (eds), *Critical Perspectives on Private Authority in Global Politics*. Basingstoke: Palgrave Macmillan, pp. 208–22.

Hansen, H. K. and Salskov-Iversen, D. (eds) (2007) *Critical Perspectives on Private Authority in Global Politics*. Basingstoke: Palgrave Macmillan.

Hansen, T. and Stepputat, F. (eds) (2001) *States of Imagination: Ethnographic Explorations of the Postcolonial State*. Durham, NC: Duke University Press.

Harrison, S. and Mort, M. (1998) 'Which champions, which people? Public and user involvement in health care as a technology of legitimation', *Social Policy and Administration*, 32 (1): 60–70.

Harrow, J. (2007) 'The third sector: underpaid, overworked but over-valued? Reflections on the risks and rewards for voluntary and community organisations providing public services', Paper to the *International Summer School for Public Managers*, Krakov, August.

Hartmann, Y. (2005) 'In bed with the enemy: some ideas on the connections between neoliberalism and the welfare state', *Current Sociology*, 53 (1): 57–73.

Harvey, D. (2005) *A Brief History of Neoliberalism*. Oxford: Oxford University Press.

Harzig, C. and Juteau, D. (2003) 'Introduction: recasting Canadian and European history in a pluralist perspective', in C. Harzig and D. Juteau with I. Schmitt (eds), *The Social Construction of Diversity: Recasting the Master Narrative of Industrial Nations*. New York, and Oxford: Berghahn Books.

Harzig, C. and Juteau, D. with Schmitt, I. (eds) (2003) *The Social Construction of Diversity: Recasting the Master Narrative of Industrial Nations*. New York, Oxford: Berghahn Books.

Hay, C. (1998) 'Globalisation, retrenchment and the logic of "no alternative": why second best won't do', *Journal of Social Policy*, 27 (4): 525–32.

Hebson, G., Grimshaw, D. and Marchington, M. (2003) 'PPPs and the changing public sector ethos: case study evidence from the health and local authority sectors', 17 (3): 481–501.

Hennessy, T. (1998) *Dividing Ireland: World War I and Partition*. London: Routledge.

Hesse, B. (ed.) (2001) *Un/settled Multiculturalisms: Diasporas, Entanglements, Disruptions*. London: Zed Books.

Hickey, S. (2002) 'Transnational NGDOs and participatory forms of rights-based development: converging with the local politics of citizenship in Cameroon', *Journal of International Development*, 14 (6): 841–57.

Hickey, S. and Mohan, G. (eds) (2004) *Participation: From Tyranny to Transformation? Exploring New Approaches to Participation*. London: Zed Books.

Hickey, S. and Mohan, G. (2005) 'Relocating participation within a radical politics of development', *Development and Change*, 36 (2): 237–62.

HM Treasury (2002) *The Role of the Voluntary and Community Sector in Service Delivery: A Cross-Cutting Review*. London: The Stationery Office.

HM Treasury (2005) *Exploring the Role of the Third Sector in Public Service Delivery and Reform*. London: The Stationery Office.

Hoggett, P. (2005) 'A service to the public: the containment of ethical and moral conflicts by public bureaucracies', in P. du Gay (ed.), *The Values of Bureaucracy*. Oxford: Oxford University Press: 165–190.

Hoggett, P. (2006) 'Conflict, ambivalence and the contested purpose of public service organizations', *Human Relations*, 59 (2): 175–94.

Hoggett, P., Beedell, P., Jiminez, L., Mayo, M. and Miller, C. (2006a) 'Identity, life history and commitment to welfare', *Journal of Social Policy*, 35 (4): 689–704.

Hoggett, P., Mayo, M. and Miller, C. (2006b) 'Private passions, the public good and public service reform', *Social Policy and Administration*, 40 (7): 758–73.

Hohnen, P. (2003) *A Market Out of Place? Remaking Economic, Social and Symbolic Boundaries in Post-Communist Lithuania*. Oxford: Oxford University Press.

Holland, D., Nonini, S., Lutz, C., Bartlett, L., Frederick-McGlathery, M., Guldbrandsen, T. and Murillo, E. (2007) *Local Democracy Under Siege: Activism, Public Interests and Private Politics*. New York: New York University Press.

Home Office (1998) *Compact on Relations between Government and the Voluntary and Community Sector in England*. London: Home Office (Cm 4100).

Home Office (2004a) *Strength in Diversity*. London: The Stationery Office.

Home Office (2004b) *Change Up: Capacity Building and Infrastructure Framework for the Voluntary and Community Sector.* www.communities.homeoffice.gov.uk/activecomms/ac-publications/pubications/290693/changeup-report-new.pdf?view+Binary.

Home Office (2004c) *Faith Groups in the Community – Working Together: Cooperation Between Government and Faith Communities.* London: The Home Office.

Home Office (2007) *Life in the United Kingdom: A Journey to Citizenship.* London: The Stationery Office (2nd edn).

Home Office (2008) *The Path to Citizenship: Next Steps in Reforming the Immigration System.* London: Home Office Border and Immigration Agency.

Honig, B. (1996) 'Difference, dilemmas and the politics of home', in S. Benhabib (ed.), *Democracy and Difference: Contesting the Boundaries of the Political.* Princeton, NJ: Princeton University Press.

Hood, C. and Peters, B. G. (2004) 'The middle ageing of new public management: into the age of paradox?', *Journal of Public Administration Research and Theory*, 14 (3): 267–82.

Hood, C., Scott, C., James, O., Jones, G. and Travers, T. (1999) *Regulation Inside Government: Waste Watchers, Quality Police and Sleaze Busters.* Oxford: Oxford University Press.

Hooghe, L. and Marks, G. (2003) *Multi-level Governance and European Integration.* Lanham, MD: Rowan and Littlefield.

Horner, L., Lekhi, R. amd Blaug, R. (2006) *Final Report of the Work Foundation's Public Value Consortium,* November 2006. London: The Work Foundation.

Hoyle, E. and Wallace, M. (2007) 'Educational reform: an ironic perspective', *Educational Management, Administration and Leadership*, 35 (1): 9–25.

Huber, R. and Stephens, J. D. (2001) *Development and Crisis of the Welfare State: Parties and Policies in Global Markets.* Chicago: University of Chicago Press.

Hudson, A. (2000) 'Making the connection: legitimacy claims, legitimacy chains and northern NGOs' international advocacy', in D. Lewis and T. Wallace (eds), *New Roles and Relevance: Development NGOs and the Challenge of Change.* Sterling, VA: Kumarian Press.

Hughes, G. (2006) *The Politics of Crime and Community.* London: Palgrave.

Hughes, G. (2007) 'Community cohesion, asylum seeking and the question of the "stranger": towards a new politics of public safety', *Cultural Studies*, 21 (6): 931–51.

Hughes, G. and Edwards, A. (eds) (2002) *Crime Control and Community: The New Politics of Public Safety.* Cullompton, Devon: Willan Publishing.

Hughes, G. and Gilling, D. (2004) 'Mission impossible? The habitus of the community safety manager and the new expertise in the local partnership governance of crime and safety', *Criminal Justice*, 4 (2): 129–49.

Hughes, G. and Lewis, G. (ed.) (1998) *Unsettllng Welfare: The Reconstruction of Social Policy.* London: Routledge.

Hughes, G., McLaughlin, J. and Muncie, J. (eds) (2001) *Crime Prevention and Community Safety: New Directions.* London: Sage.

Hughes, G. and Mooney, G. (1998) 'Community', in G. Hughes (ed.), *Imagining Welfare Futures.* London: Routledge, pp. 55–102.

Huntington, S. P. (1997) *The Clash of Civilizations: And the Remaking of World Order.* New York: Simon and Schuster.

Hutton, W. (2006) 'Developments in public value', in L. Horner, R. Lekhi and R. Blaug, *Final Report of the Work Foundation's Public Value Consortium* November 2006. London: The Work Foundation, pp. 1–6.

Huysmans, J. (2006) *The Politics of Insecurity: Fear, Migration and Asylum in the EU*. London: Routledge.

Hvinden, B. and Johannson, H. (2007) 'Conclusions: remaking social citizenship in the nordic welfare states', in B. Hvinden and H. Johannson (eds), *Citizenship in the Nordic Welfare States: Dynamics of Choice, Duties and Participation in a Changing Europe*. London: Routledge.

Hvinden, B. and Johannson, H. (eds) (2007) *Citizenship in the Nordic Welfare States: Dynamics of Choice, Duties and Participation in a Changing Europe*. London: Routledge.

Hyatt, S. B. (2001) 'From citizen to volunteer: neo-liberal governance and the erasure of poverty', in J. Goode and J. Maskovsky (eds), *The New Poverty Studies*. New York: New York University Press.

Hyland, M. (2006) 'Proud scum – the spectre of the ingrate', *Mute magazine – Culture and Politics after the Net*, 24 May (accessed at http://www.metamute.org/node/7792, 13 June 2006).

IPSOS MORI Horizons (2008) 'Senior Civil Service Leadership: the future context', *Discussion Paper for the Cabinet Office*, January.

Isin, E. (2004) 'The neurotic citizen', *Citizenship Studies*, 8 (3): 217–35.

Itzin, C. and Newman, J. (eds) (1995) *Gender, Culture and Organisational Change*. London: Routledge.

Jacobs, J. (1992) *Systems of Survival: A Dialogue on the Moral Foundations of Commerce and Politics*. London: Hodder and Stoughton.

Jameson, F. and Miyoshi, M. (eds) (1998) *Cultures of Globalization*. Durham, NC: Duke University Press.

Jenkins, S. (2008) 'The state is utterly clueless on the public-private divide', *The Guardian*, February 20: 29.

Jessop, B. (2000) 'Governance failure', in G. Stoker (ed.), *The New Politics of British Local Governance*. Basingstoke: Macmillan.

Jessop, B. (2002) *The Future of the Capitalist State*. Cambridge: Polity.

Johansson, H. and Hvinden, B. (2005) 'Welfare governance and the remaking of citizenship', in J. Newman (ed.) *Remaking Governance: Peoples, Politics and the Public Sphere*. Bristol: Policy Press: 101–118.

Johannson, H. and Hvinden, B. (2007) 'Opening citizenship: why do we need a new understanding of social citizenshp?', in B. Hvinden and H. Johannson (eds), *Citizenship in the Nordic Welfare States: Dynamics of Choice, Duties and Participation in a Changing Europe*. London: Routledge, pp. 3–17.

Johnson, T. (1973) *Professions and Power*. London: Macmillan.

Jordan, B. (2006a) *Social Policy for the Twenty-First Century*. Cambridge: Polity.

Jordan, B. (2006b) 'Public services an the service economy: individualism and the choice agenda', *Journal of Social Policy,* 35(1): 143–62.

Jowell, T. (2005) *Tackling the 'Poverty of Aspiration' through Rebuilding the Public Realm*. London: Demos.

Kalb, D. (2005) 'From flows to violence: politics and knowledge in the debates on globalization and empire', *Anthropological Theory*, 5 (2): 176–204.

Keane, J. (1998) *Civil Society: Old Images, New Visions.* Cambridge: Polity Press.

Kelly, G., Muers, S. and Mulgan, G. (2002) *Creating Public Value: An Analytical Framework for Public Service Reform.* London: Cabinet Office.

Kessl, F. (2007) 'Civil society', *Social Work & Society,* 5 (1): 110–14.

Kickert, W. (2001) 'Public management of hybrid organisations: governance of quasi-autonomous executive agencies', *International Public Management Journal,* 4: 135–50.

Kingfisher, C. (2002) *Western Welfare in Decline: Globalisation and Women's Poverty.* Philadephia: University of Pennsylania Press.

Kirkpatrick, I. and Hoque, K. (2006) 'A retreat from permanent employment? Accounting for the rise of professional agency work in UK public services', *Work, Employment and Society,* 20 (4): 649–66.

Klein, R. and Millar, J. (1995) 'Do-it-yourself social policy: searching for a new paradigm?', *Social Policy & Administration,* 29 (4): 303–16.

Klijn, E. and Kopperjan, J. (2000) 'Public management and policy networks: foundations of a network approach to governance', *Public Management,* 2 (2): 135–38.

Kooiman, J. (ed.) (1993) *Modern Governance: New Government-Society Interactions.* London: Sage.

Kooiman, J. (2000) 'Societal governance: levels, models and orders of social-political interaction', in J. Pierre (ed.) *Debating Governance: Authority, Steering and Democracy.* Oxford: Oxford University Press.

Kooiman, J. (2003) *Governing as Governance.* London: Sage.

Kramsch, O. (2002) 'Reimagining the scalar topologies of cross-border governance: eu(ro) regions in the post-colonial present.' *Space and Polity,* 6 (2): 169–196.

Kremer, M. and Tonkens, E. (2006) 'Authority, trust, knowledge and the public good in disarray', in J. W. Duyvendak, T. Knijn and M. Kremer (eds), *People, Policy and the New Professionals.* Amsterdam: Amsterdam University Press, pp. 122–34.

Kumar, K. (2001) 'Englishness and English national identity', in D. Morley and K. Robins (eds), *British Cultural Studies.* Oxford: Oxford University Press.

Larner, W. (2000) 'Neo-liberalism: policy, ideology, governmentality', *Studies in Political Economy,* 63: 5–25.

Larner, W. and Craig, D. (2005) 'After neoliberalism? Community activism and local partnerships in Aotearoa New Zealand', *Antipode,* 37 (3): 402–24.

Larner, W. and Walters, W. (eds) (2004) *Global Governmentality.* London: Routledge.

Lash, S. and Urry, J. (1994) *Economies of Signs and Space.* London: Sage.

Latour, B. (2005) *Reassembling the Social.* Oxford: Oxford University Press.

Latour, B. and Weibel, P. (eds) (2005) *Making Things Public: Atmospheres of Democracy.* Karlsruhe: Center for Art and Media; Cambridge, MA: The MIT Press.

Lawless, P. (2007) 'New deal for communities: state of knowledge', Paper to the advisory group of the Joseph Rowntree Foundation research project *Governance, Good Practice and Service Structures* (unpublished).

Lawton, A. (2005) 'Public service ethics in a changing world', *Futures,* 37 (2–3): 231–43.

Le Grand, J. (2003) *Motivation, Agency and Public Policy.* Oxford: Oxford University Press.

Le Grand, J. (2007) *The Other Invisible Hand: Delivering Public Services through Choice and Competition.* Princeton, NJ: Princeton University Press.

Leadbeater, C. (2004) *Personalisation through Participation: A New Script for Public Services*. London: Demos.

Leadbeater, C. (2008) *We-think: The Power of Mass Creativity*. London: Profile Books Ltd.

Leadbeater, C., Bartlett, J. and Gallagher, N. (2008) *Making it Personal*. London: Demos.

Leadbeater, C. and Cottam, H. (2007) 'The user-generated state: public services 2.0', in P. Diamond (ed.), *Public Matters: The Renewal of the Public Realm*. London: Methuen.

Leadbetter, C. and Goss, S. (1998) *Civic Entrepreneurship*. London: Demos.

Leece, J. and Bornat, J. (eds) (2006) *Developments in Direct Payments*. Bristol: The Policy Press.

Leibfried, S. and Zürn, M. (2005) 'Reconfiguring the national constellation', in S. Leibfried and M. Zürn (eds), *Transformations of the State*. Cambridge: Cambridge University Press, pp. 1–36.

Lendvai, N. (2005) 'Remaking European governance: transition, accession and integration', in J. Newman (ed.), *Remaking Governance: Peoples, Politics and the Public Sphere*. Bristol: The Policy Press.

Lendvai, N. and Stubbs, P. (2006) 'Translation, intermediaries and welfare reforms in South Eastern Europe', Paper Presented at the *4th ESPANET conference*, Bremen, September 2006.

Lendvai, N. and Stubbs, P. (2007) 'Policies as translation: situating transnational social policies', in S. Hodgson and Z. Irving (eds), *Policy Reconsidered: Meanings, Politics and Practices*. Bristol: Policy Press.

Levitas, R. (1998) *The Inclusive Society?* Basingstoke: Macmillan.

Lewis, G. (ed.) (1998) *Forming Nation, Framing Welfare*. London: Routledge.

Lewis, G. (2000a) 'Discursive histories, the pursuit of multi-culturalism and social policy', in G. Lewis, S. Gewirtz and J. Clarke (eds), *Rethinking Social Policy*. London: Sage.

Lewis, G. (2000b) *'Race', Gender and Social Welfare: Encounters in a Postcolonial Society*. Cambridge: Polity Press.

Lewis, G. (2007) 'Racializing culture is ordinary', *Cultural Studies*, 21 (6): 866–86.

Lewis, G., Gewirtz, S. and Clarke, J. (eds) (2000) *Rethinking Social Policy*. London: Sage.

Lewis, J. and Surrender, R. (2004) *Welfare State Change: Towards a Third Way?* Oxford: Oxford University Press.

Li, T. (2007a) 'Practices of assemblage and community forest management', *Economy and Society*, 36 (2): 263–93.

Li, T. (2007b) *The Will to Improve*. Durham, NC: Duke University Press.

Li, T. (2007c) 'Indigeneity, Capitalism and Countermovements', Paper Presented to the *American Anthropological Association* annual conference, Washington DC, November.

Lipsky, M. (1980) *Street Level Bureaucracy: Dilemmas of the Individual in Public Services*. New York: Russell Sage Foundation.

Lister, R. (2002) 'Towards a new welfare settlement?', in C. Hay (ed.), *British Politics Today*. Cambridge: Polity.

Lister, R. (2003) *Citizenship: Feminist Perspectives*. 2nd edn. Basingstoke: Palgrave Macmillan.

Lister, R. (2004) 'The third way's social investment state', in J. Lewis and R. Surrender (eds), *Welfare State Change: Towards a Third Way?* Oxford: Oxford University Press.

Lister, R. (2007) 'Inclusive Citizenship: Realizing the Potential' *Citizenship Studies*, Vol. 11(1): 49–61.

Loader, B., Hardy, M. and Keeble, L. (2007) *Wired for the Third Age: An Evaluation of an Electronic Service Delivery Project for Older People in Durham*. Final Report: see www.masc.bham.ac.uk.

Lowndes, V. and Newman, J. (2008) 'Disruptive presences: faith in public policy and governance', Paper to ESRC seminar on *Faith and the Good Citizen: key debates and perspectives*, Milton Keynes, 6–7 March, 2008.

Maasen, S. and Sutter, B. (eds) (2007) *On Willing Selves: Neoliberal Politics vis-à-vis the Neuroscientific Challenge*. Basingstoke: Palgrave

MacKinnon, C. A. (1989) *Towards a Feminist Theory of the State*. Cambridge, MA: Harvard University Press.

MacPhee, G. and Poddar, P. (eds) (2007) *Empire and After: Englishness in Postcolonial Perspective*. Oxford: Blackwell.

McDermont, M. (2007) 'Territorializing regulation: a case study of "social housing" in England', *Law and Social Inquiry*, 32 (2): 373–98.

McDonald, C. and Marston, G. (eds) (2006) *Analysing Social Policy: A Governmental Approach*. Cheltenham: Edward Elgar.

McKee, K. and Cooper, V. (2007) 'The paradox of tenant empowerment: regulatory and liberatory possibilties', *Housing, Theory and Society*, December: 1–15.

Mahajan, G. and Reifeld, H. (eds) (2003) *The Public and the Private: Issues of Democratic Citizenship*. New Delhi, Thousand Oaks, CA and London: Sage.

Mahony, N. (2008, forthcoming) *Spectaular Political Experiments: Remaking Publicness and the Political?*. Doctoral Thesis, Faculty of Social science, The Open University.

Mamdani, M. (2004) *Good Muslim, Bad Muslim: America, the Cold War and the Roots of Terror*. New York: Pantheon.

Marfleet, P. (1999) 'Europe's civilising mission', in P. Cohen (ed.), *New Ethnicities, Old Racisms*. London: Zed Books.

Marquand, D. (2004) *Decline of the Public: The Hollowing-out of Citizenship*. Cambridge: Polity Press.

Mastnak, T. (2005) 'The reinvention of civil society: through the looking glass of democracy', *Archive of European Sociology*, XLVI (2): 323–55.

Matthews, D. (1984) 'The public in practice and theory', *Public Administration Review*, 44: 120–25.

Mayo, M., Hoggett, P. and Miller, C. (2006) 'Capacities of the capacity-builders: should training frameworks include ethical and emotional dimensions?', in J. Diamond, A. Southern, J. Liddel and A. Townsend (eds), *Managing the City*. London: Routledge.

Milburn, A. (2002) *Speech to the Annual Social Services Conference*, 16 October, Cardiff. http://www.dh.gov.uk/en/News/Speeches/Speecheslist/DH_4031620. Accessed 15. 08. 2008.

Milton, S. and Phillips T. (2008) *Allocation of social Housing by Local Authorities in England and Wales* – letter to Chief Executives from Sir Simon Milton and Trevor Phillips. Local Government Association (08.04.2008): http://www.lga.gov.uk/lga/core/page.do?pageId=435478 (accessed 18/04.2008.).

Mink, G. (1998) *Welfare's End*. Ithaca: Cornell University Press.

Modood, T. (2005) *Multicultural Politics: Racism, Ethnicity and Muslims in Britain*. Edinburgh: Edinburgh University Press.

Modood, T., Triandafyllidou, A. and Zapata-Barrero, R. (eds) (2006) *Multiculturalism, Muslims and Citizenship: A European Approach.* London: Routledge.

Moe, R. (2001) 'The emerging federal quasi-government: issues of management and accountability', *Public Management Review*, 61 (3): 290–12.

Monteleone, R. (ed.) (2007) *La Contrattualizzazione nelle Politiche Sociali: Forme ed Effeti.* Rome: Officina Edizione.

Mooney, G. and Law, A. (eds) (2007) *New Labour, Hard Labour: Restructuring and Resistance Inside the Welfare Industry.* Bristol: Policy Press.

Mooney, G. and Neal, S. (eds) (2009) *Community: Welfare, Crime and Society.* Maidenhead: Open University Press/Open University.

Moore, M. H. (1995) *Creating Public Value: Strategic Management in Government.* Cambridge, MA: Harvard University Press.

Morley, D. and Robbins, K. (eds) (2001) *British Cultural Studies.* Oxford: Oxford University Press.

Morissens, A. and Sainsbury, D. (2005) 'Migrants' social rights, ethnicity and welfare regimes', *Journal of Social Policy*, 34 (4): 637–60.

Morris, M. (2002) *Managing Migration: Civic Stratification and Migrants' Rights.* London: Routledge.

Needham, C. (2003) *Citizen-Consumers: New Labour's Marketplace Democracy.* London: Catalyst Forum.

Needham, C. (2007) *The Reform of Public Services under New Labour: Narratives of Consumerism.* Basingstoke: Palgrave.

Neveu, C. (2007a) 'Deux formes de territorialisation de l'engagement dans l'espace urbain', in H. Bertheleu and F. Bourdarias (eds), *Les Formes de Manifestation du Politique.* Tours: Presses Universitaires François Rabelais.

Neveu, C. (ed.) (2007b) *Cultures et Pratiques Participatives: Perspectives Comparatives.* Paris: L'Harmattan.

Newman, J. (2001) *Modernising Governance: New Labour, Policy and Society.* London: Sage.

Newman, J. (2004a) 'Constructing accountability: network governance and managerial agency', *Public Policy and Administration*, 19 (4): 18–35.

Newman, J. (2004b) 'Modernising the State: a new style of governance', in J. Lewis and R. Surender (eds), *Welfare State Change; Towards a Third Way?* Oxford: Oxford University Press.

Newman, J. (2005a) *Going Public.* Inaugural lecture, The Open University, Milton Keynes, May.

Newman, J. (2005b) 'Introduction', in J. Newman (ed.), *Remaking Governance: Peoples, Politics and the Public Sphere.* Bristol: Policy Press.

Newman, J. (2005c) 'Re-gendering governance', in J. Newman (ed.), *Remaking Governance: Policy, Politics and the Public Sphere.* Bristol: Policy Press.

Newman, J. (2005d) 'Network governance, transformational leadership and the micro politics of public service change', *Sociology*, 39 (4): 717–34.

Newman, J. (2005e) 'Participative governance and the remaking of the public sphere', in J. Newman (ed.), *Remaking Governance? Peoples, Politics and the Public Sphere.* Bristol: Policy Press, pp. 119–38.

Newman, J. (2006a) 'Rowing, steering or out of control?', Paper to *The Scientific Council for Government (WRR)*, The Hague, February.

Newman, J. (2006b) 'Restating a politics of the public', *Soundings: A Journal of Politics and Culture*, 32: 162–76.

Newman, J. (2006c) 'Constituting trans-national governance: spaces, actors and vocabularies of power', Paper Presented to *4th ESPANET conference*, Bremen, September, 2006.

Newman, J. (2006d) 'Restating a politics of the public', *Soundings: A Journal of Politics and Culture*, 32: 162–76.

Newman, J. (2007a) 'Rethinking "the public" in troubled times: unsettling nation, state and the liberal public sphere', *Public Policy and Administration*, 22 (1): 27–47.

Newman, J. (2007b) 'Remapping the public: public libraries and the public sphere', *Cultural Studies*, 21 (6): 887–909.

Newman, J. (2007c) 'The "double dynamics" of activation: institutions, citizens and the remaking of welfare governance', *International Journal of Sociology and Social Policy*, 29 (9/10): 364–75.

Newman, J. (2007d) 'Governance as cultural practice: texts, talk and the struggle for meaning', in M. Bevir and F. Trentmann (eds), *Governance, Consumer and Citizens: Agency and Resistance on Contemporary Politics*. Basingstoke: Palgrave.

Newman, J. (2008) 'The 21st century governance challenge', paper to the *Joint Cabinet Office/National School of Government Roundtable on Leadership Vision*, London, February 2008

Newman, J., Barnes, M. and Sullivan, H. (2004) 'Public participation and collaborative governance', *Journal of Social Policy*, 33 (2): 203–23.

Newman, J., Glendinning, C. and Hughes, M. (2008) 'Beyond modernisation? Social care and the transformation of welfare governance', *Journal of Social Policy*, 37 (4): 531–558.

Newman, J. and Mahony, N. (2007) 'Democracy and the public realm: towards a progressive agenda?', *Soundings*, 36: 52–62.

Newman, J. and McKee, R. (2005) 'Beyond the new public management? Public services and the social investment state', *Policy and Politics*, 33 (4): 657–74.

Newman, J. and Mooney, G. (2004) 'Managing personal lives', in G. Mooney (ed.), *Work: Personal Lives and Social Policy*. Bristol: The Policy Press/Open University.

Newman, J., Richards, S. and Smith, P. (1998) 'Market testing and institutional change in the UK civil service: compliance, non compliance and engagement', *Public Policy and Administration*, 13 (4): 96–110.

Newman, J. and Vidler, E. (2006a) 'Discriminating customers, responsible patients, empowered users: consumerism and the modernisation of health care', *Journal of Social Policy*, 35 (2): 193–209.

Newman, J. and Vidler, E. (2006b) 'More than a matter of choice? Consumerism and the modernisation of health care', in L. Bauld, K. Clarke and T. Maltby (eds), *Social Policy Review 18*. Bristol: Policy Press.

Newman, J. and Yeates, N. (eds) (2008) *Social Justice*. Maidenhead: Open University Press/Open University.

Noordegraaf, M. (2006) 'Professional management of professionals', in J. W. Duyvendak, T. Knijn and M. Kremer (eds), *People, Policy and the New Professionals*. Amsterdam: Amsterdam University Press, pp. 181–93.

Noordegraaf, M. (2007) 'From "Pure" to "Hybrid" professionalism: present day professionalism in ambiguous public domains', *Administration and Society*, 39 (6): 761–85.

Oakeshott, M. (1996) *The Politics of Faith and the Politics of Scepticism*. New Haven: Yale University Press.

Office of Fair Trading (OFT) (2008) *OFT issues statement of objections against 112 construction companies*. http://www.oft.gov.uk/news/press/2008/52-08 (accessed 20.04.2008).

Office of Public Services Reform (2002) *Reforming Our Public Services*. London: OPSR.

O'Malley, P. (2004) *Risk, Uncertainty and Government*. London: Glasshouse Press.

O'Neill, B. and Gidengil, E. (eds) (2005) *Gender and Social Capital*. London: Routledge.

O'Neill, O. (2002) *A Question of Trust (The BBC Reith Lectures 2002)*. Cambridge: Cambridge University Press.

Ong, A. (1999) *Flexible Citizenship*. Durham, NC: Duke University Press.

Ong, A. (2006) *Neoliberalism as exception: mutations in citizenship and sovereignty*. Durham, NC: Duke University Press.

Ong, A. and Collier, S. J. (eds) (2005) *Global Assemblages*. Oxford: Blackwell.

O'Reilly, D., Wallace, M., Deem, R., Morris, J. and Reed, M. (2006) 'Developing organisational leaders as change agents in the public services: an exploratory analysis', Paper Presented at *British Academy of Management Annual Conference*, Belfast, 12th–14th September 2006. Paper available at: http://www.cf.ac.uk/carbs/research/groups/esrc/dissemination_activities.html. (accessed 18.04.2008).

Osborne, S. (2000) *Public-Private Partnerships: Theory and Practice in International Perspective*. London: Routledge.

Osborne, S. and Brown, K. (2005) *Managing Change and Innovation in Public Service Organisations*. London: Routledge

Painter, J. (2006) 'Prosaic geographies of stateness', *Political Geography*, 25: 752–74

Pandey, G. (2005) *The Construction of Communalism in North India*. Oxford: Oxford University Press (2nd edn).

Pandey, G. (2006) 'The politics of community: some notes from India', in G. Creed (ed.), *The Seductions of Community: Emancipations, Oppressions Quandaries*. Santa Fe: School of American Research Press; Oxford: James Currey.

Parekh, B. (2000a) *Rethinking Multiculturalism*. Basingstoke: Palgrave.

Parekh, B. (2000b) *The Future of Multi-Ethnic Britain (The Report of the Runnymede Trust Commission)*. London: Profile.

Pateman, C. (1987) 'Feminist critiques of the public/private distinction', in A. Phillips (ed.), *Feminism and Equality*. Oxford: Blackwell, pp. 103–26.

Paton, R. (2003) *Managing and Measuring Social Enterprises*. London: Sage.

Pearce, J. (2003) *Social Enterprise in Anytown*. London: Caloustie Gulbenkian Foundation.

Pearce, N. and Margo, J. (eds) (2007) *Politics for a New Generation: The Progressive Moment*. Basingstoke: Macmillan.

Peck, J. (2001) *Workfare States*. New York: Guilford.

Peck, J. (2002) 'Political economies of scale: fast policy, interscalar relations and neoliberal welfare', *Economic Geography*, 78: 331–60.

Peck, J. and Tickell, A. (2002) 'Neoliberalizing space', *Antipode*, 34: 380–404.

Pesch, U. (2005 *The Predicament of Publicness: An Inquiry into the Conceptual Ambiguity of Public Administration*. Delft: Eburon.

Petersen, A., Barnes, I., Dudley, J. and Harris, P. (1999) *Post Structuralism, Citizenship and Social Policy*. London: Routledge.

Phillips, A. (1993) *Democracy and Difference*. Pennsylvania: Pennsylvania University Press.

Phillips, A. (1995) *The Politics of Presence*. Oxford: Oxford University Press.

Phillips, T. (2007) 'Britishness and integration', in N. Johnson (ed.) *Britishness: Towards a Progressive Citizenship*. London: The Smith Institute.

Phillis Report (2004) *The Report of an Independent Review of Government Communications*. London: The Cabinet Office.

Pierre, J. (ed.) (2000) *Debating Governance: Authority, Steering and Democracy*. Oxford: Oxford University Press.

Pierre, J. and Peters, G. (2000) *Governance, Politics and the State*. Basingstoke: Macmillan.

Pollitt, C. (1993) *Managerialism and the Public Services*. Oxford: Basil Blackwell.

Pollitt, C. (1995) 'Justification by works or by faith? Evaluating the new public management', *Evaluation*, 1 (2): 133–54.

Pollitt, C. (2007) 'New labour's re-disorganisation: hypermodernism and the costs of reform – a cautionary tale', *Public Management Review*, 9 (4): 529–43.

Pollitt, C. and Bouckaert, G. (2004) *Public Management Reform: A Comparative Analysis*. Oxford: Oxford University Press (2nd edn).

Pollitt, C., Birchall, J. and Putnam, K. (1998) *Decentralising Public Service Management*. Basingstoke: Macmillan.

Pollitt, C., Girre, X., Lonsdale, J., Mul, R., Summa, H. and Waerness, M. (1999) *Performance or Compliance? Performance Audit in Five Countries*. Oxford: Oxford University Press.

Pollock, A. (2004) *NHS plc: The Privatisation of Our Health Care*. London: Verso.

Power, M. (1993) *The Audit Explosion*. London: Demos.

Power, M. (1997) *The Audit Society*. Oxford: Oxford University Press.

Pratchett, L. (1999) 'The new ethics of modern public service', *British Journal of Politics and International Relations*, 1 (3): 366–76.

Pratchett, L. and Wingfield, M. (1996) 'Petty bureaucracy and woolly minded liberalism? The changing ethos of local government officers', *Public Administration*, 74 (4): 613–56.

Pratt, M. (1992) *Imperial Eyes: Travel Writing and Transculturation*. London: Routledge.

Public Administration Select Committee (2005) *Choice, Voice and Public Services*. Fourth Report of Session 2004–5, Vol 1. London: House of Commons (HV 49-1).

Putnam, R. (2000) *Bowling Alone: The Collapse and Revival of American Community*. New York: Simon and Schuster.

Putnam, R. (2007) '*E Pluribus Unum*: diversity and community in the twenty-first century. The 2006 Johan Skytte Prize Lecture', *Scandinavian Political Studies*, 30 (2): 137–74.

Putnam, R., Leonardi, R. and Nanetti, R. (1994) *Making Democracy Work: Civic Traditions in Modern Italy*. Princeton, NJ: Princeton University Press.

Ramajar, P. K. and Grundy-Warr, C. (eds) (2007) *Borderscapes: Hidden Geographies and Politics at Territory's Edge*. Minneapolis, MA: University of Minnesota Press.

Rancière, J. (2006) *The Hatred of Democracy*. (Translated by S. Corcoran). London: Verso.

Rhodes, R. A. W (1994) 'The hollowing out of the state', *Political Quarterly*, 65: 138–51.

Rhodes, R. (1997) *Understanding Governance: Networks, Governance, Reflexivity and Accountability*. Buckingham: Open University Press.

Root, A. (2007) *Market Citizenship: Experiments in Democracy and Globalisation*. London: Sage.

Rosanvallon, P. (2000) *The New Social Question: Rethinking the Welfare State*. (Translated by B. Harshav). Princeton, NJ: Princeton University Press.

Rosanvallon, P. (2006) *La Contre-démocratie*. Paris: Editions du Seuil.

Rose, N. (1999) *Powers of Freedom: Reframing Political Thought*. Cambridge: Cambridge University Press.

Rosello, M. (2002) *Postcolonial Hospitality: The Immigrant as Guest*. Palo Alto, CA: Stanford University Press.

Rowe, R. and Shepherd, M. (2002) 'Public participation in the new NHS: no closer to citizen control?', *Social Policy and Administration*, 36 (3): 275–90.

Ruane, S. (2004) 'It's a leap of faith, isn't it? Managers perceptions of PFI in the NHS', in M. Dent, J. Chandler and J. Barry (eds), *Questioning the New Public Management*. Aldershot: Ashgate.

Ruppert, E. (2006) *The Moral Economy of Cities: Shaping Good Citizens*. Toronto: University of Toronto Press.

Russell, J. (2008) 'We rage at Hain and Conway but miss the real profligacy', *The Guardian*, January 30: 26.

Sachdev, S. (2004) *Paying the Cost? Public Private Partnerships and the Public Service Workforce*. London: Catalyst.

Sahlin-Andersson, K. and Engwall, L. (eds) (2002) *The Expansion of Management Knowledge*. Stanford: Stanford University Press.

Said, E. (1993) *Culture and Imperialism*. London: Chatto and Windus.

Salskov-Iversen, D., Hansen, H. K. and Bislev, S. (2000) 'Governmentality, globalisation and local practice: transformations of a hegemonic discourse', *Alternatives*, 25: 183–222.

Sandeman, I. (2007) 'David Freud's review', http://www.bbc.co.uk/dna/actionnetwork/ F?thread=3944678 (accessed 7.01.2008).

Sassatelli, R. (2007) *Consumer Culture: History, Theory and Politics*. London: Sage.

Sassen, S. (1998) *Globalization and Its Discontents*. New York: The New Press.

Sassen, S. (2006) *Territory, Authority, Rights: From Mediaeval to Global Assemblages*. Princeton, NJ: Princeton University Press.

Saward, M. (2005) 'Governance and the transformation of political representation', in J. Newman (ed.) (2005) *Remaking Governance: Peoples, Politics and the Public Sphere*. Bristol: The Policy Press.

Seeleib-Kaiser, M. (ed.) (2008) *Transforming Welfare States*. Basingstoke: Palgrave Macmillan.

Schofield, B. (2002) 'Governing the self-sustaining community', *Sociology*, 36 (3): 663–83.

Schram, S. (2000) *After Welfare: The Culture of Postindustrial Social Policy*. New York: New York University Press.

Schultz, A. and von Stein, A. (2007) 'How to govern hybrid networks in contradictory institutional settings', Paper to the CINEFOGO conference *Partnership – keystone of new governance*, Munster, Germany, January 29–30th.

Sevenhuijsen, S. (1998) *Citizenship and the Ethics of Care: Feminist Considerations of Justice, Morality and Politics*. New York and London: Routledge.

Sharma, A. (2006) 'Crossbreeding institutions, breeding struggle: women's empowerment, neoliberal governmentality, and state (re)formation in India', *Cultural Anthropology*, 21 (1): 61–95.

Sharma, A. (2008) *Logics of Empowerment*. Minneapolis, MA: University of Minnesota Press.

Sharma, A. and Gupta, A. (2006) 'Rethinking Theories of the state in an age of globalization', in A. Sharma and A. Gupta (eds), *The Anthropology of the State: A Reader.* Oxford: Blackwell Publishing.

Simon, J. (2007) *Governing through Crime.* Oxford: Oxford University Press.

Skeggs, B. (2004) *Class, Self, Culture.* London: Routledge.

Skelcher, C. (2005) 'Public-private partnerships and hybridity', in E. Ferlie, L. Lynn and C. Pollitt (eds), *Oxford Handbook of Public Management.* Oxford: Oxford University Press, pp. 347–70.

Skelcher, C., Mathur, N. and Smith, M. (2005) 'The public governance of collaborative spaces: discourse, design and democracy', *Public Administration,* 83 (3): 573–96.

Slaughter, A. (2004) *A New World Order.* Princeton, NJ: Princeton University Press.

Smart, A. (2006) *The Shek Kip Mei Myth: Squatters, Fires and Colonial Rule in Hong Kong, 1950-1963.* Hong Kong: Hong Kong University Press.

Smith, P. (1997) *Millenial Dreams: Contemporary Culture and Capital.* London: Verso.

Soederberg, S., Menz, G. and Cerny, P. (2005) *Internalizing Globalization: The Rise of Neoliberalism and the Decline of National Varieties of Capitalism.* Basingstoke: Palgrave Macmillan.

Sorenson, E., and Torfing, J. (2006) *Theories of Democratic Network Governance.* London: Routledge.

Soysal, Y. N. (1994) *Limits of Citizenship: Migrants and Postnational Membership In Europe.* Chicago: University of Chicago Press.

Squires, P. (ed.) (2006) *Community Safety: Critical Perspectives on Policy and Practice.* Bristol: Policy Press.

Stenson, K. (2000) 'Crime control, social policy and liberalism', in G. Lewis, S. Gewirtz and J. Clarke (eds), *Rethinking Social Policy.* London: Sage.

Stenson, K. (2008) 'Governing the local: sovereignty, social governance and community safety', *Social Work and Society,* vol 6(1), www.socwork.net/2008/1/special_issue.

Stoker, G. (2006) *Why Politics Matters: Making Democracy Work.* Basingstoke: Palgrave McMillan.

Strathern, M. (ed.) (2000) *Audit Cultures.* London: Routledge.

Stubbs, P. (2002) 'Globalisation, memory and welfare regimes in transition: towards an anthropology of transnational policy transfers', *International Journal of Social Welfare,* 11 (4): 321–30.

Stubbs, P. (2005) 'Stretching concepts too far? Multi-level governance, policy transfer and the politics of scale in South East Europe', *Southeast European Politics,* VI (2): 66–87.

Stubbs, P. (2006) 'Aspects of community development in contemporary Croatia: globalisation, neo-liberalisation and ngo-isation', in L. Dominelli (ed.), *Revitalising Communities.* Aldershot: Ashgate.

Stubbs, P. (2007) 'Civil society or Ubleha?', in H. Rill, T. Šmidling and A. Bitoljanu (eds), *20 Pieces of Encouragement for Awakening and Change: Peacebuilding in the Region of the Former Yugoslavia.* Belgrade: Centre for Nonviolent Action, pp. 215–28.

Sullivan, H. (2003) 'New forms of accountability: coming to terms with "many hands"', *Policy and Politics,* 31 (3): 353–70.

Sullivan, H. and Skelcher, C. (2002) *Working across Boundaries: Partnerships in Public Services.* Basingstoke: Palgrave.

Taguieff, P-A. (2007) *L'Illusion Populiste.* Manchecourt: Editions Flammarion (1st edn, 2002).

Taylor, C. (2004) *Modern Social Imaginaries*. Durham, NC: Duke University Press.

Taylor, M. (2003) *Public Policy in the Community*. Basingstoke: Palgrave Macmillan.

Taylor, M. (2007) 'Across the great divide – dilemmas of new governance spaces', Paper to the seminar *Between states and citizens – the role of civic elements in the governance and production of social services*, Berlin, 30–31st March.

Taylor, M. and Wilks-Heeg, S. (2007) 'Localism and Local Governance'. ESRC seminar series: *Mapping the public policy landscape*. Swindon: ESRC.

Taylor-Gooby, P. (ed.) (1998) *Choice and Public Policy: The Limits to Welfare Markets*. Basingstoke: Macmillan/ESRC.

Taylor-Gooby, P. (ed.) (2001) *Welfare States Under Pressure*. London: Sage.

Taylor-Gooby, P. (2005) 'Is the future American? Or, can left politics preserve European welfare state from erosion through growing "racial" diversity?', *Journal of Social Policy*, 34 (4): 661–72.

Taylor-Gooby, P. (2008) 'Choice and values: individualised rational action and social goals', *Journal of Social Policy*, 37 (2): 167–86.

Townsend, J. et al (2002) 'The role of the transnational community of nongovernment organisations: governance or poverty reduction?', *Journal of International Development*, 14 (6): 829–39.

Travers, M. (2007) *The New Bureaucracy: Quality Assurance and its Critics*. Bristol: Policy Press.

Triandafyllidou, A., Modood, T. and Zapata-Barrero, R. (2006) 'European challenges of multicultural citizenship: Muslims, secularism and beyond', in T. Modood, A. Triandafyllidou and R. Zapata-Barrero (eds), *Multiculturalism, Muslims and Citizenship: A European Approach*. London: Routledge.

Tronto, J. C.(1993) *Moral Boundaries: A Political Argument for an Ethic of Care*. New York and London: Routledge.

Uberoi, P. (2003) 'Feminism and the public–private distinction', in G. Mahajan and H. Reifeld (eds), *The Public and the Private: Issues of Democratic Citizenship*. London and New Delhi: Sage.

Valkenburg, B. (2007) 'Individualising activation services: thrashing out an ambiguous concept', in R. Van Berkel and B. Valkenburg, *Making it Personal: Individualising Activation Services in the EU*. Bristol: Policy Press, pp. 25–44.

Van Berkel, V. and Valkenburg, B. (2007) 'The individualization of activation services in context', in R. Van Berkel and B. Valkenburg, *Making it Personal: Individualising Activation Services in the EU*. Bristol: Policy Press, pp. 3–24.

Van Houten, H., Kramsch, O. and Zierhofer, W. (2005) 'Prologue', in H. van Houten, O. Kramsch and W. Zierhofer (eds), *Bordering Space*. Aldershot: Ashgate.

Van Zoonen, L. (2005) *Entertaining the Citizen: When Politics and Popular Culture Converge*. Lanham, MD: Rowan and Littlefield.

Vidler, E. and Clarke, J. (2005) 'Creating citizen-consumers: New Labour and the remaking of public services', *Public Policy and Administration*, 20 (2): 19–37.

Wajcman, J. and Martin, B. (2002) 'Narratives of identity in modern management: the corrosion of gender difference?', *Sociology*, 36 (4): 985–1002.

Wallace, M. (2008) 'Acculturating public service leaders as change agents? Mediatory responses to leadership development in England', Paper Presented to the 12th *International Research Symposium on Public Management* (IRSPM XII), Brisbane, March.

Wallace, M. and Hoyle, E. (2007) 'An ironic perspective on public service change', in M. Wallace, M. Fertig and E. Schneller (eds), *Managing Change in the Public Services.* Oxford: Blackwell.

Walters, W. (2004) 'Some critical notes on "governance"', *Studies in Political Economy*, 73 (Spring/Summer): 27–46.

Walzer, M. (ed.) (1995) *Towards a Global Civil Society.* Providence, MA and Oxford: Berghahn Books.

Ware, V. (2007) *Who Cares about Britishness? A Global View of the National Identity Debate.* London: Arcadia Books.

Warner, M. (2002) *Publics and Counterpublics.* New York: Zed Books.

Webb, J. (1999) 'Work and the new public service class?', *Sociology*, 33: 747–66.

Wedel, J. (2001) *Collision and Collusion: The Strange Case of Western Aid to Eastern Europe.* New York: Palgrave.

Wedel, J. (2009) *The Shadow Elite.* New York: Basic Books.

Weintraub, J. A. (1997) 'The theory and politics of the public/private divide', in J. A. Weintraub and K. Kumar (eds), *Public and Private in Thought and Practice.* Chicago: University of Chicago Press.

West, H. and Sanders, T. (eds) (2003) *Transparency and Conspiracy: Ethnographies of Suspicion.* Durham, NC: Duke University Press.

West, P. (2005) *The Poverty of Multi-Culturalism.* London: Civitas.

Wetherell, M., Lafleche, M., and Berkeley, R. (eds) (2007) *Identity, Ethnic Diversity and Community Cohesion.* London: Sage.

Whitehead, M. (2007) 'The architecture of partnerships: urban regeneration in the shadow of hierarchy', *Policy and Politics*, 35 (1): 3–23.

Williams, F. (2000) 'Principles of recognition and respect in welfare', in G. Lewis, S. Gewirtz and J. Clarke (eds), *Rethinking Social Policy.* London: Sage.

Williams, M. (2004) 'Discursive democracy and New Labour: five ways in which decision-makers manage citizen agendas in public participation initiatives', *Sociological Research Online*, 9 (3).

Williams, R. (1988) *Keywords: A Vocabulary of Culture and Society.* London: Fontana (2nd edn).

Wolch, J. (1990) *The Shadow State: Government and the Voluntary Sector in Transition.* New York: The Foundation Centre.

Wright, S. (2002) 'Activating the unemployed: the street-level implementation of UK policy', *Tijdschrift voor Arbeid en Participie*, 24 (2): 105–24.

Wright, S. (2006) 'The administration of transformation: a case study of implementing welfare reform in the UK', in P. Henman and M. Fenger (eds), *Administering Welfare Reform: International Transformations in Welfare Governance.* Bristol: Policy Press, pp. 161–82.

Yeates, N. (2001) *Globalisation and Social Policy.* London: Sage.

Young, I. M. (1990) *Justice and the Politics of Difference.* New Jersey: Princeton University Press.

Yuval-Davis, N. (1999) 'Ethnicity, gender relations and multiculturalism', in R. D. Torres, L. F. Miron and J. X. Inda (eds), *Race, Identity and Citizenship: A Reader.* Oxford: Blackwell.

Index